THE COMPLETE ENCYCLOPEDIA OF

STEAMSHIPS

MERCHANT STEAMSHIPS 1798-2006

THE COMPLETE ENCYCLOPEDIA OF
STEAMSHIPS
MERCHANT STEAMSHIPS 1798-2006

JOHN BATCHELOR & CHRIS CHANT

REBO
PUBLISHERS

Published by Rebo International b.v., Lisse, The Netherlands in association with Publishing Solutions (www) Ltd. England.

© 2007 Rebo International b.v., Lisse, The Netherlands and Publishing Solutions (www) Ltd., England

Text: Christopher Chant
Illustrations: John Batchelor
Production, layout and typesetting: The Minster Press, 5 Mill Lane, Wimborne, Dorset, BH21 1JQ, England
Cover design: AdAm Studio, Prague, Czech Republic
Pre-press Services: Amos Typographical Studio, Prague, Czech Republic
Proofreading: Erin Ferretti Slattery

ISBN 978 90 366 1720 8

Contents

Introduction

The term "merchant vessel" is used for the types of river, lake, sea and ocean vessel utilized by elements of the world's shipping industry, which is economically based on the movement of things and persons by water. As of the start of the twenty-first century, it is estimated that more than 90% of all international trade is transported by sea, and every year the merchant fleets of the world's maritime nations are responsible for the delivery, in bulk form, of several billion tons of raw materials such as crude oil, refined petroleum products, mineral ores, coal, timber and grain, and for the movement of a vast quantity of manufactured goods, mostly in the type of standard container which facilitates loading and unloading in terms of ease and speed.

While air transport has almost totally replaced long-haul passenger services once operated by celebrated ocean liners, very large numbers of passengers and vehicles are nonetheless still carried by ferries, usually over short distances, and it should be added that the rapid increase during the last 50 years in the popularity of holidays at sea, with the voyage as an end in itself, has led to the construction of many large cruise liners.

The origins of many of the features characteristic of the modern shipping industry can be found in the nineteenth century as the Industrial Revolution began to make its effects felt in a major fashion. In 1818, for example, the Black Ball Line initiated the first scheduled service with the sailing of the *James Monroe* between New York and Liverpool. In the next year, the *Savannah* crossed the Atlantic Ocean, using steam propulsion for much of the way, and in 1838 the British vessel *Sirius* made the first transatlantic crossing entirely under steam. Some 10 years later, the concepts of ship design and ship construction were revolutionized by the innovations of Isambard K. Brunel in his *Great Western*, *Great Britain* and *Great Eastern*.

The completion of the Suez Canal in 1869, thus connecting the Mediterranean and Red Seas and removing the need to pass round the

Cape of Good Hope, considerably shortened the trade routes between Europe, the Middle East, and the Far East. At about this time, the sailing vessel *Elizabeth* carried the first mineral oil cargo, and in 1886 the *Glückauf* entered service as the world's first modern ocean-going tanker. At this time the most important freight vessel was the tramp steamer, which did not have any form of fixed schedule, or operate between published ports of call.

In the last two decades of the nineteenth century, growing numbers of large passenger liners were built to satisfy the increasing demand for international travel by the affluent and by emigrants seeking better lives in other countries and, especially, in other continents. The steam turbine, invented by Sir Charles Parsons in 1884, enabled some passenger vessels to achieve speeds of more than 20 knots (kt).

In 1912 the Danish *Selandia* became the first sea-going motor ship; that is, one with an internal combustion engine (specifically the diesel engine) rather than steam-powered machinery. Although the diesel engine was not accepted widely at first, this type of engine matured rapidly in and after World War I (1914-18), largely as the engine for submarines running on the surface, and in the first part of the twenty-first century, most merchant ships have diesel engines, usually connected to a single propeller. This process was most evident from the middle of the twentieth century, and the rise of diesel propulsion was mirrored by the decline in steam propulsion, which had now all but disappeared. Nuclear propulsion, installed experimentally in vessels such as the U.S. *Savannah*, the West German *Otto Hahn*, the Japanese *Mutsu* and the Soviet *Sevmorput*, has not been generally welcomed for mercantile purposes, although it is still extensively used in warships, especially submarines.

The trend since World War II (1939-45) had been toward ever larger, faster and more specialized merchant ships. Many tankers of more than 200,000 tons deadweight have been built. The French *Batillus*, one of the largest, was built in the 1970s and was more than 600,000 tons deadweight. Bulk ore carriers of more than 100,000 tons deadweight are now perfectly standard.

Most manufactured goods are now transported by ships specially designed to carry standard containers, which are of several sizes. The largest container ships, such as the Danish *Regina Mærsk*, are some 1,150 ft (350 m) in length and carry more than 6,000 containers.

The shipping industry, like most large modern industries, is extremely competitive, concentrating primarily on the demands of international trade. The industry is highly international-ized in terms of its organization and the nature of its services. Thus, most shipping companies are comparatively specialized in markets such as dry bulk, oil and liner. In the nineteenth century and up to about 1950, most of the world's merchant fleet operated under either the British flag or that of one of the long-established maritime trading nations such as France, Germany, Japan and Norway. Since 1950, however, the flag flown by any ship is not necessarily an indication of the country in which the ship is beneficially owned. Many ships now fly a flag of convenience, typically those of Liberia, Panama, Cyprus and a number of Central American republics. This offers the owner a number of financial advantages including reduced or even obviated corporate tax liability in its home nation. A large proportion of the world's merchant fleet is therefore currently registered in "open-registry" nations, even though the owner is probably based in Europe, North America or South-East Asia.

In the first decade of the twenty-first century, the world's merchant fleet comprises almost 100,000 vessels, about half of which are cargo-carrying ships, and the other half in activities not related to trade, such as fishing, support of the offshore resources-exploitation industries and

the provision of ancillary services such as towage, dredging and surveying.

The composition of the world's current merchant fleet is notably from that of the period immediately following World War II. The typical dry cargo ship of the earlier period was a 10,000-ton deadweight general-purpose vessel such as the "Liberty" ship built in large numbers during World War II and used to carry bulk or general cargoes. The typical tanker of the same time was on the order of 15,000 tons deadweight, like the many "T2" standard vessels constructed in the U.S. during World War II. Today's merchant fleet reflects the introduction of several types of specialized cargo ships, many of them customized and also extremely large, to satisfy the needs of a global and very diversified market.

Today's ships are considerably larger than their predecessors, and have also become markedly more complex as technological developments in automation, and also in computers and communications, have radically changed the manner in which ships are worked. The result of this process is a reduction in the size of crews, which nonetheless have greater productivity. The other side of this coin is the virtual disappearance of many traditional navigation and seafaring skills.

Stepping back in time, one of the first types of merchant ship to emerge in the period after steam supplanted sail was the ocean liner. This was the type of ship which carried people, freight (including high-value material such as bullion), and mail on a scheduled basis between the ports of predetermined trans-oceanic routes. The typical ocean liner was sturdily built with high freeboard to withstand sea states and adverse conditions encountered in the open ocean, and

had large capacities for fuel and the host of other stores required on voyages that might last several days or several months.

The ocean liner was the primary means of intercontinental travel for more than one hundred years between the mid-nineteenth century and the 1960s, when its place was assumed by the jet airliner.

The busiest route for liners was that across the North Atlantic, which was plied by ships travelling between Europe and North America. The fastest, largest and most confortable liners were built for this route, which attests to its commercial importance. However, it should not be imagined that the great liners of the North Atlantic were in any way typical of the breed: most liners were of medium size and worked in the everyday role of transporting passengers and cargo between empires and their colonies in the era before the advent of air travel as a means of mass transportation. Thus, the average liners were those which maintained the physical link between European nations and their African and Asian colonies, and also carried the emigrant traffic from Europe to the Americas in the nineteenth century and first twenty years of the twentieth century, and to Australia, New Zealand and Canada after World War II.

In 1818 the Black Ball Line, which operated only sailing vessels, offered the first regular passenger service with emphasis on passenger comfort, between the U.S. and UK. The domination of the sailing vessel for such services was challenged after Brunel's *Great Western* began her first Atlantic service in 1837. The large load of cargo and the steady power of the steam engines allowed a crossing time of some 15 days in a period when the vagaries of wind, strength and direction might cause a sailing vessel to require two months. The steam-powered vessel could therefore offer a schedule with a realistic expectation of success. The first steamships still had sails, it should be noted, which allowed vessels such as the *Great Western* to take advantage of a favourable wind to coal consumption without any serious degradation of speed.

In 1840 the Cunard Line began its first regular steam ship passenger and cargo service with the *Britannia*, which operated between Liverpool and Boston. At this stage the scheduling advantage of the steamships was offset to a great extent by the greater economy of the sailing vessel and, in some cases, a reluctance by some members of the traveling public, to entrust themselves to "new-fangled" and somewhat dirty devices such as steamships. The balance was steadily turned toward the steamship as its proved reliable and its operating costs fell, and in 1847 the *Great Britain* became the first propeller-driven and iron-hulled ship to cross the Atlantic. From this time on, its growing efficiency and reduced vulnerability to sea conditions meant that the propeller steadily relegated the paddle wheel to obsolescence for ocean propulsion.

During 1870 a new era in the comfort of ocean travel was pioneered by the White Star Line's *Oceanic*, which had her first-class accommodation midships for reduced reaction to the ship's pitching. The accommodation also included large portholes, running water and electrical lighting.

From 1880 the size of ocean liners increased steadily to provide for the ever-swelling numbers of persons wanting to emigrate from Europe to the U.S. By this time, steam propulsion was completely proved for reliability and fuel economy, and the sister ships *Umbria* and *Etruria* were the last two transatlantic liners completed with auxiliary sails. These two ships were notable as the largest liners of their day, and worked between Liverpool and New York.

The period between the start of the twentieth century and the outbreak of World War II in 1939 is generally considered to have been the "golden age" of the ocean liner. Grounded economically on the base provided by the great emigrant market to the U.S. and Canada, the great shipping lines vied strongly with each other, and placed ever greater emphasis on the size (and thus the capacity) and speed of their liners, which included extremely luxurious accommodation for the wealthy, travelling more readily and frequently between Europe and North America.

Since the 1830s, ships had competed to achieve the fastest crossing of the North Atlantic, in a contest which became known as the Blue Riband. In 1897 Germany become predominant in the Blue Riband "market" with a series of new liners beginning with the *Kaiser Wilhelm der Gross*. Then in 1905 the Cunard Line installed steam-turbine propulsion in its *Carmania*, which revealed speed and economy somewhat better than the *Caronia*, which differed only in being powered by triple-expansion steam engines. The two vessels were then Cunard's largest ships, and the different propulsion methods in otherwise-identical ships allowed the company to evaluate the merits of both. The *Carmania*'s turbines clearly offered great advantages, and in 1907 Cunard therefore introduced the somewhat larger *Lusitania* and *Mauretania*, both with turbine propulsion. The *Mauretania* soon captured the Blue Riband, and then held it for twenty years.

Cunard's hold on the Blue Riband did not keep other lines from fighting back with size and luxury. In 1910 the White Star Line launched the *Olympic* of more than 45,000 gross

registered tons, and she was soon complemented by her sister ships *Titanic* and *Britannic*. Each of these liners was almost 15,000 tons larger and 100 ft (30.5 m) longer than the *Lusitania* and *Mauretania*. At much the same time the Hamburg-Amerika Linie also ordered the *Imperator*, *Vaterland* and *Bismarck*, each of more than 51,500 gross registered tons. The first of these, the *Imperator*, was launched in 1912, and the largest, the *Bismarck*, was the world's largest ship until 1935. The ships were little-used by the company before World War I's were seized as war reparations allocated to British and American lines.

It should be noted that the rapid growth in the size of ocean liners in the first years of the twentieth century was not without its problems, especially as safety regulations failed to keep pace. A first result of this tendency occurred in 1912, when the *Titanic* sank after hitting an iceberg, with the loss of more than 1,500 lives as a result of many factors, including the inadequate number of lifeboats demanded by the regulations. The catastrophe of the *Titanic* resulted in a swift revision of the regulation to require ocean liners to carry lifeboats for their full passenger and crew numbers.

In the 1920s the U.S. started to place severe limits on the number of immigrants it would accept, which was a major blow to the transatlantic passenger trade. Many of the ships built primarily for the migrant trade were diverted to the cruise-ship role, at least during the winter months, and the cheapest accommodation was revised from third- to tourist-class standard. The downturn of the transatlantic trade was then exacerbated by the effect of the Depression, which resulted in the

bankruptcy of many shipping lines.

Even so, several lines ordered still larger and faster ships. In 1929 the German ships *Bremen* and *Europa* finally exceeded the crossing record set by the *Mauretania* 20 years earlier with an average speed of almost 28 kt. The ships used bulbous bows and oil-fired boilers to reach these high speeds while maintaining economical operating costs. In 1935 the French liner *Normandie* used a new type of hull shape and powerful turbo-electric propulsion to take the Blue Riband from the Italian *Rex*. For economic reasons the British government arranged a forced marriage of the Cunard and White Star Lines, and partially financed the *Queen Mary* and *Queen Elizabeth*. The former held the Blue Riband from 1936-37 and 1938-52.

The period following the end of World War II notably included transatlantic liners such as the *United States*, the last ocean liner to hold the Blue Riband, and the *France*, which was the longest passenger ship from the time she entered service in 1961 until the advent of the *Queen Mary 2* in 2003. The period after World War II was also characterized by government-sponsored immigration to Australia, and this spurred a resurgence in the migrant trade with vessels such as the *Oriana* and *Canberra*. Operating on the P & O-Orient Line service, these were the last, largest and fastest liners built for the Australian route.

In 1953, the de Havilland Comet became the world's first commercial jet airliner, but it was with aircraft such as the Boeing Model 707 and Douglas DC-8 from the later 1950s that long-range aircraft came to threaten the liner's position as queen of the transatlantic and other long-distance passenger routes. Airliners steadily eroded the dominance of the liner during the 1960s, and by the early 1970s, the advent of very large aircraft, typified by the Boeing Model 747 "jumbo" jet, meant that the large passenger ship had been relegated almost exclusively to a cruising role. Many ships survived in this task, and even as late as 2003 a few former liners were still operational. By 2006 the only large liner still used on scheduled line voyages was the Cunard Line's *Queen Mary 2*, which in 2004 succeeded the same line's *Queen Elizabeth 2*, a ship which had operated the transatlantic service from 1969 and was then devoted solely to cruising.

Stepping back in time to the first half of the twentieth century, it should be recorded that the ocean liners played a major role in World Wars I and II. Larger liners were used for troops and as hospital ships, while smaller liners were converted

into armed merchant cruisers for the protection of trade routes. The *Britannic*, sister of the *Titanic* and *Olympic*, never actually served in the liner role for which she had been built, instead entering war service as a hospital ship as soon as she was completed; she sank one year later after striking a mine.

Large liners such as the *Queen Mary* and *Queen Elizabeth* were also used in World War II, again mostly as troopships and hospital ships. Most of the "super-liners" of the 1920s and 1930s fell victim to mines or to attacks by submarines or warplanes; a notably unfortunate victim of this type, the *Empress of Britain*, was damaged by air attack and then sunk by submarine attack as she was being towed to safety. This was the largest British ocean liner to succumb in World War II. Italy's most important liners, the *Rex* and *Conte di Savoia*, fell victim to British air attack and to

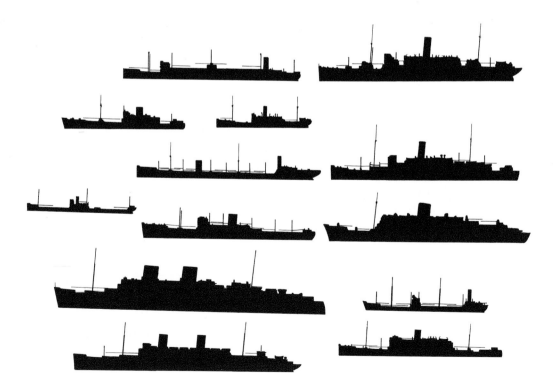

the retreating Germans respectively. The U.S. lost the American President Lines' *President Coolidge* to a mine (ironically, laid by the Allies) in the South Pacific.

As late as the 1980s, moreover, a similar process resulted in three ships being "taken up from trade" for British service during the Falklands war in 1982. Cunard's *Queen Elizabeth 2* and P & O's *Canberra* served as troop ships, while P & O's educational cruise ship and former British India Steam Navigation Company liner *Uganda* became a hospital ship during the conflict before being used as a troop ship until an air base was built at Port Stanley to handle trooping flights.

Despite the lessons learned in the tragic loss of the *Titanic* during 1912, ocean liners were still lost in circumstances involving heavy loss of life. In 1914 the *Empress of Ireland* sank in the St Lawrence River in eastern Canada with the loss of 1,012 lives, and the *Lusitania* was lost in 1915 to a German submarine during World War I while on passage from the U.S. to Britain. But the worst disasters were the loss of Cunard's *Lancastria* in 1940 off St Nazaire to German bombing while attempting to evacuate troops of the British Expeditionary Force from France, with the loss of over 3,000 lives; and the sinking of the *Wilhelm Gustloff* in the Baltic Sea in 1945 with the loss of more than 9,000 lives. As late as 1956 the Italian liner *Andrea Doria* sank after colliding with the Swedish liner *Stockholm* in heavy fog, despite the fact that she was fitted with radar.

The cruise ship or cruise liner is a passenger ship used for pleasure voyages, where the voyage itself and the enjoyment of the ship's amenities are considered an (if not the) essential part of the experience. Cruising has become a major part of the tourism industry, with millions of passengers each year. The rapid growth of the industry has resulted in the introduction of nine or more newly built ships for the North American trade each year since 2001, as well as others to cater for the European market. The tendency is for smaller markets such as that of the Asian and Pacific region to be served by older vessels replaced by new ships in the most important markets.

Cruise ships operate in two ways: either a round-trip course (starting and ending at the same port), or a one-way course with their passengers arriving and/or departing by air.

The first vessel constructed specifically as a cruise ship was the German *Prinzessin Victoria Luise*, commissioned by Albert Ballin, general manager of Hamburg-Amerika Linie, and completed in 1900. But the type of cruising so much a feature of the modern holiday industry emerged out of the concept of transatlantic travel. A crossing

was seldom scheduled for less than four days, and to attract passengers in the face of intense competition, the companies offering transatlantic travel relied increasingly on the comforts which their ships could provide: well-appointed staterooms, fine dining with high-quality wines, dancing in magnificent ballrooms, and extras such as libraries. This opened the way for longer voyages with comfortable travel as important as the destination, especially during the winter months when transatlantic crossings were not popular. Late in the nineteenth century, the Hamburg-Amerika Linie became the first company to use its transatlantic liners for lengthy cruises into the warmer and less stormy southern latitudes. The success of Hamburg-Amerika was considerable, and other companies started to offer similar cruises. Some even went so far as to construct ships specifically designed for easy transformation between summer crossings and winter cruising.

With the arrival of mass air transport and the collapse of the transatlantic liner trade, it became clear that there was still a major market for luxurious cruises. Such voyages initially catered to a limited market, but the cruise then became more popular after the early 1980s. Adapted liners were at first the norm, but then there appeared the first dedicated cruise ships. These were initially of small size, but after the success of the *Norway* (ex-*France*) from 1980 as the first "super-ship" cruise liner in the Caribbean, cruise ship size began to grow rapidly until the latest examples are the largest passenger ships ever built.

The development of the cruise ship market was at first centred on the U.S. demand for cruises around the Caribbean, Mexico, and Alaska, but is now global. By the middle of the first decade of the twenty-first century, there were several hundred cruise ships, some of them carrying more than 3,000. Modern cruise ships are in fact floating hotels, with separate hospitality and standard ship's crews. In such circumstances, therefore, it is hardly surprising that cruise ships are sometimes used

for other tasks which can exploit their capabilities. A shortage of hotel accommodation for the 2004 Olympic Games in Athens led to the use of several cruise ships at Piraeus to provide tourist accommodation, and in September 2005 the Federal Emergency Management Administration arranged the use of three Carnival Cruise Lines' vessels to house evacuees from Hurricane Katrina in the southern U.S.

Further down the range ladder, and most often the capacity ladder, from the ocean liner is the ferry. This is dedicated to the movement over short distance, such as a strait or other short sea crossing, of passengers and sometimes their cars, in many cases freight-carrying trucks, and in some cases railway carriages or freight wagons.

On the smallest scale, ferries can include waterbuses or water taxis providing transport for small numbers of passengers in cities, such as St Petersburg and Venice, divided by waterways. Such ferries form a part of the public transport infrastructure of many waterfront cities, providing direct transit between points at a capital cost much lower than that which would otherwise result from the construction of bridges or tunnels.

The busiest seaway in the world is that connecting the UK with the mainland of Europe across the Strait of Dover at the eastern end of the English Channel. British ferries operate mainly to French ports such as Boulogne, Calais, Cherbourg-Octeville and Le Havre, but also to destinations in Belgium, Denmark, the Netherlands, Norway and Spain. Some of the services carry mainly tourist traffic together with a limited quantity of freight, but others are for the exclusive use of freight trucks.

Large "cruiseferries" operate in the Baltic Sea between Finland, Sweden, Germany and Estonia, and, in the Mediterranean Sea, connect southern Italy with Albania and Greece. As suggested by their names, such cruise ferries are akin to cruise ships inasmuch as they provide levels of comfort and service higher than might have been expected, but they can also carry hundreds of cars on car decks.

In Australia, two (originally three) *Spirit of Tasmania* ferries carry passengers and vehicles 185 miles (300 km) across the Bass Strait between Melbourne in the Australian mainland state of Victoria and

Devonport in the north of the island of Tasmania. This is primarily an overnight service, but includes day crossings at peak periods.

In New Zealand, ferry services offered by Interislander and Bluebridge connect Wellington in the North Island with Picton in the South Island, across Cook Strait.

As a result of their many large freshwater lakes and the length of the Canadian coast, many Canadian provinces and territories have ferry services. BC Ferries of British Columbia carries travellers between Vancouver Island and the mainland of British Columbia, and also provides services to other islands including the Gulf Islands and the Queen Charlotte Islands. Typical of many such services in large number of cities around the world, the 12-minute harbor ferry service in Halifax, Nova Scotia is used by more than 3,000 commuters per day as a means of avoiding traffic congestion on the Macdonald and Mackay bridges. A similar concept is embodied by the *Chi-Cheemaun* passenger and freight ferry in Toronto, which carries beach-goers, tourists and aircraft passengers between downtown Toronto, Toronto Island beach, and the city's airport.

In the U.S., Washington State Ferries undertakes the country's most extensive ferry system, with 10 routes on Puget Sound and the Strait of Juan de Fuca serving terminals in Washington and Vancouver Island; in 1999 Washington State Ferries carried no fewer than 11 million vehicles and 26 million passengers. The Staten Island Ferry in New York City, linking the boroughs of Manhattan and Staten Island, is the nation's single busiest ferry route in numbers of passengers.

The specific design of any ferry depends on the length of the route being operated, the passenger or vehicle capacity required, the cruising speed required and the prevalent water conditions.

For some services hydrofoils and hovercraft (air-cushion vehicles) are appropriate, but fall outside the compass of this book. The catamaran type of vessel is generally associated with high-speed ferry services. A Swedish company, the Stena Line operates the largest catamarans in the world, the "*Stena HSS*" class, between the UK and mainland Europe or Ireland. Driven by waterjets and with a displacement of 19,638 tons, these ferries are considerably larger than most catamarans, and can accommodate 1,500 passengers and 375 cars for high-speed runs.

The "standard" type of modern ferry, if there can be said to be any such thing, is the "Ro/Ro" or roll-on/roll-off type, in which vehicles enter the vehicle via the bow or stern ramp and door and then exit in an essentially identical arrangement at the ferry's other end. This system maximizes the volume available for vehicle accommodation as there is no need to provide for turning, and also minimizes loading and unloading times to allow a higher frequency of service and thus open the way to greater utilization of the vessel.

Offering both vehicle and passenger capability, the "RoPax" ferry combines substantial vehicle volume with a comparatively large passenger capacity. Such ferries typically have conventional diesel propulsion and propellers, and are capable of speeds greater than 25 kt. The first such vessels were introduced by the Superfast Ferries subsidiary of the Attica Group with its *Superfast I* in 1995 for services between Greece and Italy.

Ferries frequently operate to and from a ferry slip, which is a dedicated port facility created specifically to position the vessel for loading and unloading, generally with the aid of an adjustable ramp, or apron, on the slip if the ferry carries road vehicles or railway cars, but otherwise part of the vessel. This is lifted to serve as a wave guard before the vessel departs, and is lowered at the terminus to meet a fixed ramp, which is a portion of road extending into the water.

As noted above, two of the world's largest ferry systems are located in the Strait of Georgia in the Canadian province of British Columbia, and Puget Sound in the U.S. state of Washington. BC Ferries of British Columbia has 34 vessels and serves 47 destinations. Washington State Ferries has 28 vessels and serves 20 destinations round Puget Sound. Another large ferry operator, in terms of passenger numbers, is the Sydney Ferries Corporation of Sydney, New South Wales, in Australia, which has 31 passenger (catamaran and other) ferries in Port Jackson (Sydney harbor) and carries some 18 million passengers per year. Metrolink Queensland operates 21 passenger ferries on behalf of the city council of Brisbane, the capital of Queensland, Australia: 12 of the vessels are of the single-hull type, and the other nine are CityCat (catamarans).

The cargo ship, otherwise known as the freighter, is any type of vessel dedicated to the carriage of cargo, goods, and materials from one port to another. Thousands of such vessels work the world's oceans, seas, larger lakes and major rivers and carry most of the world's international trade. In general, the cargo ship is designed specifically for its task, and is often equipped with cranes and/or other mechanisms to load and unload. Specialized cargo vessels include container ships and bulk carriers, and while tankers and super-tankers are technically cargo ships, they are generally considered to constitute a separate category of merchant vessel because of their size and specialized role.

While for practical purposes, cargo and freight can be considered as synonymous, in purist terms, "cargo" comprises goods carried aboard the ship for hire, and "freight" refers to the payment the ship owner or charterer receives for carrying the cargo.

In basic terms the modern shipping business is divided into two classes. First, there is the liner business in which container vessels (loaded with 20- or 40-ft [6.1- or 12.2-m] "cargo boxes" carrying general cargo) is a "common carriers" calling at a predetermined list of ports. The term "common carrier" refers to a regulated service in which any member of the public may book cargo for shipment, according to long-established international rules. Second, there is the tramp-tanker business in which, for the most part, a private arrangement is negotiated between the sender and receiver, and facilitated by the owner or operator of the relevant vessel, who offers his vessels for hire to carry bulk (dry or liquid) or break bulk (cargoes with individually handled pieces) to any suitable port in the world.

The larger types of cargo ship are generally operated by dedicated shipping lines, which are companies that specialize in the handling of cargo in general, while smaller vessels, such as coasters, are often owned by their operators.

There have been many types of celebrated cargo ship, but perhaps the single best-known type is the "Liberty" ship of World War II. Based largely on a British design, "Liberty ships" were built in large number by U.S. shipyards by assembling pre-fabricated sections made in many parts of the country. This process of making the parts of the ships simultaneously opened the way to

rapid assembly and completion of standardized vessels which met exact requirements and were simpler to maintain and repair than cargo vessels individually designed and built. The Liberty ships were assembled by builders in an average of six weeks but, in one record-breaking instance, in only a little more than four days. The availability of numbers of Liberty ships allowed the Allied powers to replace sunken cargo vessels at a rate greater than the German submarine arm could sink them, and the Liberty ship therefore made a huge contribution to the Allied war effort and eventual victory.

Another and more specialized type of cargo vessel is the lake freighter built for service on the Great Lakes in North America. These have a particular design and structure different from those of oceanic cargo vessels because of the difference in wave size and frequency on the Great Lakes, and some of these highly specialised vessels are so large that they cannot leave the Great Lakes because they are too big to fit into the locks of the joint U.S.-Canadian St Lawrence Seaway connecting the Great Lakes with the Atlantic Ocean.

Cargo ships are defined in part by their capacity, in part by their weight and in part by their size. This last is of more importance than might at first be thought, for it determines whether any given vessel can make use of the locks on important waterways such as the Panama and Suez Canals, and also the St Lawrence Seaway.

Some common definitions for modern ships include the Small Handy size carrier (20,000 to 28,000 tons deadweight); Handy size carrier (28,000 to 40,000 tons deadweight); Handymax carrier (40,000 to 50,000 tons deadweight); Seawaymax, the largest size which can traverse the St Lawrence Seaway; Aframax oil tanker (75,000 to 15,000 tons deadweight); Suezmax, the largest size which can traverse the Suez Canal; Panamax, the largest size which can traverse the Panama Canal and thus with a width of less than 105 ft 8 in (32.2 m); Capesize vessel, larger than the Panamax and Suezmax and which must traverse the Cape of Good Hope and Cape Horn in order to travel between oceans; Very Large Crude Carrier super-tanker (150,000 to 320,000 tons deadweight); and the Ultra Large Crude Carrier super-tanker (320,000 to 550,000 tons deadweight).

Container ships are cargo vessels designed and built specifically to carry all their load in truck-size containers. The first container ships were converted tankers, built up from surplus "T2" type tankers after World War II. The first of these conversions was the *Ideal-X* owned by Malcom McLean, and this carried 58 metal containers between Newark, New Jersey, and Houston, Texas, on the first container service in April, 1956. Modern container ships are all purpose-built, and are exceeded only by crude oil tankers as the biggest cargo vessels on the oceans.

The container ship is designed for minimum waste of space, and its capacity is calculated in TEUs (20-ft Equivalent Units). This is the maximum number of 20-ft (6.1-m) containers which the vessel in question

can accommodate. It is worth noting, though, that most containers today are typically of the 40-ft (12.2-m) type.

Above a certain size, container ships do not carry their own loading/unloading gear, and such vessels are therefore limited to services between ports equipped with the right type of loading and unloading gear. Smaller ships, with a capacity of up to 2,900 TEUs, are often equipped with their own cranes.

Colloquially known as the "box boat," the container ship carries most of the world's dry cargo (manufactured goods), while cargoes such as mineral ores, coal and grain are carried in bulk carriers with large conventional holds. The large main-line vessels ply the deep sea routes between major ports with their own onshore provision for the loading and unloading of containers, and containers are moved in smaller numbers, between their ports of origin or final destination by smaller "feeder" ships which carry their own loading/unloading equipment and work to and from the main hub ports. Most container ships are powered by diesel engines, and have a crew of between 20 and 40. The container ship is generally characterized by a single large accommodation block located well aft, straight above the engine room, in an arrangement that leaves the majority of the vessels and its decks free for the carriage of containers. Modern container ships carry up to 15,000 containers at any one time. The construction of large container ships, classifiable as those of more than 7,000 TEUs, is a specialised task, and the world's most important constructors of such vessels are the Odense Steel Shipyard of Denmark; Hyundai Heavy Industries, Samsung Heavy Industries and Daewoo Heavy Industries of South Korea; and Ishikawajima-Harima Heavy Industries and Mitsubishi Heavy Industries of Kure and Nagasaki respectively in Japan.

As of September 2006, when the new *Emma Mærsk* departed on her maiden voyage, a new standard was set in the container trade. When launched, this ship was the largest the largest container ship yet built at 170,974 gross tons, and, as of 2007 is the longest ship in use at an overall length of 1,302 ft 6 in (397.0 m). The largest ship ever built was the supertanker *Knock Nevis*, but now it serves as a floating storage and offloading unit. According to the Mærsk line,

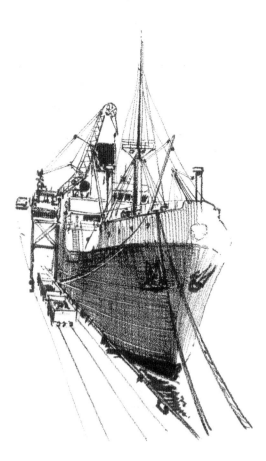

As can be imagined, this means that the total value of the cargo carried by this and comparable vessels can reach as much as US$300 million. At any one time there are between 5 and 6 million containers at sea somewhere in the world, and this represents huge risks.

Some of the risks are linked to the loading and unloading of the containers, and the carriage of so many containers by a single vessel requires ports which handle large container ships to have a sophisticated system of identifying and tracking containers so that they are not lost or misrouted. The containers are usually loaded and unloaded by a portainer and, as there must be as little vibration of the loaded container as possible, the operator has to be well-qualified and experienced to operate the equipment efficiently.

While port operations can be dangerous, the container ship faces other dangers at sea. Storms can cause the loss of containers, which may break free and be washed overboard, and high winds adversely affect the handling of these large vessels with containers packed high above the deck.

Cargo too large for containerization can be handled using flat racks, open-topped containers and platforms. There are also Ro-Ro container ships which make use of shore-based ramp systems for loading and unloading. Ro-Ro vessels are generally involved with shorter trade routes as they cannot carry the volume of containers typically embarked on container ships. As a result of its operational versatility and high speed, the Ro-Ro ship is often used in today's container market.

Economies of scale have dictated a steady growth in the size and payload of the container ship in

the *Emma Mærsk* is rated at 11,000 TEUs, a figure about 1,400 more than that any other ship currently afloat. In normal calculation, however, her cargo capacity is considerably greater, at 13,500 to 14,500 TEUs. The difference between the official and estimated number results from the fact that Mærsk calculates the cargo capacity of a container ship by using the number of containers with a weight of 14 tons that can be carried on a vessel, and for the *Emma Mærsk* this is 11,000. Other companies calculate the cargo capacity of a ship according to the maximum number of containers that can be put on the ship, independent of the weight of the containers. This number is always greater than the number calculated by the Mærsk company.

order to introduce major economy of scale. There are limits on the growth, however, one constraint being that which defines the Suezmax standard for the largest ship theoretically able to pass along the Suez Canal. This limits the load to 14,000 TEUs, and such a vessel would displace no more than 137,000 tons deadweight, be no more than 1,312 ft 4 in (400.0 m) in length, 164 ft (50 m) in width and 49 ft 2 in (15.0 m) in draft. Such a ship would require more than 114,000 hp (85000 kW) to make 25.5 kt. This specification is met by the *Emma Mærsk*.

Beyond the Suezmax limit there are the Malaccamax limits related to the Strait of Malacca between Malaysia and the Indonesian island of Sumatra. One of the busiest waterways in the world, this limits the payload to 18,000 TEUs in a vessel displacing no more 200,000 tons deadweight with dimensions no more than 1,542 ft (470 m) in length, 196 ft 10 in (60 m) in width and 52 ft 6 in (16 m) in draft. Such a vessel would need more than 134,120 hp (100,000 kW) for 25.5 kt. Such is likely to remain the limit unless a major restructuring of world container trade routes is introduced.

Another problem with ships of so great a size was the power needed, preferably in large single diesel engines, which led to the development of the MAN B&W K108ME-C engine, which could be produced to yield a maximum of 136,000 hp (101400 kW). A related problem was the creation of a propeller to handle and make effective use of such power. This demands a very carefully balanced unit with a diameter of some 32 ft 10 in (10,0 m) and weight of about 130 tons. Such a propeller has been made for the *Emma Mærsk*. Another constraint on the building of still larger ships is the acutely limited numbers of hub ports able to accommodate such vessels.

The tanker is a ship designed

for the bulk transport of liquids. Tankers can range in size from a few hundreds of tons (intended primarily to service small harbors and coastal settlements), to several hundred thousands of tons, intended for long-distance deliveries. Tankers carry a wide range of products including hydrocarbons such as oil, liquefied petroleum gas and liquefied natural gas, chemicals such as ammonia and chlorine, fresh water, and even wine. As different products require specific types of handling and movement, there have inevitably appeared specialized types of tanker such as chemical tankers and oil tankers.

Within the oil tanker category, the super-tanker was created to deliver oil from the Middle East around the Cape of Good Hope to destinations in Europe and the Americas. This category of vessel includes the world's largest ship, the *Knock Nevis*. This Norwegian-owned super-tanker, formerly known as the *Seawise Giant*, *Happy Giant* and *Jahre Viking* is 1,502 ft 8 in (458.0 m) long and 226 ft 4 in (69.0 m) wide, and was built in Japan between 1979 and 1981. The vessel was damaged during the Iran-Iraq War of the 1980s, refloated in 1991, and repaired at Dubai to become an immobile offshore platform for the oil industry. The *Knock Nevis* has a deadweight of 555,834 tons and a displacement of 637,711 tons when carrying nearly 4.1 million barrels (650,000 m³) of oil, at which load the vessel draws 80 ft 8.5 in (24.6 m). This draft prevented the ship from passing along the English Channel, let alone the Suez and Panama Canals.

Together with overland pipelines, super-tankers are the only means available for the movement of very large quantities of oil, but they can threaten major ecological disaster when something goes wrong in coastal regions, as happened when tankers such as the *Exxon Valdez, Braer,*

Prestige, Torrey Canyon and *Erika* went aground or were wrecked.

Like container ships, tankers are classified according to their payload, in this case liquid rather than loaded metal containers. The origins of this classification system can be found in 1954, when, for financial reasons, the Shell Oil Company, with the aid of the London Tanker Brokers' Panel, developed the Average Freight Rate Assessment (AFRA) system. This allowed tankers to be grouped in different sizes, which were initially GP (general-purpose) tankers for vessels of less than 25,000 tons deadweight tons, MR (medium-range) tankers for ships between 25,000 and 45,000 tons deadweight, and LR (large-range) for what were then the largest vessels of more than 45,000 tons deadweight.

During and after the 1970s, tankers became ever larger and the list of categories was extended to include the greater sizes: thus vessels between 10,000 and 24,999 tons deadweight are GP tankers, between 25,000 and 44,999 tons deadweight MR tankers, between 45,000 and 79,999 tons deadweight are LR1 (Large Range 1) tankers, between 80,000 and 159,999 tons deadweight are LR2 (Large Range 2) tankers, between 160,000 and 319,999 tons deadweight are VLCC (Very Large Crude Carrier) tankers, and between 320,000 and 549,999 tons deadweight are ULCC (Ultra Large Crude Carrier) tankers.

Another system classifies vessels by the following arrangement: those between 10,000 and 60,000 tons deadweight are Product tankers; between 60,000 and 80,000 tons deadweight, Panamax tankers; between 80,000 and 120,000 tons; deadweight, Aframax tankers, between 120,000 and 200,000 tons; deadweight, Suezmax tankers, between 200,000 and 315,000 tons; deadweight, VLCC tankers, and between 320,000 and 550,000 tons deadweight, ULCC tankers.

The unofficial term "super-tanker" is generally applied to the world's largest tankers, those of more than 250,000 tons deadweight and thus able to carry between 2 and 3 million barrels of oil. In practice the super-tanker is used almost exclusively for the transport of crude oil.

Primitive Paddle Boats (1472)

Man's first attempts to propel a boat were based on the pole, paddle and oar. Then the sail was invented, and the size of craft could be increased. But sailing depends on the presence of wind, and often its strength and direction are inconvenient. Thought thus turned to propulsion not reliant on the wind: the paddle wheel. It remains uncertain whether the paddle wheel was developed from paddling, or from the use of wheels given greater "bite" in the water by blades.

The means by which the paddles were first turned remains unknown. The first paddle-wheel apparatus was probably driven by human muscles, and in its initial form was probably a smooth, straight pole extending outside each side of the boat and carrying two radial paddle wheels. The wheels probably each comprised two poles tied at right angles at their middles, where they were fastened to

the axle ends with planks or strips of bark attached at the extremities of the radial poles as the blades. The axle was probably positioned by pairs of pins in the gunwales, and a rope was passed twice round the centre of the axle and its ends tied together; hauling on this rope then turned the axle.

Two of the earliest records of a paddle-wheel vessel are to be found in a 1472 book, the *De Re Militari* of Robertus Valturius. One boat had five pairs of paddle wheels and the other, just one. The installation of two or more wheels in tandem is inefficient, with all of the wheels but the forward unit ineffective. But late in the fifteenth century the wheels were so limited that serious degradation was not likely. The wheels each had four blades, and revolved by cranks on their axles, the cranks of the 10-wheeled boat being connected by a rope to give uniform action.

Valturius' two types of man-powered paddle-wheel boats.

Barque à roues

The paddle-wheel boat was developed in the Far East, probably before its appearance in Europe. In a paper read at the Society of Arts in April 1858, a barrister fascinated by early mechanical appliances, John McGregor, said that an old work on China contained a sketch of a vessel powered by two sets of paddle wheels, used perhaps in the seventh century. In the *Memoires* of the Jesuit Fathers at Peking, published in Paris in 1782, there appears the description of *barque à roues* (wheeled boat) with a length of 42 ft (12.8 m) and beam of 13 ft (4.0 m). The paddle wheels were located with their upper parts in sturdy boxes outboard of the gunwales, and from the axle or centre of the wheels "any number of spokes radiate which act like teeth for the wheels. They enter the water to the depth of a foot. A number of men make the wheels turn round." Other features included a tall stern from which extended the steering oar, a short mast above the bow section, and a propulsion compartment covered by an awning or planked roof to keep the sun and rain off the propulsion crew. These men were also soldiers, and emerged from the compartment after the leather-covered side boards, painted with tiger heads. The boxes outboard of the gunwale served as buffers to protect the otherwise vulnerable paddle wheels as the boat drew alongside its target.

The authors of the *Memoires* recommended that the French royal authorities should consider their report with a view to adopting or developing the basic concept for French warships. The authors added their opinion that even if the extra speed generated by the paddle wheels was only very slight, it might nonetheless prove useful in extricating a vessel, otherwise limited to the thrust of its sails, from a dangerous situation. This seems highly unlikely, for the paddle wheels would have been too vulnerable to broad-side cannon fire or heavy weather to have offered any significant advantage.

Whatever the practicality of the system, it indicates that the use of paddle wheels was not just a Western concept, but had been elevated to a limited utility by the Chinese, probably for river use.

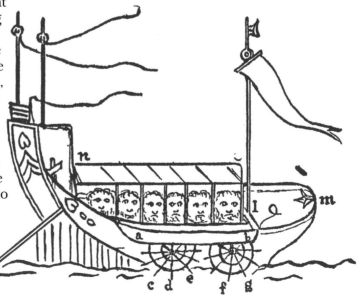

The Chinese barque à roues as described by French Jesuits in China during 1782.

Pyroscaphe (1783)

An effective source of mechanical power became available only in the last quarter of the eighteenth century in the form of the steam engine, which became a prime mover for river, coastal and maritime vessels. The first vessel to make successful use of the new form of motive power was a French paddle-wheel boat, the *Pyroscaphe* ("fire vessel") designed by the Marquis Claude de Jouffroy d'Abbans. After an unsuccessful experimental boat in June 1783, at Ecully, the marquis completed the *Pyroscaphe* with a steam engine driving a pair of 13.1-ft (4-m) diameter eight-paddle side wheels. The horizontal double-action engine was devised and made by the firm of Frères Jean et Compagnie in Lyons. On July 15th, the *Pyroscaphe* steamed up the Saône river against the current for 15 minutes before the engine failed.

Jouffroy's application for a 15-year patent to build steam boats in France was then rejected. Revolution and war next intervened, and Jouffroy built his second vessel, the *Charles-Philippe*, only in 1816 and thus well after the introduction of steam power in other countries.

The Pyroscaphe under way on a French river.

Pyroscaphe

Type:	steam-powered paddle-wheel boat
Tonnage:	163 tons
Dimensions:	length 140 ft (42.7 m); beam 14 ft (4.25 m)
Propulsion:	one horizontal double-acting steam engine
Complement:	not available

Charlotte Dundas (1801)

The first steam-powered vessel to enter commercial service was the Scottish *Charlotte Dundas*. In 1801 Lord Dundas approached Symington for an engine for the Forth & Clyde Canal Company, and Symington responded with an engine whose piston rod was attached by a connecting rod to a crank on the paddle shaft. This proved very effective, and became standard for paddle wheel shafts. Fitted with such an engine, the wooden tug *Charlotte Dundas* (named for the lord's daughter) in March 1802 towed two 70-ton barges 19.5 miles (31.5 km) in six hours against a strong headwind.

So impressed was the Duke of Bridgewater that he ordered eight vessels for use on the canal. But the Duke's death soon after ended the project as other canal officials felt that the wash of steam tugs would erode the canal's banks. The *Charlotte Dundas* was left in a backwater until 1861, and was then broken up.

The Charlotte Dundas was the world's first steam-powered commercial vessel, and showed the way forward in the use of steam propulsion for waterborne service.

Charlotte Dundas

Type:	steam-powered tug
Tonnage:	not available
Dimensions:	length 56 ft (17.1 m); beam 18 ft (5.5 m); draft 8 ft (2.4 m)
Propulsion:	one Symington horizontal steam engine delivering about 10 hp (7.5 kW) to one recessed stern wheel for 3.5 kt
Complement:	not available

Comet (1812)

While the *Charlotte Dundas* of 1801 has the distinction of being the first steam-powered vessel designed and constructed anywhere in the world for planned commercial service, the vessel never earned its keep in such a task. Thus the distinction of being the first steam-powered vessel to have entered commercial service in Europe falls to the *Comet*,

Symington, who was responsible for the design and then supervised the construction of the *Charlotte Dundas*, and of Fulton. Bell first installed a steam engine in a boat in 1802, and as early as 1803 was attempting to persuade the Admiralty to consider the large-scale employment of steam propulsion in the warship fleet of the Royal Navy. After failing to

which emerged five years after the appearance of Robert Fulton's *North River Steam Boat*, later known as the *Clermont*, in the U.S.

A man with a lengthy interest in steam power for waterborne purposes, the Scottish engineer Henry Bell was familiar with the work of William

secure any significant interest from the British naval authorities, Bell corresponded with Fulton, and then ordered the *Comet* from a Glasgow firm of shipbuilders on the lower reaches of the River Clyde, John Wood & Company. This vessel was to be completed with an engine of

Bell's own design and manufactured by another Glasgow company, John Robertson, with a boiler built by David Napier.

Completed on the basis of a wooden hull, the *Comet* was built in 1812 with four paddle wheels on two shafts, but this configuration was found to be completely inefficient as the two after wheels turned in the turbulent water streaming aft from the two forward wheels and therefore failed to provide any real boost in propulsive effort. One pair of wheels was therefore removed, saving weight and complexity, allowing the power of the engine to be used more efficiently, and suffering no degradation in performance. A notably unusual feature of the *Comet* was the single tall funnel, which was strong enough to double as a mast.

After trials in August 1812, the *Comet* entered commercial service on the ferry route along the Clyde between Glasgow on the northern bank and Greenock farther downstream, but did not prove successful in this task. Far greater success attended the vessel's subsequent tour of Scotland, which was specifically intended to create and increase the level of interest in the use of steam-powered vessels for commercial purposes. Largely as a result of the *Comet*'s efforts, by 1815 there were 10 steam-powered vessels in operation on the Clyde.

In 1816 the *Comet* herself was based in the Firth of Forth, on the other side of Scotland, and she was later put into service between Glasgow and the West Highlands. On December 13, 1820, while en route to Fort William, she ran aground at Craignish Point.

The *Comet*'s vertical single-cylinder engine is preserved at the Science Museum in London.

Comet

Type:	steam-powered paddle-wheel boat
Tonnage:	25 gross registered tons
Dimensions:	43 ft 6 (13.25 m); beam 11 ft 4 in (3.45 m); draft 5 ft 6 in (1.7 m)
Propulsion:	one single-cylinder double-acting jet condensing steam engine delivering some 4 hp (3 kW) to two side paddle wheels for 6 kt
Complement:	not available

Stockholmshaxan (1816)

The *Stockholmshaxan* ("witch of Stockholm") was produced in 1816 as a conversion of a sailing sloop. The first steam-powered vessel to be produced in Sweden, she was also notable for the fact that she was driven by a propeller rather than the paddle-wheel arrangement that was otherwise standard at this time.

The iron works created at Bergsund in Sweden by Thomas Lewis, an expatriate Scotsman, in the first decade of the nineteenth century, built the first Watt steam engine made in Sweden and also a large sheet rolling mill, both designed by another expatriate. Samuel Owen had been born in the Shropshire village of Northon in 1774, and at the age of 20 was employed as a pattern maker in the Boulton & Watt works at Soho near Birmingham. Here Owen struck up a friendship with Abraham Storey, who taught Owen the rudiments of the steam engine and its workings. Four years later Owen moved to another steam engine manufacturing firm, Fenton, Murray & Wood. In 1804 the Swedish Baron A. N. Edelcrantz arrived in England to buy four Watt steam engines, three of which he ordered from Owen's employer. The company then suggested that Owen travel to Sweden to assemble the engines. Owen arrived in Sweden during 1804, and settled in that country after a second visit in 1806, the year in which he was appointed manager at the Bergsund works. Owen soon proved his capabilities as an engineer and, after just 30 months at Bergsund, laid the foundations of his own engineering works at Kungsholmen in Stockholm. From a small start, Owen rapidly created a flourishing and very influential business which could soon

A funnel as tall as this was required to create a good up-draft for the fire in the boiler room.

draw on the services of its own hearth and puddling furnace with a blooming hammer for making wrought iron blooms and large forgings, a rolling mill for sheets and plates, and a steam-driven helve hammer for bar iron.

At a tangent, but not altogether removed from his primary sphere of endeavour, Owen established a ship-building yard, where he created the *Stockholmshaxan* as the first Swedish steamer. The *Stockholmshaxan* was adapted from a two-masted sloop and, given its weight, the rudimentary steam engine with a single cylinder, fabricated from wrought and cast iron, the engine was installed in the centre of the vessel and characterized by a notably tall funnel. As noted above, one of the key features of the vessel was its propulsion by a propeller. This was a simple unit with four wooden blades, and was fitted into a cast iron frame. The technical success of the little steamer in the Stockholm area brought welcome attention and sales to Owen's engineering works and ship-building yard.

Owen's construction in 1817 of the paddle steamer *Amphitrite* in the same yard attests to this. It was also a technical success, and operated the regular passenger route linking Stockholm with Uppsala and Vasteras along inland waterways.

Through this and other steamers of later construction, Sweden became one of the European pioneers in the application of steam propulsion to ships for maritime as well as inland applications. The Kungsholmen engineering works fulfilled a great number of orders during the 33 years in which it remained in existence. Among its products were 60 steam engines, of which about half were installed in ships. Some of the engines were also exported to countries such as Brazil and Russia.

An immensely sturdy and notably large beam engine of Owen design and manufacture was used to power the drainage pumps at the Hoganas coal mines in southern Sweden from 1832 to 1903, and it is now on display at the Technical Museum in Stockholm. The Owen Company also built more than 1,000 threshing machines, many other kinds of mechanical contrivances of which a substantial proportion was exported, and made several rolling mills for Swedish iron works.

Owen was also interested in powered land vehicles, and in 1819 received a 30-year exclusive right from the Crown to develop steam-powered road vehicles and sleighs. Owen also started to make a steam-powered car, but did not complete it. Despite his successes, Owen started to lose money, and in 1843 he was compelled to close the engineering works, and became bankrupt, thereafter working as a consulting engineer.

Stockholmshaxan

Type:	steam-powered sloop conversion
Tonnage:	not available
Dimensions:	length 50 ft 4 in (15.3 m); beam 14 ft 6 in (4.4 m); draft 6 ft (1.8 m)
Propulsion:	one single-cylinder steam engine delivering 4.5 hp (1.4 kW) to one propeller for 2.6 kt under steam
Complement:	4

Sirius (1837)

Built for the St George Steam Packet Company (later the City of Cork Steam Packet Company) by Robert Menzies and Son, of Leith on the Firth of Forth in Scotland, the *Sirius* is celebrated as the first ship to cross the Atlantic under sustained steam power. Among the ship's features, the most important was the use of surface condensers of the type patented by Samuel Hall in 1834. This type of condenser meant that the boilers did not become caked with salt from the seawater used to cool the steam. The vessel was scheduled for service on the route linking Cork and London.

In 1836 the British Queen Steam Navigation Company had been formed for the specific task of undertaking transatlantic services under steam power, and in the same year had contracted with Messrs Curling and Young of Blackwall, London, for the construction of a steam ship to carry the name *British Queen*. However, the bankruptcy of Messrs Claude Girdwood and Company of Glasgow, which had received the order for the engines, occasioned considerable delay in the completion of the *British Queen*. Seeing and seizing the opportunity, a group of entrepreneurs in Bristol created the Great Western Steamship Company to build and operate the *Great Western*, which they determined to get into service before the completion of the delayed *British Queen*. To save the honor and commercial viability of their own company, the directors of the British Queen Steam Navigation Company hired the *Sirius* from the St George Steam Packet Company to make the first steam-powered transatlantic voyage.

Commanded by Lieutenant Richard Roberts, of the Royal Navy, the *Sirius* left London on March 28, 1838, loaded coal in Cork and then departed across the Atlantic on April 4. The ship reached New York on April 22 after a passage of 18 days and 10 hours with an average speed of 6.7 kt. The *Great Western* arrived on the following day after crossing at an average speed of 8.8 kt.

It was known that the *Sirius* was too small for regular service across the Atlantic, and even before she started on her first voyage it had been announced that the ship would undertake only two transatlantic voyages. Like those of all other vessels of the period, the engines were of the side-lever type with cylinders characterized by a diameter of 5 ft (1.52 m) and a stroke of 6 ft (1.83 m), and the engines drove two side paddles with a diameter of 24 ft (7.3 m). The wooden-hulled vessel had one funnel and two masts, with three square sails on the foremast and fore-and-aft sails on the after mast.

The *Sirius* departed from East Lane Stairs in London carrying only passengers. Steaming down the Thames, she overtook the *Great Western* on her trials, and thereafter drew ahead of her. Shortly after 10 o'clock on the morning of April 4 the *Sirius* left Cork, and on April 8 was reported in Liverpool by the newly arrived Watt, as having been in 51° N and 12° W three days earlier, steaming through a westerly gale. During the voyage there was a measure of difficulty, and Roberts reported that it was only as a result of "stern discipline and the persuasive arguments of loaded firearms" that the crew was restored to order after becoming demoralized by continual head-winds and the men's concern that it was mad to press on in so small a vessel. There were 94 passengers on board, of whom 30 were in the state-cabin, 29 in the fore-cabin, and 35 in steerage.

The ship's engines burned 24 tons of coal per day, in which an average of 161 miles (259 km) was achieved. The arrival of the *Sirius* in New York met with great excitement, which was only heightened by the news that the *Great Western*, at this time the largest steam ship to have reached North America, had been sighted in the approaches to the port. Delayed by the need for repairs after a fire as the ship steamed from London to Bristol, the *Great Western* had left Bristol three days after the departure of the *Sirius* from Cork, and had made a somewhat faster crossing to arrive only hours later than the smaller ship.

The *Sirius* departed New York again on May 1 and reached Falmouth on the south coast of England on May 18. After a second return voyage across the Atlantic, in July of the same year, the *Sirius* returned to her original type of short crossings. On January 29, 1847, while bound from Glasgow for Cork under Captain Moffett, she became a total loss in Ballycotton Bay, with the loss of 19 of her 90 passengers and crew.

Intended only for short crossings, the Sirius completed the first transatlantic crossing under steam.

Sirius

Type:	paddle wheel steam ship
Tonnage:	703 gross registered tons
Dimensions:	208 ft (63.4 m); beam 25 ft 8 in (7.8 m) or 47 ft 3 in (14.4 m) over the paddle wheels; draft 15 ft (4.6 m)
Propulsion:	two side-lever steam engines delivering 320 hp (239 kW) to two paddle wheels for 9 kt
Complement:	40 or more passengers and 35 crew

Great Britain (1843)

The *Great Britain* was the second of three ships designed by Isambard Kingdom Brunel: she was preceded by the *Great Western* and succeeded by the *Great Eastern*. For several reasons the *Great Britain* was a major turning point in ship design and construction. By a considerable margin, she was the largest ship of her day (33% longer than the largest

July 19, 1843 by Prince Albert, the husband of Queen Victoria.

The ship which became the *Great Britain* was in fact designed as something altogether different: a companion for the *Great Western*, and thus a wooden-hulled paddle steamer which was to

have carried the name *City of New York*. Always wanting to improve on his own work, Brunel soon decided that great enhancements were possible (especially in the coal bunkerage) through the use of a larger hull. Brunel then assessed the sea-keeping qualities of the iron-hulled short sea paddle steamer *Rainbow*, and decided that iron rather than wood would be a superior material for the larger hull.

ship serving with the Royal Navy); the first sea-going ship built of iron; and the first ocean-going ship with propeller rather than paddle-wheel propulsion. The *Great Britain* was not a financial success for her builder, the Great Western Steamship Company of Bristol in the west of England, but many of the vessel's innovative features became standard in the years after the ship's launch on

The Great Western Steam-ship Company could find no taker for the new ship, and therefore decided to build the vessel itself. The size of the *Great Britain* demanded the construction of a dry dock, known as the Great Western Dock (later the Wapping Dock). The company also decided to build the engines for the huge paddle wheels intended for

of a drive chain, drove the propeller at 53 revolutions per minute. The propeller was fabricated of iron, had a diameter of 15 ft 6 in (4.72 m), and turned the scales at more than 3 tons. In all, the engines and boilers massed 520 tons of iron, and 1,040 tons of the same material were used for the hull. The engines exhausted via a single funnel, and also rising above the deck were six masts: five of these were rigged with fore-and-aft sails, while the one second from the bow carried square sails. The hull was divided into six compartments by watertight bulkheads, the first time this safety feature had been incorporated in any ship, and also

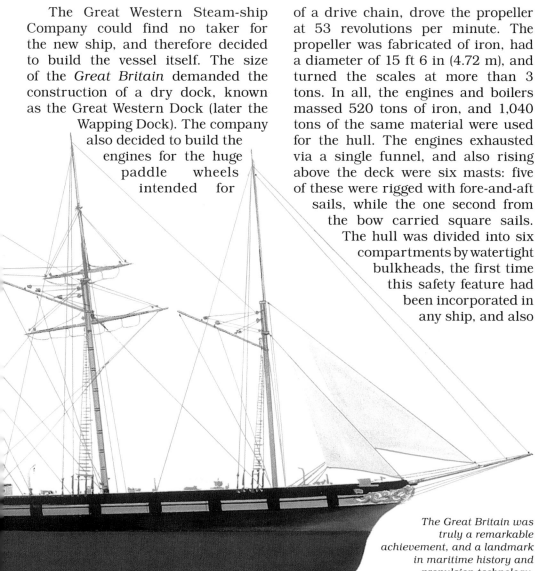

The Great Britain was truly a remarkable achievement, and a landmark in maritime history and propulsion technology.

the ship, which was currently known as the *Mammoth*. In 1840 Brunel further reassessed his design and decided to change the propulsion to a single large propeller. The revised propulsion configuration also entailed a major revision of the engine, which was completed with four cylinders, each with a diameter of 88 in (2.24 m). The engine turned at 18 revolutions per minute and, by means

had bilge keels. The *Great Britain's* accommodation included 26 single and 113 double rooms; there were also holds for 1,000 tons of cargo and bunkers for 1,000 tons of coal.

It was only after the ship had taken to the water that it was discovered that the locks of Bristol's Floating Harbor were too narrow for the *Great Britain* to traverse, so the company had to widen the locks. The *Great*

Great Britain *continued*

Britain embarked on her sea trials on December 13, 1844, and in the course of these trials recorded a speed of 11 kt. After a six-month stop in London, where she was visited by many thousands of people including Queen Victoria, the *Great Britain* departed in June 1845 to Liverpool and loaded 60 first-class passengers, a full complement of steerage-class passengers and 600 tons of cargo for New York. She sailed on July 26 with the veteran Captain James Hoskens in command, and reached New York on August 10 after a crossing of 14 days and 21 hours. Her return to Bristol took about the same time.

During her second voyage, the *Great Britain* lost most of the blades off her propeller, and a new four-blade propeller was then fitted. Propeller blades fell off and a new four-bladed screw had to be fitted. The engine was also revised by Maudslay Sons and Field, resulting in an increase of power from 686 to 1,663 hp (511 to 1240 kW). The following voyages were beset by a number of technical problems, large and small, but while outward bound with 180 passengers from Liverpool on her fifth voyage, the *Great Britain* ran aground during September 1846 in Dundrum Bay south of Belfast Lough in the north of Ireland. No one was killed, but the ship remained aground until August 27, 1847, when she was freed with the aid of steam frigate HMS *Birkenhead*. Lacking the financial resources to pay for the repairs which were needed, the

Four images of the Great Britain awaiting careful restoration to her former glory as a fitting tribute to Isambard K. Brunel and British maritime history. Photos: John Batchelor.

Great Western Steamship Company put the ship on the market. Three years later, the ship was bought by Gibbs, Bright & Co.

Fitted with a new three-blade propeller driven by a two-cylinder engine via a simple gear drive, and the number of her masts reduced to four (square-rigged on the middle pair), the ship returned to the transatlantic run, but was switched to the Australian route after only one voyage. Departing Liverpool on August 21, 1852, with 650 passengers, the *Great Britain* reached Melbourne on November 1 of the same year after 82 days. The ship left Australia in January with 260 passengers and £550,000 in gold.

Once more revised, in this instance to a three-masted ship rug, the *Great Britain* was bought by the Liverpool & Australian Navigation Company, and sailed from Liverpool with more than 1,000 passengers. Except for service as a troop transport during the Crimean War (1855-56) and one voyage during the Indian Mutiny (1857), the ship remained in the Australian passenger trade until she was laid up in Birkenhead during February 1876. In the following year, the ship was bought by Antony Gibb, Sons and Co., for service on the bulk trade route between the UK and San Francisco after she had been stripped of her engines and had her hull sheathed in wood. On her third voyage out, on February 25, 1886, the *Great Britain* was forced back to Stanley, Falkland Islands, and there condemned. After 47 years as a coal and wool storage ship, the Falkland Islands Company moved her from Stanley to nearby Sparrow Cove, and abandoned her.

In 1967 a *Great Britain* Project Committee was formed to bring the ship back to Bristol for restoration to her original condition. In April 1970 the ship was towed from Stanley aboard a pontoon barge, reaching Bristol on July 19, the place and anniversary of her launch. The ship has since been restored, this including replicas of the original engines and boilers.

Great Britain

Type:	steam ship
Tonnage:	2,936 gross registered tons
Dimensions:	length 322 ft (98.1 m); beam 50 ft 6 in (15.4 m); draft 16 ft 4.9 m)
Propulsion:	one direct-acting steam engine delivering 686 ihp (511 kW) to one propeller for 11 kt
Complement:	260 passengers and crew

British Queen (1838)

Appropriately for a ship of this name, the *British Queen* was launched on the birthday of Queen Victoria in 1838, and first made the transatlantic crossing, from London to New York, during July 1839 under the command of Lieutenant Richard Roberts, who had earlier skippered the *Sirius*, which the British Queen Steam Navigation Company had chartered because of delays in the completion of the *British Queen*. At the time of her completion,

perfectly ignorant of Steam and Steam Vessels. I have made the passage from Portsmouth to New York shorter than ever performed, only 13 d. 11 h. from Pilot to Pilot. Let *Great Western* do that if she can, though she has ten hours' shorter distance to run. I sail at 1 p.m. this day with full cargo and every berth taken, and sincerely do I wish to make a short passage...I intend trying for some shore berth... but will not leave till I command the

the *British Queen* was the largest and fastest steam-powered ship anywhere in the world. Writing to a friend from New York on June 1, 1840, Roberts said, "I can only state there is not a faster seagoing vessel in the World, and time will tell. We have beat the *Great Western* every voyage this year and... last year; therefore whoever gave you the idea of our Speed and Power were

first iron vessel to steam across the Atlantic." This was not to be, for he was in command of the *President* when she departed New York with 136 passengers on March 12, 1841 and then disappeared without a trace.

The *President* was launched on December 7, 1839 from the same Thames yard, Messrs Curling and Young, which had built the *British*

Queen. The two ships were in effect sister vessels in terms of their appearance and general equipment, but the 1,840-ton *President* was 10 ft (3.05 m) shorter and 7 ft (2.13 m) narrower in the beam, and had slightly more powerful engines offering 540 hp (403 kW).

These two wooden-hulled, barque-rigged (fore-and-aft sails on all three masts, and also square sails on the fore mast) vessels were further characterized by their square sterns and carried a long white funnel with a black top. Characterized by a diameter of 30 ft 6 in and 31 ft (9.3 and 9.45 m) in the *British Queen* and *President* respectively, the paddles were placed almost amidships, with the funnel aft the paddle boxes, whose upper curves extended well above deck level. The two vessels had engines of the side-lever type, but while those of the *British Queen* were supplied by Napier from Clyde, those of the President were made by Fawcett and

Preston of Liverpool. Each vessel's engines, boilers, and water weighed 500 tons, each carried 750 tons, of coal, sufficient for 20 days of steaming; and the cargo capacities were 500 and 750 tons for the *British Queen* and *President.*

The *President* was built of oak planked with fir, and had a flush upper deck between the bow and stern, the latter decorated with the British and U.S. coats of arms, supported by a lion and an eagle. The *President*'s figurehead was a bust of George Washington and each of the paddle boxes was decorated with a five-point star. The first attempt to float the *President* was not a success as the attempt was made with an inadequate tide; the second attempt on the next day also failed, but on the third day, December 9, 1839, the ship floated and was towed out of the dock and down the Thames to Blackwall.

After the loss of the *President,* the British and American Steam Navigation Company sold the *British Queen* to a Belgian company and pulled out of the shipping business, leaving the *Great Western* in what was effectively the sole possession of the North Atlantic for the next few years.

British Queen

Type:	paddle wheel steam ship
Tonnage:	2,016 tons
Dimensions:	275 ft (83.8 m); beam 40 ft (12.2 m) or 64 ft (19.5 m) over the paddle boxes; draft not available
Propulsion:	side-lever steam engines delivering 500 hp (373 kW) to two paddle wheels
Complement:	not available

Robert F. Stockton (1839)

In 1837 the great Swedish-born but Britain-based engineer John Ericsson launched the small *Francis B. Ogden* in England as an experimental propeller-driven vessel. This little vessel performed moderately well, as had been expected, but despite the fact that the vessel had towed the Admiralty barge with the Lords of the Admiralty on board, on the Thames, the Admiralty was not impressed: a later American biographer of Ericsson claimed that the engineer's concepts were "so novel they confused the mind of the average Englishman"! Even so, Ericsson was awarded £4,000 of a £20,000 prize which had been put up by the Admiralty in an effort to kick-start the development of an effective means of propeller propulsion. Shortly after this, however, Ericsson met Lieutenant (later Captain) Robert F. Stockton of the U.S. Navy (who was visiting the UK in an effort to secure monetary backing for the Delaware and Raritan Canal, located in New Jersey and which the Stockton family owned) and Stockton asked Ericsson to design and build a second propeller-driven vessel, which was to be named after him.

The resulting steam tug was built by the John Laid company at Birkenhead on the southern side of the Mersey, and launched in 1838. The new vessel's machinery comprised a two-cylinder steam engine with direct drive of a two-propeller system patented by Ericsson and comprising, in its original form, one propeller on a solid shaft slipped inside a hollow outer shaft carrying another propeller that rotated in the opposite direction. This arrangement proved unwieldy, and one of the propellers was soon removed. During the trials of the *Robert F. Stockton*, the machinery proved notably capable and efficient.

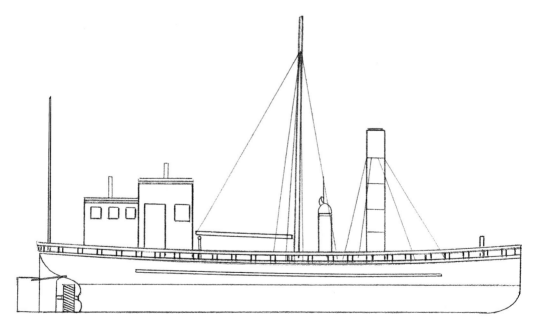

The Robert F. Stockton was a thoroughly practical steam-powered vessel.

Towing a 650-ton ship against a 2-kt current, the *Robert F. Stockton* covered 3.5 miles (5.6 km) in 40 minutes, or about 4.5 kt in real terms.

Temporarily rigged as a two-masted schooner for her transatlantic crossing, for which sufficient coal could not be carried, the *Robert F. Stockton* sailed to New York in April 1839, reaching the city after a 46-day passage. The *Robert F. Stockton* was rechristened as the *New Jersey* in 1840, and worked successfully on the Delaware and Raritan Canal as a tug for a period of some 30 years. Belatedly appreciating the importance of the tug's British-made machinery in of what would today be called technological history, the British Patent Office attempted to purchase the original machinery for its museum for exhibition alongside Henry Bell's steam engine for the pioneering *Comet* and other revolutionary inventions of British interest, but the *New Jersey* and its machinery were scrapped in 1871 and therefore lost to the world.

In 1839, it is worth noting, Stockton had persuaded Ericsson to quit his position as the superintending engineer of the Eastern Counties Railway and emigrate to the U.S., where Ericsson became a major figure in the development of American steam propulsion, iron for ship construction, armor protection, and ultimately the turreted gun for ship armament.

With propulsion by a propeller rather than paddle wheels, the Robert F. Stockton was better able to operate in choppy water.

Robert F. Stockton

Type:	steam tug
Tonnage:	32 tons
Dimensions:	length 70 ft (21.3 m); beam 10 ft (3,05 m); draft 6 ft 8 in (2.0 m)
Propulsion:	one direct-acting steam engine delivering 50 hp (37 kW) to two (later one) propellers for 6 kt
Complement:	5

Central America (1853)

Of classic paddle-wheel layout, with one paddle wheel on each beam in a substantial box for protection, the wooden-hulled vessel first known as the *George Law* was built in New York in 1853 by the William H. Webb yard specifically for service between New York and in Panama in connection aft sails on all three masts, and also with square sails on her foremast), carried many of those prospectors who had managed to "strike it rich" and were returning from the Californian gold fields, and also consignments of gold consigned to the New York money markets.

with the Californian gold rush which had started in 1849. At this Central American port, the gold prospector passengers had to leave the vessel and cross the Isthmus of Panama to the Pacific coast, where they boarded another ship bound for San Francisco in California. On her return passages to New York, the *George Law*, which was rigged as a barquentine (fore-and-

Shortly after being renamed the *Central America* in 1857, the vessel departed on her 44th passage from Panama to New York, via Havana, with passengers and some 5,000 lb (2268 kg) of gold, with an estimated value of US$1,6 million at the price of the time. Commanded by Captain William Lewis Herndon, the vessel was steaming north off the coast of South Carolina on September 8 when she was caught in a hurricane. The roughness of the attendant seas caused the hull to start leaking, but for three days the crew managed to keep the vessel both afloat and moving in mountainous seas and violent winds. Then the vessel's engines broke down, and on the following day the brig *Marine of Boston*, also badly mauled in the hurricane, took on board 148 of the *Central America*'s complement, including all of the women and children. During the night which followed, the *Central America* sank stern-first, taking with her the other 423 passengers and crew.

This was the worst maritime disaster which the U.S. had suffered up to this date. The cost was measured not just in lives but in the loss of the month's shipment of gold from the San Francisco mint to New York banks. This helped to spark the panic which crippled the U.S. economy in 1857.

For the next 130 years, the vessel lay in 8,000 ft (2440 m) of water off the South Carolina coast. In the 1980s, Tommy Thompson, Bob Evans and Barry Schatz formed the Columbus-America Discovery Group and, working from the research vessel *Arctic Discoverer*, located the wreck about 160 miles (260 km) east of Charleston, South Carolina. Using a remotely-operated vehicle, the group recovered an undisclosed quantity of gold, now valued at some US$1 billion, as well as several artifacts including two trunks full of clothing and other personal effects. In 1992, a Federal court of Appeals ruled that the group lacked clear title to the recovered treasure, in the face of claims by eight of the cargo's original insurers. Further work on the site was suspended pending the dispute's resolution.

The Central America was a barquentine-rigged side paddle-wheeler of very elegant lines.

Central America

Type:	paddle-wheel steam ship
Tonnage:	2,141 gross registered tons
Dimensions:	length 278 ft (84.7 m); beam 40 ft (12.2 m); draft 32 ft (9.75 m)
Propulsion:	steam engines powering two side paddle wheels
Complement:	545 passengers and crew

Great Eastern (1858)

Designed by Isambard K. Brunel, the *Great Eastern* was the single most stupendous vessel of the nineteenth century. The ship was designed to steam, without taking on more coal, between the UK and Australia or India, with up to 4,000 passengers and 6,000 tons of cargo, around the Cape of Good Hope. This notion appealed to the new Eastern Steam Navigation Company. Brunel collaborated in the design with John Scott Russell, a gifted but possibly unscrupulous marine engineer and shipbuilder. Russell's yard, on the Isle of Dogs in east London, built the vessel. Brunel made use of engineering concepts he had developed in bridge design and, as in his earlier ships, ensured that the ship had great longitudinal strength. The vessel was double-hulled, with cellular internal subdivisions along her length, and this undoubtedly saved her in 1862 when she struck an unmarked reef, ripping a gash 85 ft (25.9 m) long but 5 ft (1,5 m) high in her outer hull. Bulkheads created 10 watertight compartments.

The propulsion was based on a single propeller and two box-protected side paddle wheels. With diameters of 24 ft (7.3 m) and 56 ft (17.1 m), respectively, these were the largest yet made, and the propeller diameter was exceeded only late in the twentieth century. The layout was adopted to exploit current engine capabilities, but had the very useful extra benefit of improving agility. The propeller was powered by a four-cylinder horizontal direct-acting engine made by James Watt & Co., and the paddle wheels by a four-cylinder oscillating engine made by Russell. The vessel was also the first to incorporate a steering engine, and had six masts.

The vessel was built on an inclined slipway parallel with the Thames, for launch sideways. Russell's financial mismanagement almost killed the project, and the vessel's completion was finally made possible only by the direct supervision of Brunel, whose efforts are though to have caused his death in 1859.

The first but unsuccessful attempt

*Right:
Under steam and short sail, the Great Eastern in stormy seas.*

*Left:
The iconic image of Isambard Kingdom Brunel.*

Credit:
Brunel 200

to launch the vessel was made on November 3, 1857; it was January 31 of the following year before the *Great Eastern* finally took to the water. The fitting out of so large a vessel was a long process completed only in September 1859, with Brunel again supervising personally. Four days before Brunel's death, on September 5, the *Great Eastern* suffered a major explosion during her trials.

In June 1860 the *Great Eastern* entered service with a transatlantic voyage. The vessel made 10 such passenger voyages, suffering two non-fatal but costly accidents, and proved uneconomic. In 1864 the

Great Eastern was sold to the new Great Eastern Steamship Company and, after alterations including the removal of one set of boilers and one of her five funnels, began a second career as a cable-laying ship. The Telegraph Construction Company chartered the vessel, and on June 24, 1865, the *Great Eastern* lay off the south coast of Ireland with 7,000 tons of cable and a crew of 500. The European end of the cable was laid near Valentia in Ireland by HMS *Caroline*; the *Great Eastern* then sailed in company with HMS *Terrible* and HMS *Sphinx*. On August 2, at a point some three-quarters of the route to Newfoundland, the cable broke and the *Great Eastern* returned to port. The ship sailed once more on July 13, 1866, and the cable was completed 12 days later. By her career's end, the ship had laid five transatlantic cables, and one between Bombay and Suez.

In 1874 the vessel was sold to a French company for first-class passenger services between New York and France, but the project was abandoned after one voyage. Laid up in 1875-86, the *Great Eastern* was sold as an exhibition ship but broken up two years later.

Great Eastern

Type:	paddle-wheel and propeller steam ship
Tonnage:	18,915 gross registered tons
Dimensions:	length 692 ft (210.9 m); beam 82 ft 7 in (25.2 m) over the hull and 117 ft (35.7 m) over the paddle boxes; draft 30 ft (9.15 m)
Propulsion:	one horizontal-acting steam engine driving one propeller and two oscillating steam engines driving the paddle wheels, a total of 4,890 ihp (3646 kW) for 13 kt
Complement:	200 first-, 400 second- and 2,400 steerage-class passengers, plus crew

Coringa (1861)

Appearing in some records of the time as the *Cooringa*, the *Coringa* was designed for the carriage of passengers and cargo, and was built on the Clyde river in Glasgow at the yard of Alexander Stephens and Sons. Launched on January 24, 1861, the *Coringa* was of iron-hulled construction and fitted with a simple

The fore and main masts each carried two square sails (course and topsail), while the mizzen mast

steam engine designed and built by the same well-known company which built the ship. A particular feature of the design was the lifting propeller, an arrangement which was designed to reduce drag and thereby boost performance when the vessel was under sail, for which the vessel was barque-rigged.

carried only a fore-and-aft sail. There was also provision for the carriage of several jibs and staysails. The whole of the sailing rig was optimized for the exploitation of the generally strong winds available in the Indian Ocean and Bay of Bengal, which were the areas in which the *Coringa* was designed to serve. The arrangement therefore reduced the vessel's reliance on coal, and thereby effected significant improvement in her operating economics. The single funnel, which was tall and slender in the fashion of the time, and therefore stayed in two dimensions, was located just aft the main mast, and a pair of boats was carried in davits on the sides of the ship farther abaft the main mast.

The vessel had two decks and four holds, and was delivered to the Calcutta and Burmah Steam Navigation Company Ltd. in January 1861 for use on the trade routes extending to and from Madras on the south-

east coast of India. On October 28 of the following year, the *Coringa*'s owner was restyled as the British India Steam Navigation Company Ltd. In 1863 the vessel was driven ashore near Muscat after her anchors had dragged in a storm, but suffered only comparatively minor damage. Five years later, the vessel undertook her first voyage taking Moslems on the Haj pilgrimage to Mecca, sailing from Bombay in western India to Jeddah, the port of Mecca, on the western side of the Arabian peninsula.

In 1869 the *Coringa* was transferred to the Denny shipbuilding company in part exchange for a new ship, the *Abyssinia*. Denny rebuilt the vessel, reducing her to a two-masted configuration, and in 1872 sold her to the Clyde Shipping Company, which rechristened the vessel as the *Arklow*. The *Arklow* had only a comparatively short career, for she was lost on October 22, 1880 when she went aground on St Alban's Head, near Portland Bill in Dorset, on the south coast of England, while on passage from the Clyde to Southampton.

Coringa

Type:	steam ship
Tonnage:	765 gross registered tons
Dimensions:	199 ft 8 in (60.85 m); beam 27 ft 6 in (8.4 m); draft 15 ft 8 in (4.8 m)
Propulsion:	one Alexander Stephens and Sons two-cylinder simple steam engine delivering 150 hp (112 kW) or, from 1875, one D. & W. Henderson two-cylinder compound steam engine delivering 150 hp (112 kW) to one propeller for 10 kt
Complement:	not available

Republic (1865)

Built by John A. Robb of Baltimore, Maryland, the two-masted steamer *Tennessee* was launched on August 13, 1853. Installed after the launch by the machine works of Charles A. Reed & Sons, her vertical beam engine was powered by a steam cylinder with a diameter of greater than 6 ft (1.83 m) and a height of 9 ft (2.75 m), and drove two side paddle wheels with a diameter of 28 ft (8.53 m). The *Tennessee* began life with a trial voyage early in 1854 between Baltimore and Charleston, South Carolina, carrying freight and interested parties, before returning with 88 passengers. The vessel had been built for James Hooper specially for service in South Carolina and Maryland, but the U.S. economy slumped soon after the *Tennessee* had entered service, and Hooper tried to sell the vessel, but without success. In June 1855, therefore, he sent the vessel across the Atlantic in the hope of finding business, and on August 19 the *Tennessee* departed Le Havre with a useful cargo, but then suffered damage to one of her paddle wheels in a hurricane and on September 4 entered Halifax, Nova Scotia, for repairs and coal, reaching New York three days later.

Late in the year, the vessel was bought by S. de Agreda Jove & Co. for the first U.S. steamship service to South America but in October 1856 changed hands once more, being bought by Charles Morgan to carry to Nicaragua, where there was a civil war, mercenaries and gold prospectors, the latter en route to California. Nicaragua's ports were closed to U.S. ships late in 1856, and on her last voyage before this, the *Tennessee* was forced to put into Charleston with damage caused by a hurricane. With the insurrection in Nicaragua defeated, Morgan found another market in the Caribbean, where the *Tennessee* operated a service linking New Orleans and Vera Cruz in Mexico. In 1860 the vessel was sheathed with copper, and had her engines overhauled and her boilers replaced.

The whole appearance of the Republic was dominated by her paddle wheel boxes and funnel.

At the outbreak of the Civil War in 1861, the *Tennessee* was one of six Morgan ships seized by the Confederacy in New Orleans. Union ships were despatched to hunt down the *Tennessee* before she left for France to be outfitted as a warship. The ship was unable to slip out of New Orleans, however, and was seized when the Union took the city on April 28, 1862, soon being commissioned into the U.S. Navy. The *Tennessee* was armed and became Admiral David Farragut's flagship for the Union's Mississippi river campaign until mid-1863. The *Tennesse* was then reallocated to the blockade of the Confederacy's ports in the Gulf of Mexico. The vessel was also involved in the reduction of Fort Morgan within the Battle of Mobile Bay, and in September 1864 became the USS *Mobile*. In the following month, she was again caught in a hurricane near the mouth of the Rio Grande river, suffering hull damage. She reached New York before the end of the year, but in March 1865 surveyors reported the ship too severely damaged for economic repair.

The vessel was then sold to investors headed by Russell Sturgis, who had her repaired and refitted as the *Republic*. With the Civil War over, there was a great demand for a resumption of commercial shipping services, and the *Republic* was to serve on the route linking New York and New Orleans, after being chartered to William H. Robson. The *Republic* departed on her first such voyage on May 13, 1865. She sailed again from New York on June 15 and July 19. During July the H. B. Cromwell shipping line acquired the charter but left the *Republic* on the same profitable route. The vessel left New York on her fifth voyage to New Orleans on October 18, 1865. She passed Cape Hatteras on October 22, and off Savannah on the following day encountered the fourth hurricane of her career. The vessel was effectively lost when her engine broke down and her pumps failed two days later. During the afternoon of October 25 the crew and passengers abandoned ship onto four ship's boats and one raft. Some 66 persons were eventually rescued, but 14 of the 16 people on the raft died.

Early in the 1990s, Greg Stemm and John Morris of Odyssey Marine Exploration, in Florida, started to look for the wreck of the *Republic*, which had sunk with more than US$400,000 in gold coin on board. The company was successful in July 2003, and later recovered many artifacts and much coinage.

Treasure from the Republic. Courtesy: www.shipwreck.net

Republic

Type:	paddle wheel steam ship
Tonnage:	1,149 tons
Dimensions:	length 210 ft (64.0 m); beam 33 ft 11 in (10.3 m); draft not available
Propulsion:	one vertical beam steam engine driving two paddle wheels
Complement:	100 passengers, plus crew

Servia (1881)

Many have claimed that the *Servia*, launched in 1881, was in effect the world's first "superliner," a term not coined until 1929. The vessel was indeed a major and remarkable advance in the science of naval architecture and the art of translating the theoretical science into a real and useful article of commercial use. Coming just 41 years after the *Britannia*, which was completed in 1840 for the Cunard line, more formally known as the British and North American Royal Mail Steam Packet Company, the *Servia* was a huge advance in technical and performance terms, but reflected her owner's dedication to its original concept of operating scheduled services across the North Atlantic between the UK and U.S. with

a fleet of ships offering comparable performance and reliability.

Able to carry 115 passengers as well as a modest cargo load, the 1,156-ton *Britannia* was propelled through the water by side paddle wheels at a maximum speed of 8.5 kt, and also had three masts. The *Servia* was built by the Glasgow yard of J. & G. Thompson Ltd,, and recorded a speed of 17.8 kt on her trials. The ship could carry 450 first- and 600 third-class passengers, and her main dining saloon, which was 74 ft (22.6 m) long and 49 ft (13.7 m) wide, could accommodate 350 passengers at each sitting.

Built of metal and notable for her excellent, indeed elegant, lines, the *Servia* was propelled through the water by a single propeller driven

The servia had a "turtle back" over the poop deck to make her more seaworthy.

by a compound steam engine, which exhausted its smoke and spent gases by means of two slightly raked funnels, and in service could maintain 17 kt. The vessel also carried three masts for a full set of square sails (though normally restricted to a course, topsail, and topgallant sail on the fore mast and a topsail and topgallant sail on the main mast), fore-and-aft sails on each mast and a full suit of headsails. The two funnels were widely spaced between the fore and main masts.

Most significantly of all, though, were the facts that the *Servia* was the first of the Cunard line's ships to be constructed of steel, and also the "Cunarder" to be lighted entirely by electricity. There can be no doubt that the *Servia* represented the emergence of a new generation of Cunard liners.

Even with her sails set, the *Servia* looked like a steam ship with supplementary sails rather than a sailing ship into which a steam propulsion arrangement had been shoe-horned. Characteristic features of the vessel's elegant appearance were her straight stem and her nicely contoured and graceful rounded (counter) stern. Another comparatively novel feature, and quite new for the period, was the "turtle-back" sterncastle, whose rounded upper lines, without any obstructions, made it easy for water to slide off it. Located ahead of the fore funnel, the bridge was low and very inconspicuous, and along each beam, from a point abreast the fore mast to the mizzen mast, were six white-painted life boats in davits.

The sailing of the vessel and the care of her passengers were the responsibility of a crew totalling 200 officers and men. The *Servia's* passenger accommodations, in the very widest sense of the word, were considerably more elegant than those which had characterized earlier "Cunarders," and included no fewer than 202 first-class passenger cabins as well as a saloon. The best staterooms, or rather suites, included a double bed, a dressing area, and one or more wardrobes.

The *Servia* embarked on her commercial career with a maiden voyage from Liverpool to New York starting on November 26, 1881, and the vessel quickly gained plaudits for her comfort, speed and good seakeeping qualities. However, this superb ship remained commercially viable on the prestigious North Atlantic service for only 20 years, in the course of which the *Servia* completed 171 round-trips between the UK and U.S. Appearing very old-fashioned with her three masts in the first years of the twentieth century, the vessel was then retired from Cunard service and sold. Her new owner was Thomas W. Ward, whose sole interest in the vessels was her materials, and the *Servia* was towed to Preston, where she was dismantled for scrap.

Servia

Type:	transatlantic passenger steam ship
Tonnage:	7,391 gross registered tons
Dimensions:	length 532 ft (162.2 m); beam 52 ft (15.8 m); draft not available
Propulsion:	one compound steam engine driving one propeller
Complement:	1,050 passengers and 200 crew

Glückauf (1886)

In the last quarter of the nineteenth century, petroleum products started to become an increasingly important part of the economy of the Western nations. Sources of oil were generally far removed from the facilities at which they could be refined and the markets which they served created the need for a new class of vessel, the tanker or liquid bulk carrier. Up to 1888 the agent in Germany for the Standard Oil Company was Heinrich Riedmann of Bremen, who in 1884 arranged for the conversion of the 1,871-ton sailing vessel *Andromeda* into a tanker by building 72 steel tanks into the vessel:

In 1886 the naval architect Colonel Henry Swan was a director of Armstrong Mitchell & Co. on Wallsend on the Tyne river in north-eastern England. This shipbuilder had constructed for Nobel and other organizations several tankers for service in the Caspian Sea, while Swan, who had become fascinated by the problems of bulk oil carriage, had developed a design including the best features of existing vessels. In this design the oil was carried right out to the shell, and provision was incorporated for the taking on of water ballast for return voyages. Other

two rows of tanks were fitted in each of the holds, orlop deck and between deck, and there was an expansion tank on each deck. The *Andromeda* proved very successful and remained in service until February 1919 when, renamed the *Helene*, she was run down and sunk by a steamer.

notable features were a cofferdam at each end of the tank section, operation of all the cargo valves from the main deck, the location of the cargo main right through the tanks just above the floor level, vapor lines at the top of each expansion tank, pumps for loading and discharging the oil below main deck level, and counter-sunk riveting in the construction of the oil-tight bulkheads.

The Armstrong yard began building Swan's vessel as a private venture before Riedmann saw and bought her for service as the *Glückauf* ("good luck"), and at the same time contracted with the yard for the building of several similar vessels. The *Glückauf* is now generally considered to have been the true ancestor of the modern tanker. The vessel was considered largely experimental but in 1891, after five years in service, the vessel was

Designed and built in the UK, the Glückauf was bought by a German operator before completion, and is of considerable historical importance as the world's first "true" oil tanker.

surveyed and found to need only minor additions to the structure, notably the stiffening of some of the stringers.

Thus the *Glückauf*'s first difficulties were not mechanical but human, for when on her maiden voyage she reached Philadelphia to load 2,880 tons of petroleum products for delivery to Germany, there was a violent protest from American stevedores after they learned that their services were not needed. Other protests came from barrel and tinplate manufacturers, who were concerned about job security. It was six or seven weeks before two coal barges could be brought secretly from Halifax, Nova Scotia, to top up her bunkers. The *Glückauf* then proceeded to Halifax to complete bunkering for the return voyage. After discharging her cargo, the vessel returned to the Tyne for the extension of her spar deck forward to the fore mast, so increasing the bunker space and enabling her to take on enough fuel for the return voyage.

The *Glückauf* was lost in 1893 when she ran aground during a storm on Fire Island, off Long Island, New York. The Standard Oil Co. formed a British subsidiary in 1888 as the Anglo-American Oil Company. Before this the company had chartered vessels, but then began to buy tankers from other companies, in particular the Riedmann fleet, which included the *Glückauf*.

Glückauf

Type:	steam-powered tanker
Tonnage:	2,307 gross registered tons
Dimensions:	length 300 ft 6 in (91.6 m); beam 37 ft 2 in (11.3 m); draft 19 ft (5.8 m)
Propulsion:	one triple-expansion steam engine driving one propeller for 11 kt
Complement:	not available

Mount Washington (1890)

The first powered transport on Lake Champlain, the long but narrow body of water lying on the border between the states of New York and Vermont, came with the appearance in 1808 of the *Vermont I* as the first of an eventual 29 steam vessels to operate on the lake. This and other steamers of the period still faced strong competition from sailing craft, which with fair winds were just as fast, and always more reliable and cheaper to operate. Even so, there was a rash of steamer construction in the first part of the nineteenth century. Early vessels were little more than open-decked vessels with an awning to protect the passengers, but steamers improved steadily in quality, size and payload, and by the middle of the nineteenth century were optimized for passengers rather than cargo. The Champlain steamer then became very popular, and thus became larger and more comfortable.

In the middle of the century, there was strong (and occasionally violent) competition between the steamer companies, sometimes as many as five. The Champlain Transportation Co., for instance, resorted to price fixing and buy-outs as well as races with its competitors in its effort to secure a monopoly. The company eventually managed to buy out the Lake Champlain Steamboat Co., Champlain Ferry Co., St Albans Steamboat Co., and Ross-McNeil Line. Smaller commercial ferry and pleasure boat companies also operated around or, more commonly, across the lake.

From the late nineteenth century the larger Champlain steamers were magnificent side paddle wheelers with promenade decks fore and aft. There were powered by walking beam

engines, which were reliable and powerful, easily outliving the wooden hulls in which they were installed. Most of the larger steamers were built at the Shelburne Shipyard in Shelburne, Vermont, and all but three had wooden hulls. The steel hulls of

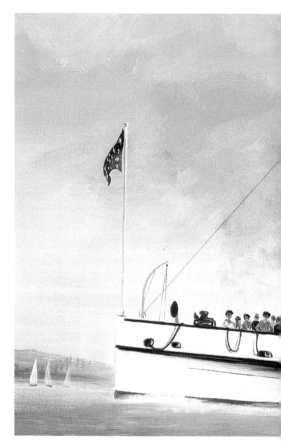

the *Chateaugay* of 1888, *Vermont III* of 1903, and *Ticonderoga* of 1906 were prefabricated by iron works outside Vermont and assembled at Shelburne by gangs of riveters who came with the hull "kits." The engines were also imported from firms near New York City. The 1,195-ton *Vermont III* was the largest of the steamers with a length of 262ft (76.8 m) and outfitted with 50 staterooms.

The launch of the steel-hulled *Ticonderoga* on April 18, 1906, was the start of the steamers' finale. She was built as successor to the wooden-hulled *Maquam* of 1881 and, though similar in size to the *Chateaugay* and *Vermont III*, was slightly less grand. The new 892-ton vessel was 220 ft (67.1 m) long and could carry some 1,070 passengers. The *Ticonderoga*

moved to Lake Winnipesaukee in New Hampshire and reassembled as the basis of the diesel-powered *Mount Washington*. The *Ticonderoga* went back into service for the latter half of the 1936 season, but before the start of the 1937 season, the Delaware & Hudson Railroad (by then owner of Champlain Transportation) sold the business.

served for almost 50 years, but from the start faced social, financial and technical challenges in a period of rapid change until the 1920s. The steamers managed to cope, but during the Depression, the Champlain Transportation Co. was forced to mothball most of its larger steamers. The *Vermont III* and *Chateaugay* were retired. In 1939 the latter had her hull divided into 20 sections, which were

In the period between 1937 and 1953, steam travel on Lake Champlain was undertaken only by the *Ticonderoga*, first in the hands of Horace Corbin. Corbin saw the boat's future as an excursion craft converted for cruises and parties. Since 1955, the steamer has been on permanent exhibit in Shelburne.

Campania (1893)

Built for Cunard by the Fairfield Shipbuilding & Engineering Co. Ltd. at Govan for launch on September 8, 1893, the *Campania* and her sister ship *Lucania* have often been said to be among the first "real" steamships, with substantial, raked funnels of good proportion and with a height nicely dominating the overall appearance. The funnels were 19 ft (5.8 m) in diameter, and were 130 ft (39.6 m) tall from the keel. Other characteristic features of the design were the sharp, straight stem and the elegant counter stern. The *Campania* and *Lucania* marked a high point in steamship development at the end of the nineteenth century, and gave Cunard a decisive edge over its rivals.

More prosaically, her engines were supplied with steam by 13 boilers fired by 100 furnaces consuming 20.5 tons of coal per hour. Even so, the *Campania* was not as large as the *Great Eastern* of 1858, whose displacement and length were not to be exceeded until 1903 and 1899 respectively.

The *Campania* started her first transatlantic voyage on April 22, 1894, setting an eastbound record of 5 days, 17 hours and 27 minutes on the voyage's return leg. The *Campania* was the first Cunard liner with the two-propeller propulsion arrangement pioneered in French vessels and by the steamers of the Inman Line. The omission of all pretension of a sailing rig allowed the creation of a tall superstructure of several decks, including a five-deck forward bridge allowing the captain to see over the bow.

The turn of the century was a difficult time for Cunard, for at this time the American magnate J. P. Morgan sought to gain a monopoly on Atlantic shipping. He bought the White Star Line and several other major companies, and reached special agreements with major Belgian, Dutch and German shipping lines. So concerned was the British government that it provided Cunard with very substantial subsidies to build and operate new ships, the largest and fastest vessels on the North Atlantic

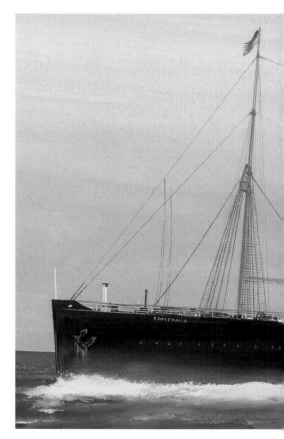

routes. These were the *Lusitania* and *Mauretania*, which entered service some 10 years after the *Campania* and *Lucania*. The two new ships were almost three times as large as their predecessors, and could thus offer greater comfort as well as greater speed.

Less than 16 years old, the *Lucania* was burned out at her pier at Liverpool, though her engines were not damaged and she was thus able to steam to the breaker's yard to be scrapped. The *Campania* was sold for breaking in 1914, but had lost only her deck fittings when the outbreak of World War I persuaded the Admiralty to buy her for conversion as a primitive aircraft carrier with a 120-ft (36.6-m) flying-off deck forward, a hangar and workshops midships and a short landing-on deck aft. A later change was the replacement of the fore funnel by a side-by-side pair of narrow smokepipes to allow the lengthening of the forward platform to 200 ft (61 m). The *Campania* was commissioned into naval service on April 17, 1915. On November 5, 1918 the *Campania* dragged her anchor in the Firth of Forth during a gale, drifted across the bows of the battleship HMS *Revenge*, and foundered.

Campania

Type:	transatlantic passenger ship
Tonnage:	12,950 gross registered tons
Dimensions:	length 622 ft (189.6 m); beam 65 ft (19.8 m); draft 26 ft (7.9 m)
Propulsion:	two triple-expansion steam engines delivering 30,000 ihp (22368 kW) to two propellers for 22 kt
Complement:	600 first-, 400 second- and 1,000 third-class passengers, plus crew

Virginian (1904)

In 1914 a Glasgow-based shipping line, Allan Bros & Co. UK Ltd., placed contracts for a pair of notable sister ships. These were completed in 1905 as the *Victorian* and *Virginian*, and became the first liners on the North Atlantic route with steam turbine machinery. Offering high reliability and smoother operation than the reciprocating engines of the type used in earlier transatlantic liners, the more modern machinery came to be seen as a considerable advance, and the two sister ships came to be highly regarded. This is one of the reasons why the Cunard line shortly thereafter opted for steam turbine machinery for its 19,500-ton *Carmania*. With this type of machinery provided in the *Carmania*, within two years Cunard specified steam turbine machinery for a pair of considerably large liners, the *Lusitania* and *Mauretania*, each with a displacement of more than 30,000 tons and intended for high-speed transatlantic service which would oppose the efforts of the American entrepreneur and financier J. P. Morgan to secure an effective monopoly on the North Atlantic route.

Both of the Allan line ships were ordered from Workman, Clark & Co. of Belfast, but the contract for the *Virginian* was then switched to Alexander Stephens and Sons Ltd. of Linthouse on the Clyde river when it became evident that the Northern Irish yard might not be able to complete two turbine-driven ships at the same time. Despite this fact, the two ships differed only in minor details, such as slight differences in displacement and the *Virginian*'s lack of any bridge opening aft.

Of the direct-drive rather than geared type, the steam turbines of the two Allan line ships initially suffered from a number of problems. The three turbines each powered a single small propeller, with a diameter of 9 ft 6 in (2.89 m), at the high speed of 280 revolutions per minute. This caused cavitation and a pronounced strumming vibration aft. The speed at which the turbines operated most efficiently was considerably too fast for the propeller and the design of the hull, and the vibration also resulted in a high rate of coal consumption. As a result, the sister ships built by Stephens in the following year, the *Grampian* and *Hesperian*, reverted to reciprocating machinery. The lesson of matching turbine speed and propeller revolutions was swiftly learned, however, and the *Lusitania* and *Mauretania* were nicely balanced in this respect.

The *Virginian* was launched on December 22, 1904, and after completion set off from Liverpool during April 6, 1905 on her maiden voyage to St John, New Brunswick, on the east coast of Canada. With this proving voyage completed, the ship was then committed to her definitive service, which linked Liverpool and Montreal. In June of the same year, the *Virginian* set a speed record for the route between Cape Race and Moville of 4 days and 4 hours. In September of the same year, the ship went gently aground on Cape St Charles in the St Lawrence river while steaming through the smoke resulting from a forest fire, but came off without difficulty and suffered no damage.

The *Virginian* continued with her schedule sailing linking the UK and Canada right to the start of World War I in August 1914, the only episode of note in the period between 1905 and 1914 being connected with the loss of the White Star liner *Titanic* on April 14, 1912. The *Virginian* was one of the ship that received the greater liner's radioed SOS message, but proceeded on passage when a Cunard liner, the *Carpathia*, signalled that she was only 57 miles (92 km) distant from the *Titanic*.

On the outbreak of World War I, the *Virginian* was taken over by the British authorities for service as a troopship, but on November 13 of the same year was taken in hand for conversion with limited armament as an armed merchant cruiser. In this capacity the *Virginian*, together with the similarly adapted *Victorian*, was attached to the 10th Cruiser Squadron, remaining in this role even after the Canadian Pacific Ocean Services had taken over the Allan line on January 10, 1916. The *Virginian* remained in British service until July 16, 1917, when she was transferred to the CPOS as part of the Liner

Virginian continued

Requisition Scheme. On December 23, 1918, the *Virginian* arrived at the Stephens yard for refurbishment, declared surplus to requirement and was offered for sale. On February 14, 1920, the ship was bought by the Swedish America Line, renamed as the *Drottningholm*, and in May placed in service on the route linking Gothenburg in south-western Sweden with New York.

During 1922 the ship was taken in hand at Gothenburg for modernization with De Laval single-reduction geared

the ship was repainted with a white hull, and this became the Swedish line's standard livery.

Between 1940 and 1946 the ship was used, together with the same owner's *Gripsholm*, by the International Red Cross for the exchange of diplomatic personnel, civilians and wounded prisoners of war during and immediately after World War II. These ships were some of the very small number of vessels which steamed with the maximum number of lights lit. The

turbines delivering 10,500 shp (7829 kW) and making it economical for the ship to cruise at 17 kt. The bridge deck was also extended to the main mast. In this form the ship returned to service in 1923 with accommodation for 532 cabin- and 854 third-class passengers. In 1937

Drottningholm completed 30 voyages for the Red Cross organization, and in the course of these voyages carried some 25,000 people. When another ship, the *Stockholm*, became available as a replacement, in 1945, the *Drottningholm* was sold, together with an obligation to complete her current commitments, to the Panama-based Home Lines, in which the Swedish America Line had a 50% share.

The ship was delivered to Home Lines in 1948 and renamed as the *Brasil*. On July 27 of the same year the ship started her first service for her new owner, a voyage between Genoa and Rio de Janeiro, a service on which she was complemented by the *Argentina* (ex-*Bergendfjord*). In 1950 the *Brasil* switched to the route linking New York and Naples during the Roman Catholic church's holy year, and carried large numbers of Italian Americans between the two countries. The ship was modernized in Italy during the following year, and was renamed the *Homeland* with a 10,043-ton displacement and provision for 96 first- and 846 tourist-class passengers. The *Homeland* recorded her first service, between Hamburg and New York via Southampton and Halifax, on behalf of the Hamburg America Line, on June 16.

In 1952 the ship, now owned by Mediterranean Lines Inc., a subsidiary of Home Line, returned to the service between Genoa and New York via Naples and Barcelona. On March 29, 1955, the *Homeland* reached Trieste, where after 51 years of steady service she was scrapped.

A ship which served under four names and several flags, the vessel built as the Virginian remained in fruitful service for 51 years.

Virginian

Type:	transatlantic passenger liner
Tonnage:	10,757 gross registered tons
Dimensions:	length 538 ft (164.0 m); beam 60 ft 4 in ((18.4 m); draft 38 ft (11.6m)
Propulsion:	three Parsons steam turbines delivering 15,000 shp (11184 kW) to three propellers for 18 kt
Complement:	426 first-, 286 second- and 1,000 third-class passengers, plus crew

Kronborg (1906)

The ship which had her life terminated in 1915 with the Danish name *Kronborg* had been built in the UK as the *Rubens*, whose owner was the Bolton Shipping Company, an organization which named its vessels after celebrated painters.

blockade and deliver urgently needed coal and ammunition to the warship, and also undertake the supply of much needed equipment, ammunition and medical necessities to Colonel von Lettow-Vorbeck's troops, small in number but superbly led in a guerrilla

On the outbreak of World War I in August 1914, the ship was in the north German port of Hamburg, and was thereupon impounded and her crew interned. When the German navy's light cruiser SMS *Königsberg*, operating on the east coast of Africa, was trapped in the delta of the Rufiji river of what was then the colony of German East Africa, plans were implemented to break the British

campaign which tied down a vastly superior number of allied troops right to the end of the war in November 1918.

Late in 1914 the *Rubens* was altered to represent the Danish (and therefore neutral) freighter *Kronborg*, and departed for East Africa on February 19, 1915 round the Cape of Good Hope. But on April 8, when she was off the coast of the island of Madagascar, the ship sent a radio message to the *Königsberg*, and this was intercepted and passed to Admiral King-Hall, commanding the Royal Navy squadron off the East African coast.

The *Kronborg* arrived off Manza Bay, to the north of Tanga, on April 14, but was intercepted by the light cruiser HMS *Hyacinth*, which gave

chase. The cruiser suffered an engine failure and the *Kronborg* escaped into the bay. Here the crew beached the ship and set fire to the timber deck cargo in the hope of persuading the British that they had destroyed the ship. The British cruiser sent a party aboard the burning German ship but could not get the fire under control, so the British left the ship and the *Hyacinth* fired a few shells into her.

The Germans returned and managed to extinguish the fires. They then salvaged the cargo of arms and ammunition, but lacked the means to bring the coal ashore and therefore abandoned it. Some months later the light cruiser HMS *Challenger*, escorted by a small force of minesweepers, anchored in Manza Bay and sent an armed party to inspect the wreck, The party swiftly discovered that the cargo had been discharged. It was a costly mistake by the Allies as the supplies were of major importance to von Lettow-Vorbeck.

The *Kronborg* rested in Manza Bay until 1956. In that year an Italian salvage company, Mawa Handels Anstalt, started to repair the many holes in the ship's hull. After an operation lasting 70 days, the ship was towed to Dar-es- Salaam, the capital of what had become Tanganyika (now Tanzania), by the tugs *Simba* and *Nyati*. The 1,600 tons of coal were sold to East African Railways and Harbors, and the hull was broken up for scrap.

Kronborg

Type:	steam-powered cargo ship
Tonnage:	3,587 gross registered tons
Dimensions:	length 343 ft (104.5 m); beam 49 ft (14.9 m); draft not available
Propulsion:	one triple-expansion steam engine delivering 188 hp (140 kW) to one propeller
Complement:	not available

Mauretania (1908)

By the start of the twentieth century, the preeminent position of the UK's passenger lines was facing a double threat. Since 1897, the Germans had produced a succession of fast and increasingly luxurious transatlantic liners, and J. P. Morgan had much increased the size of his International Mercantile Marine, not least through gaining control of two German lines, the Hamburg-Amerika Linie and Norddeutscher Lloyd, and by buying the White Star Line of the UK. These events persuaded the British government that Morgan was trying to create a monopoly on North Atlantic passenger traffic, and it therefore offered Cunard, the other "main player" on the North Atlantic route, a loan of £2.6 million for the construction of two fast and very comfortable passenger liners. In return the government demanded that Cunard should remain in British ownership for a period of 20 years, and that the ships could be requisitioned in the event of war. The proposed deal was further sugared by the offer to Cunard of a guaranteed mail subsidy amounting to £75,000 per year for each ship.

The immediate result of this process was the 1904 order, placed with Swan, Hunter & Wigham Richardson, Ltd. of Wallsend-on-Tyne in north-east England, for the design and building of a pair of sister ships. These were the *Lusitania* and *Mauretania*, the largest, fastest and most luxuriously appointed liners of the period.

The *Mauretania* was laid down in 1904, launched on September 20, 1906, and revealed her capabilities on her maiden voyage, which started on November 16, 1907. On the return crossing from New York, the *Mauretania* took the Blue Riband from the slightly earlier *Lusitania* with an eastward crossing from Sandy Hook to Queenstown at an average 23.69 kt. In was only on September 26-30, 1909, that the *Mauretania* seized the westward record from the Lusitania with a time of 4 days, 10 hours and 51 minutes, but then her average speed of 26.06 kt remained unbeaten for some 20 years before being wrested into German hands by the *Bremen*. In eastward crossings, the *Mauretania* improved her own record seven times, culminating in a time of 5 days, 1 hour and 49 minutes between the Ambrose Light and Cherbourg, for an average of 26.25 kt, on August 20-26, 1924.

The *Mauretania* was 5 ft (1.5 m) longer than the *Lusitania*, and had cowl vents rather than the *Lusitania*'s oil drum-shaped vents. The *Mauretania* was also fitted with four-blade propellers of greater diameter than the *Lusitania*'s three-blade units, and was therefore slightly faster than the *Lusitania*. The two ships were the only vessels with direct-drive steam turbines to hold the Blue Riband, and their four turbines provided 68,000 shp (50701 kW) for a designed speed of 25 kt. Furnace smoke was discharged via four large, evenly spaced and slightly raked funnels.

The *Mauretania* quickly became the favoured mode of transport across the Atlantic for passengers of all nationalities and types. The *Mauretania* remained on the transatlantic run until just after the outbreak of World War I in August 1914, but was then taken in hand for conversion as a troopship. In this capacity the vessel at first operated

The Mauretania steams toward the New World under an Atlantic sunset.

between the UK and the British bases of operation in the Mediterranean. After brief service as a hospital ship to bring wounded men home from the ill-fated Gallipoli campaign, the vessel reverted to trooping duty in 1916, ferrying Canadian and, from 1917, U.S. troops to Europe. She remained in this work until shortly after the Armistice which ended World War I in November 1918, and reverted to commercial service during 1919.

The *Mauretania* was damaged by fire in July 1921, and Cunard took the opportunity to replace the coal-fired furnaces with oil-burning units, allowing a major reduction in engine room crew and greatly facilitating both the speed and cleanliness of rebunkering. The accommodation was also revised to reflect the decline in the number of steerage-class passengers after the U.S. had imposed immigration quotas. In North Atlantic service, therefore, the *Mauretania* now carried 589 first- 400 second- and 767 third-class passengers. As the Depression of the 1920s worsened, the *Mauretania* was withdrawn from transatlantic service for use as a cruise liner in the Mediterranean and Caribbean Seas. In 1935 the *Mauretania* was sold to the breakers and scrapped at Rosyth in 1936.

Mauretania

Type:	transatlantic passenger liner
Tonnage:	31,938 gross registered tons
Dimensions:	length 790 ft (240.8 m); beam 88 ft (26.8 m); draft not available
Propulsion:	four direct-drive steam turbines delivering 68,000 shp (50701 kW) to four propellers for 27 kt
Complement:	563 first-, 464 second- and 1,138 third-class passengers, plus a crew of 802

Anchises (1911)

Alfred Holt of Liverpool, in the north of England, began as a ship owner with Thomas Ainsworth in 1852, and the two bought their first new ship in 1854. The owners quickly chartered this to the French government for use in the Crimean War (1853-56). The company started sailing to the West Indies in 1855, but in the face of strong competition withdrew from this route. In 1864 they began sailing to China and the Far East. The company was registered as the Ocean Steamship Co., generally known as the Blue Funnel Line, in 1865. In an 1866 leaflet, Holt announced, "I beg to inform you that I am about to establish a line of Screw Steamers from Liverpool to China...The first vessel will be the *Agamemnon*, now nearly ready for sea, and intended to sail about the twentieth of March. The exact day of sailing will be advertised when I obtain delivery from the builders, but I expect it will not be far from this date...The *Agamemnon* will be followed by the *Ajax* and *Achilles*, similar vessels. The service I propose these vessels to perform is somewhat as follows...non-stop run to Mauritius then on to Penang, Singapore, Hong Kong and Shanghai with a call at Foochow to pick up a cargo of tea on the return voyage."

In 1891, the Blue Funnel Line established a Dutch subsidiary, the Nederlandsche Stoomboot Maatschappij "Ocean" to compete with Dutch companies serving the East Indies, and also formed the Singapore-based East Indian Ocean SS Co. In the same year. The China Mutual Steam Navigation Co. was taken over in 1902, adding 13 steamers to the Blue Funnel Line's fleet and a service between China and the west coasts

of Canada and the U.S. In 1915 the Blue Funnel Line bought the Indra Line of seven ships, together with its service linking New York and the Far East, and in 1917 the Knight Line. A joint passenger service to Australia with the White Star Line was started in 1924, and this was complemented by the Aberdeen Line in 1926. The

Glen and Shire Lines followed into the ownership of the Blue Funnel Line in 1935 after the collapse of the Royal Mail group, and a controlling interest in the Straits SS Co. was acquired in the same year. Shaw, Savill had taken over the joint service to Australia from White Star Line, and the Blue Funnel Line pulled out of the joint effort in 1939.

The Blue Funnel Line steadily built up a large fleet of cargo liners

combining excellent accommodation with a sizeable cargo load. Though most of the line's vessels were freighters with accommodation for up to 12 passengers, some of the vessels offered greater passenger capacity for the line's services to the Middle East, Australia and the Far East. Three sister ships built in 1910-11 for the Australia service were the *Aeneas*, *Ascanius* and *Anchises*. Unlike most ships on this run, these had accommodation for a few first-class passengers rather than larger numbers of emigrants. The *Aeneas* was bombed and sunk off Plymouth in 1940, the *Ascanius* was sold in 1949 to an Italian company and renamed as the *San Giovannino*, and the *Anchises*, which had been built by Workman, Clark & Co. Ltd. of Belfast in northern Ireland during 1911, was bombed and sunk off the Mersey in 1941 with the loss of 12 lives.

The Anchises was designed to operate between the UK and Australia with cargo and modest numbers of first-class passengers.

Anchises

Type:	steam-powered cargo liner
Tonnage:	10,046 gross registered tons
Dimensions:	509 ft (155.1 m); beam 60 ft (18.3 m); draft not available
Propulsion:	triple-expansion steam engines driving two propellers for 14 kt
Complement:	288 first-class passengers, plus crew

Selandia (1911)

Built by Burmeister & Wain at Copenhagen in Denmark for launch on November 4, 1911, the *Selandia* was one of three sister ships ordered by the East Asiatic Company of Denmark for service between Scandinavia, Genoa, Italy, and Bangkok, Thailand. The other two ships were the *Fionia*, from the same yard as the Selandia, and the *Jutlandia*, built on the Clyde river by

combustion engine, and in 1895 bought the Danish rights to the engine and started to improve and perfect it for great reliability.

By December 1910, H. N. Andersen of the East Asiatic Co. was so sure of the diesel engine's advantages over the steam engine that he placed the order for the *Selandia* as a pioneering motor ship bearing a latinized form

Barclay, Curie & Co. The vessels were of considerable historical importance as the world's first ocean-going motor ships (diesel-engined ships). From an early stage Burmeister & Wain had been confident of the great maritime future which could be expected of this new German type of internal

of Sjaelland, the island on which Copenhagen is located, as her name. The new vessel's fitting out proceeded so smoothly that she was ready for delivery by mid-February and on February 22 the *Selandia* departed for London as the first port of call on her notably long maiden voyage to

Bangkok. The crown prince and other members of the Danish royal family travelled in the *Selandia* as far as Elsinore, and while she was berthed in London the vessel was visited by hordes of interested persons.

Some 1,056 tons of oil fuel was carried in the vessel's double bottom and in tanks abreast the shaft tunnel, and in appearance the vessel marked a departure from the current norms in having no funnel but merely exhausts for her engines. The layout of the

Her lack of funnels gave the Selandia an unusual appearance by the standards of the first half of the twentieth century.

Selandia's hull was also unusual, the use and spacing of four islands giving one long and two short well decks. The vessel had two continuous decks, and beneath the between deck spaces existed five holds, in the form of three forward and two abaft the machinery space. The holds were served by 11 derricks and (another new feature), electric winches. Of the crew, the men were berthed in the poop and officers and engineers in cabins abreast the engine casing. The vessel also had accommodation for 26 first-class passengers beneath the bridge: on the centerline the vessel also had the main saloon (forward), the dining saloon and the galley. Above these were the captain's cabin, one or two passenger cabins, and the passengers' smoking room.

The *Selandia* had been built for a very long route, so it was June 26, 1912, before the vessel reached Copenhagen once more after an entirely successful maiden voyage to and from Siam. During her first 12 years of service, the *Selandia* logged more than 600,000 miles (965580 km), and in this entire period was kept in port for a mere 10 days by engine problems.

The *Selandia* was sold in 1936 to a Norwegian company, which renamed the vessel the *Norseman* and in 1940 sold her to the Finland Amerika Linjen O/Y of Helsingfors as the *Tornator*. In January 1942 the *Tornator* was wrecked in Japan.

Selandia

Type:	diesel-powered passenger and cargo vessel
Tonnage:	9,800 tons
Dimensions:	length 386 ft (117.7 m); beam 53 ft 2 in (16.2 m); draft not available
Propulsion:	two Burmeister & Wain four-stroke diesel engines delivering 2,500 ihp (1864 kW) to two propellers for 12 kt
Complement:	64 first-class passengers, and a crew of about 70

Aquitania (1914)

Cunard's great *Aquitania* was built to boost the line's presence on the all-important North Atlantic service linking Liverpool and New York, and operated in the period immediately before the start of World War I in August 1914 by the *Lusitania* and *Mauretania*. There was no intention that the new liner should seek to secure the Blue Riband, for which her older companions had vied, but she was to be some 50% larger than the sister ships, and history suggests that the *Aquitania* was the most successful transatlantic liner.

Built by John Brown & Co. Ltd. of Clydebank in Scotland and launched on April 21, 1913, the *Aquitania* departed on her maiden voyage to New York on May 30. Three months later World War I started and the new liner was taken over for conversion as an armed merchant cruiser. The ship was involved in a collision during this same month, however, and the Admiralty switched her to the troop transport and, briefly, hospital ship roles. The ship was laid up during most of 1917, and returned to troop service during 1918.

In June 1919 the *Aquitania* resumed her mercantile career. During World War I great strides had been made in propulsion technology, so when the ship was taken in hand for a major overhaul in 1920, her original coal-fired furnaces were replaced with oil-fired units, which reduced engine room personnel requirements, and at the same time removed the need for the time-consuming and very dirty process of coaling. The overhaul also provided the chance to bring the ship's original luxury-trade fittings out of store and restore the ship to her pre-war elegance. In 1926 the accommodation was for 610 first-, 950 second- and 640 tourist-class passengers.

For some 20 years the *Aquitania* was undoubtedly the most popular liner on the Atlantic route, in which

The Aquitania was one of Cunard's celebrated "four-stacker" liners, and the much successful of all transatlantic liners.

she operated in tandem with the *Berengaria* and *Mauretania*, and during the winter off-season months the *Aquitania* was employed for cruises to Mediterranean ports. From 1936-39 the *Aquitania* partnered with Cunard's newest liner, the *Queen Mary*. The *Aquitania* was to have been withdrawn after the *Queen Elizabeth*'s completion in 1940, but this plan was shelved after the outbreak of World War II in September 1939. The ship returned to her World War I role of troop carrying, for which she was adapted with provision for up to 7,725 men. The *Aquitania* was the only ship built before World War I to serve as a troopship right through World War II. Between 1939 and 1945, the ship carried more than 300,000 men, primarily between Australia and Egypt and later between the U.S. and UK.

The *Aquitania* was returned to Cunard in 1948, and completed 25 voyages between Southampton and Halifax, Nova Scotia, carrying emigrants, displaced persons and repatriated soldiers. In December 1949 the *Aquitania* arrived in Southampton and was retired after completing no fewer than 443 transatlantic crossings in a 35-year career. The ship moved to Faslane and was scrapped in February 1950.

Aquitania

Type:	transatlantic liner
Tonnage:	45,647 gross registered tons
Dimensions:	length 901 ft (274.6 m); beam 97 ft (29.6 m); draft not available
Propulsion:	four geared steam turbines delivering 59,000 shp (43990 kW) to four propellers for 23 kt
Complement:	(1914) 618 first, 614 second- and 1,998 third-class passengers, plus a crew of 972

Lapland (1908)

The International Navigation Co. of Philadelphia, Pennsylvania, came into being in 1871, and was better known as the Red Star Line. In 1872 it established a Belgian subsidiary, the Société Anonyme de Navigation Belge-Americaine, which from January 1873 operated a weekly service between Antwerp and Philadelphia. The INCo (New Jersey) and INCo (Liverpool) were set up in 1893 to run the four surviving Inman Line ships, in 1902 the former becoming the International Mercantile Marine Company, and in 1927 the latter being taken over by Frederick Leyland & Co. Continuing to 1934 before going out of business, the company operated between Antwerp and Philadelphia (1872-1902), Antwerp and New York (1876-1904), Antwerp and New York via Southampton (1902-04), and Antwerp and New York via Dover (1904-14). The ships' funnels were painted black with broad white band containing a red star in 1873, changing to buff with a red star and black top in 1884, and black with a white band in 1893.

The Lapland was built for the Red Star Line in 1908 by Harland & Wolff Ltd., primarily for the emigrant trade. The ship was launched on June 27, 1908, and departed on her maiden voyage to New York via Dover on April 10, 1909. She started her last voyage on this service on July 4, 1914, and on September 1, 1914, after most of Belgium had been overrun by the Germans at the start of World War I, operated from Liverpool under the British rather than Belgian flag, and on charter to Cunard. In April 1917 the ship was mined off the Mersey Bar Lightship, but managed to reach Liverpool. She was repaired, and in June 1917 requisitioned as

a troopship. On November 23, 1918 she departed on her first post-war voyage, sailing from Liverpool for New York for the White Star Line. On August 2, 1919 the Lapland began her

sixth and final return voyage on this service before being transferred to the route between Southampton and New York under charter to the White Star Line, for which she completed three return voyages in the period to December 1919, after which she was refitted with accommodation for 389 first-, 448 second- and 1,200 third-class passengers. The Lapland re-entered service with the Red Star Line, although still under the British flag, on January 3, 1920, when she left Antwerp for Southampton and New York. In April 1927 the vessel was revised for cabin-, tourist- and third-class passengers, and on April 29, 1932, departed on her final trip to Antwerp, Southampton, Le Havre and New York, where she arrived on May 8 before sailing once again on June 11 to Antwerp. In 1932-33 the ship was used for cruises to the Mediterranean, but in October 1933 she was sold and scrapped in Japan in 1934.

The Lapland sailed mainly under the Belgian and British flags.

Lapland (as completed)

Type:	passenger liner
Tonnage:	17,540 gross registered tons
Dimensions:	length 605 ft 8 in (184.6 m); beam 70 ft 4 in (21.4 m); draft not available
Propulsion:	two quadruple-expansion steam engines driving two propellers for 17 kt
Complement:	394 first-, 352 second- and 1,790 third-class passengers, plus crew

Carpathia (1902)

The *Carpathia* was ordered by the Cunard Line in 1902 for a transatlantic passenger role between Liverpool and Boston, and was built by Swan Hunter Ltd. at its yard at Wallsend on the Tyne river in northeast England for launch on August 6 of the same year. The ship was a slightly smaller half-sister of the same line's *Saxonia* and *Ivernia*, from which she could readily be distinguished by her shorter funnel, and was typical of the ships of the period in having four masts. Her hull also had pronounced sheer from bow to stern and, like all other Cunard Line vessels, she was given a notably elegant appearance by the narrow white boot-topping just above the waterline. The ship was built of steel, had one funnel and the standard arrangement of four masts, and had passenger accommodation, mostly for persons emigrating to the U.S., on three decks.

The *Carpathia* departed on her maiden voyage on May 5, 1903, and her typical transatlantic crossing took nine days. The ship also operated services between New York, Trieste and a number of other Mediterranean ports.

The *Carpathia* became celebrated when she rescued survivors of the *Titanic* after this unhappy vessel sank on April 15, 1912. The *Carpathia* was on passage from New York when her wireless operator, Harold Cottam, picked up distress signals from the *Titanic*. Cottam woke Captain Arthur Henry Rostron, who immediately altered course and increased speed toward the *Titanic*'s last known position, about 57 miles (92 km) distant. Though the *Carpathia*'s legend speed was 14 kt, Rostron managed to squeeze his ship up to 17 kt, which was a remarkable feat in itself but posed dangers as a result of the risks of vibration-induced damage or a boiler explosion from too high a pressure. At 4:00 a.m. the *Carpathia* arrived at the scene after working her way through dangerous ice fields, and was able to save 706 survivors.

For his effort, Rostron was awarded a silver cup and gold medal by survivors, was later a guest of President William Howard Taft at the Whitc House, and was presented with the Congressional Gold Medal, the highest honour which the U.S. Congress could confer upon him.

The *Carpathia* was part of a convoy in World War I when she was torpedoed on July 17, 1918 near Bishop Rock, off the east coast of Ireland, by the German submarine U-55. The *Carpathia* was struck by three torpedoes, the detonation of which instantly killed five men in her boiler room as the ship's side was ripped open and water started to pour in. Some 157 passengers and the surviving 218 members of the crew were rescued on the following day by the 1,210-ton fleet minesweeping sloop HMS *Snowdrop*.

The American author and diver Clive Cussler found the wreck in 1999. The wreck has been claimed by Premier Exhibitions Inc. (formerly RMS Titanic Inc.). This company also owns the salvor-in-possession rights of the *Titanic*, from which artifacts have been salved for display in exhibitions worldwide.

The Carpathia was one of several transatlantic liners which succumbed to attacks by German submarine-launched torpedoes in World War I.

Carpathia

Type:	transatlantic passenger liner
Tonnage:	13,603 gross registered tons
Dimensions:	558 ft (170.1 m); beam 64 ft (19.5 m); draft not available
Propulsion:	two quadruple-expansion steam engines driving two propellers for 14 kt
Complement:	204 first- and 1,500 third-class passengers, plus crew

Titanic (1912)

The *Titanic* was one of three sister ships built for the White Star Line, which was then a British subsidiary of American financier J. P. Morgan's International Mercantile Marine. Unlike their Cunard rivals on the transatlantic route, which were comfortable and more utilitarian, the White Star Line's *Olympic*, *Britannic* and *Titanic* had been conceived as "no expense spared" examples of what could be achieved in technical terms, and were luxuriously appointed to an extraordinary degree. The ships introduced a number of innovative features, and much was made of the "unsinkability" of the *Titanic*, whose hull was divided into watertight compartments by 15 transverse bulkheads with electrically actuated watertight doors. These bulkheads extended vertically from the ship's double bottom through four or five of her nine decks. There were other safety features but, perhaps in the belief that she was truly unsinkable, the ship carried only 16 lifeboats and four collapsible boats, sufficient for just 1,178 people, which was a

mere 35% of the maximum passenger and crew complement of 3,511. Even so, the number of lifeboats was nonetheless greater than that demanded by the Board of Trade's requirements, which dated from 1894 and demanded lifeboats to carry just 962 persons. (In 1894 the largest ship afloat displaced only 12,950 tons and carried a much smaller number of passengers and crew.)

The *Titanic* was ordered from the northern-Irish Harland & Wolff shipyard in Belfast, laid down on March 31, 1909, and launched on May 31, 1911. Just under 11 months later, on April 10, 1912, the *Titanic* departed from Southampton for New York on her maiden transatlantic voyage. The facilities and fame of the great ship had attracted a large, but by no means maximum, number of passengers, including many wealthy and celebrated people, but the departure was nonetheless and somewhat surprisingly muted. Among the 329 first-class passengers, collectively worth more than US$500 million, were John Jacob Astor, Isidor and Ida Strauss, Harry Widener, Margaret "Molly" Brown, and J. Bruce Ismay, the managing director of the White Star Line. These VIP passengers were supplemented by 285 second- and 710 third-class

The great transatlantic liner, Titanic, of the American-owned White Star Line in company with a tug.

passengers, and the crew totalled 899. The ship was commanded by Commodore Edward J. Smith, who had served the White Star Line for 25 years and had postponed his retirement to make the voyage.

As the *Titanic* left her berth, the suction of her propellers pulled the Inman Line's *New York* from her berth and snapped her mooring lines like string. The *Titanic* then steamed to Cherbourg in northern France and Queenstown in southern Ireland, where the last passengers joined the ship.

The voyage proceeded smoothly and enjoyably for the passengers, but on April 14 the ship's wireless operators, Jack Phillips and Harold Bride (Marconi rather than White Star employees) picked up warnings of a field of ice in the ship's planned course. The wireless operators picked up six such warnings (transmitted by the *Baltic*, *Noordam*, *Amerika*, *Mesaba*, *Californian* and *Caronia*) after 1:40 p.m., but posted only one of these on the bridge. Smith neither slowed his ship nor diverted to the warmer south.

At 11:40 p.m. the *Titanic* was cruising at more than 22 kt into a moonless night when a look-out in the crow's nest reported an iceberg straight ahead. The officer of the watch on the bridge was First Officer William Murdoch, who immediately ordered a turn to port so that the ship would leave the iceberg to starboard. But it was too late, and some 200 ft (61 m) of the *Titanic*'s forward section

Too late, the Titanic's look-outs and bridge crew see the iceberg and attempt to take evasive action, but in the process scrape the port side against an ice shelf and rupture the hull below the water line.

Titanic *continued*

still with her lights blazing. The ship at last broke apart between the third and fourth funnels, and sank in 13,000 ft (3960 m) of water.

scraped along a submerged spur of the iceberg. This buckled the ship's hull plates along their riveted seams, and a hastily launched examination of the damage found that the forward six watertight compartments had been breached. The problem now was the fact that because the bulkheads did not extend up to the full height of the hull, each compartment would flood and spill into the next abaft as the bow started to settle and the ship began to sink. Smith appears not to have grasped the severity of the situation, and it other officers took the initiative in firing distress rockets and launching the lifeboats.

It was only at 12.15 a.m. on April 15 that the first distress call was broadcast from the *Titanic*, and at 12.45 a.m. that the first of an eventual eight distress rockets was fired in an in an attempt to catch the attention of a nearby vessel, later thought to be the Leyland Line's *Californian*, about 19 miles (30.5 km) distant. By 2:20 a.m. the last of the lifeboats had got clear and the ship had reared with her stern right out of the water, though

Many of the lifeboats had pulled way from the stricken ship while still only partially full, and it was later discovered that the lifeboats had 473 empty seats when the *Carpathia* arrived at 3:30 a.m., after a maximum-speed dash through the ice field, to rescue 706 survivors. The number of dead has been estimated at between 1,500 and 1,635 persons, but was probably 1,496. Second Officer Charles H. Lightoller went largely by the "women and children first" concept, and though this segment amounted to only 24% of the number of persons on board,

BHUTAN

R.M.S. TITANIC 1912   25nu

30th Anniversary International Maritime Organisation

The Titanic settles bow-down in the freezing waters of the North Atlantic.

As the last lifeboats pull way, the Titanic starts to go down, her lights still blazing and her funnels pouring out smoke.

they constituted 53% of those who survived. There was also a great class divide among the 712 survivors: 60% of the first-class passengers survived, 42% of the second-class passengers, 25% of the third-class passengers, and 24% of the crew.

The circumstances of the tragedy were the subject of immense speculation, and because the *Titanic* was owned by a U.S. consortium but regulated by the British Board of Trade, inquiries were convened in Washington and London. No explicit blame was ever assigned, but strong recommendations were made about basic issues such as adequate lifeboat capacity for all on board, proper lifeboat drills and crew training, full-time wireless operation, and the creation of the International Ice Patrol.

Over the years, several teams tried to locate the *Titanic*'s wreck, but it was only in 1985 that an expedition led by Dr. Robert Ballard of the Woods Hole

Oceanographic Institution succeeded with the aid of a manned submersible, a deep-towing camera sled and a remotely operated vehicle. Ballard's team found and photographed the *Titanic* in two sections: the stern engine room section, largely destroyed, and the bow section 1,930 ft (588 m) away, more intact and surrounded by a huge debris field.

Titanic

Type:	transatlantic passenger liner
Tonnage:	46,328 gross registered tons
Dimensions:	length 882 ft 9 in (269.1 m); beam 92 ft 6 in (28.2 m); draft 34 ft 7 in (10.5 m)
Propulsion:	two triple-expansion steam engines delivering 32,000 hp (23859 kW) to the two outer propellers, and one steam turbine delivering 18,000 shp (13421 kW) to the central propeller for 23 kt
Complement:	(maiden voyage) 324 first-, 285 second- and 708 third-class passengers, plus a crew of 891

Calamares (1913)

The connection between the ship-builder Workman Clark & Co. of Belfast in northern Ireland and the United Fruit Co. of Boston, Massachusetts, began in 1903 and lasted for almost 30 years, resulting in several of the most "exotic" destinations in conditions akin to those of the modern cruise liner. The first three vessels had provision for 18 passengers, but so successful was this aspect of the company's operation that most of the later ships

The Calamares was a 'banana boat' with excellent first-class accommodation.

popular combined passenger and cargo vessels ever built. The most important task allocated to these vessels was the delivery of bananas from ports in Central America and Caribbean to the U.S., but a useful secondary task was the carriage of passengers to and from had accommodation for 100 or more first-class passengers, as well as public rooms such as the dining saloon and entrance hall, music room, lounge and smoking room.

The ships of the United Fruit Co. were all painted in a crisp white, and were collectively known as the "Great White Fleet." The ships were initially registered to the Tropical Fruit S.S. Co. Ltd. of Glasgow because U.S. law of the time denied American registration to all but U.S.-built ships. Changed legislation then allowed the ships to be reregistered in the U.S., and in this latter period the owner company became the United Fruit Co. Line in 1920, by 1939 was the United Fruit S.S. Corporation.

The *Calamares* was completed in 1913, and after initial mercantile service, was chartered by the U.S. Army in 1917 for World War I. The vessel was turned over to the U.S. Navy during April 1918 and commissioned for service first as a troop transport, making five voyages to France for this purpose. In October 1918 the vessel was reassigned to the Naval Overseas Transportation Service and carried provisions from the U.S. to France on three more trips. The *Calamares* was restored to transport duty in March 1919 and made five voyages repatriating more than 10,000 U.S. service personnel to the U.S. by mid-August 1919. One month later, the ship was restored to her owner.

In December 1941 the ship was reacquired by the U.S. Navy for use in World War II and converted as a storeship before being recommissioned into naval service in April 1943. Her first naval voyage was from the U.S. west coast to the south Pacific and back between April and August 1943. After several months of operations between the mainland and Hawaii, the *Calamares* returned to the south Pacific in November 1943 and operated there and in the western Pacific for the rest of the conflict and indeed into 1946. She then steamed to the U.S. East Coast, where she was decommissioned in April 1946, turned over to the Maritime Commission, and sold for scrapping in December 1947.

Calamares

Type:	combined passenger and refrigerated cargo vessel
Tonnage:	7,782 gross registered tons
Dimensions:	470 ft (143.25 m); beam 55 ft (16,75 m); draft not available
Propulsion:	two quadruple-expansion steam engines driving two propellers for 15 kt
Complement:	143 first-class passengers, plus crew

Vaterland and *Leviathan* (1914)

In the latter part of the nineteenth century, the German empire, formally created in 1871 by the unification of the host of German states that had existed up to that time, began to build itself up into a global power. This involved the whole nation, and was based on the rapid revitalisation and expansion of German industry. Germany was already a major land power and a growing force in the economy of Europe. The country's authorities wished to match this land power with a similar power at sea, both naval and mercantile, the latter designed to open the markets of the world to German manufacturing and to source the materials needed by German industry.

Motivated by commercial ambitions as well as the desire to see their nation emerge as a major player on the world stage, existing German mercantile companies expanded and new ones came into existence and, in many cases, growing rapidly. One of the former was the Hamburg-Amerika Linie, which had been established in the great Hanseatic port of Hamburg during 1847 as HAPAG (Hamburg Amerikanische Packetfahrt Actien Gesellschaft) to undertake shipping operations across the Atlantic. HAPAG swiftly grew into the largest German and, on occasion, the world's largest and most important shipping company, and among its most important raisons d'être was the servicing of the market created by the large-scale emigration of Germans to the U.S.

In the first years of the twentieth century, a new generation of turbine-powered and steel-hulled liners, characterized by high speed, great size and the type of luxurious accommodation demanded by the

wealthy of the Western world's elite, emerged in response to the commercial rivalry of the UK and U.S.. This was a time of burgeoning transatlantic travel by all classes, and German shipping lines were determined to compete. Under the driving leadership of its

chairman, Albert Ballin, the Hamburg-Amerika Linie was in a good position to order the largest and the best there was. The line therefore contracted for three huge "super-liners" as the

Imperator, Europa and *Bismarck*. The first became the Cunard Line's *Berengaria* after World War I, the second was launched and completed as the *Vaterland* at the suggestion of Kaiser Wilhelm II; the third was launched but not completed before World War I, and, after the war, was completed as the White Star Line's *Majestic*.

to a German company, the Blohm & Voss yard of Hamburg. Blohm & Voss introduced a number of refinements to the ship's basic concept. Among those which attracted the most widespread interest and general approval were the divided uptakes from the engine room to the first two of the three funnels, of which the aftermost was a dummy. This permitted the creation of an

The Vaterland enters New York harbor with the aid of steam tugs.

The *Vaterland* was originally to have been ordered from the Harland & Wolff yard in the northern Irish city of Belfast, but the contract for her construction was eventually allocated

uninterrupted public space some 300 ft (91.4 m) long. Another significant feature was the use of forced draft ventilation, which all but eliminated the need for cowled deck openings. The

Vaterland and *Leviathan* continued

Vaterland's other advanced features also included a double bottom and watertight bulkheads. These were not innovative, but their importance had been emphasized by the loss of the *Titanic* in 1912.

The largest ship in the world at the time of her construction, the *Vaterland* was formally launched by Kronprinz Rupprecht of Bavaria on April 13, 1913, and was completed on April 29, 1914. Just over a fortnight later, on May 14, the ship departed Hamburg on her maiden voyage to New York via Southampton in the south of England and Cherbourg in the north of France, However, the career of the *Vaterland* as the pride of the German mercantile marine was destined to be very short. As the ship was completing the preparations to sail for Hamburg from New York in July 1914, the virtual inevitability of the outbreak of World War I became evident to the German authorities, who instructed the ship's captain, Kommodore Hans Ruser, to keep his ship at her pier at Hoboken rather than risk interception and seizure by British and French cruisers lying off New York. Thus the *Vaterland* became the largest of 35 Hamburg-Amerika Linie vessels interned in the U.S., seven of them in and around New York. Many of the ship's crew remained on board the *Vaterland* until the U.S. entered World War I on the Allied side on April 6, 1917, when the ship was seized.

Two months later, the *Vaterland* was transferred to the U.S. Navy for conversion as a troopship, and in July the ship was formally commissioned as the USS *Leviathan*, which was a name chosen personally by President Woodrow Wilson. The *Leviathan* made 16 round-trip voyages to Brest in north-western France and three to Liverpool in north-western England between 1917 and 1919, and, in the course of the trips, carried 119,000 men of the American Expeditionary Forces to Europe. After the end of the war and final service in the repatriation of American troops to the U.S., the *Leviathan* was decommissioned in October 1919, and passed into the hands of the U.S. Shipping Board, which planned to dispose of the ship to the financier J. P. Morgan's International Mercantile Marine organization. However, this plan was defeated by a strident opposition orchestrated by William Randolph Hearst, an opponent of Morgan who maintained that the IMM was a British concern and that the sale of the U.S.'s largest ship would benefit "Anglo-Wall Street" interests rather than the U.S.. In 1920 the *Leviathan* was chartered to the United States Mail Steamship Company. A reconstruction lasting some three years was carried out at Newport News under the auspices of William Francis Gibbs, the leading U.S. naval architect of the time but without the aid of the original blueprints, for which Germany wanted US\$1 million, and then re-emerged at 59,965 gross registered tons, 5,000 more than her sister ship *Majestic* completed after World War I. Large tonnages were prestigious in sales and promotional terms, but were also the yardstick by which port dues were calculated, so in 1931 the *Leviathan* was remeasured and emerged this time with at 48,943 gross registered tons.

The *Leviathan* re-entered service on the transatlantic passenger route on July 4, 1923, sailing from New York for Cherbourg and Southampton. By this time, the ship was being operated

The USS Leviathan operated as a troopship in World War I,
and for some of this time sported an impressive "dazzle paint" scheme.

by the United States Lines on behalf of the U.S. Shipping Board and, as one of the largest and most celebrated liners of the period after World War I, was the flagship of the U.S. merchant marines. The fact that the ship was operated by a quasi-governmental concern meant that no alcohol could be served during the Prohibition period, but she nonetheless remained a very popular and successful ship throughout the 1920s. In 1925 the ship was revised to include "tourist third-class" accommodation, and this proved very popular, most particularly to students making the transatlantic crossing to Europe.

Financial losses during the later stages of the Depression era led the laying-up of the *Leviathan* in 1933, but in the following year the ship was restored to full service at the demand of the U.S. Department of Commerce. After only five round-trip voyages, the continued scale of the losses resulted in the *Leviathan* being withdrawn later in 1934. Three years later, the ship was sold to Metal Industries Ltd. She then sailed from New York for the last time to Rosyth on the eastern side of Scotland, where she was scrapped during 1938.

Leviathan

Type:	transatlantic liner
Tonnage:	54,282 gross registered tons
Dimensions:	length 950 ft (289.6 m); beam 100 ft 4 in (30.6 m); draft not available
Propulsion:	four Parsons geared steam turbines driving four propellers for 26 kt
Complement:	1,165 passengers as complete, or 14,000 men as a troop transport, plus crew
Armament:	(World War I only) eight 6-in (152-mm) guns, two 1-pdr guns and two machine guns

Lusitania (1907)

When one thinks of the *Lusitania*, one is drawn mostly to the tragic manner of her loss on May 7, 1915 to the torpedo attack of the German submarine U-20. However, this ignores the importance of the *Lusitania* in the fascinating and indeed dramatic history of passenger shipping from the end of the nineteenth century into the first decade, or slightly longer, of the twentieth century. One of the key figures in this process was the American financier J. P. Morgan, who had become increasingly concerned that the U.S.'s shipping interests and shipbuilding were being eclipsed in a European dominance. In 1904, therefore, Morgan established the

The Cunard Line's Lusitania was a vessel whose impressive external appearance was complemented by good performance and all manner of luxuries for the better-paying passengers.

on British commercial and trade interests, but also with the longer-term possibility that the UK would no longer have available to it all the shipping it might need in time of war, the British government offered the Cunard Line a loan of £2.6 million and an annual mail subsidy of £75,000 per ship if it would order two new passenger liners, guarantee that the company would remain in British ownership for 20 years, and make the two ships available for wartime requisition for adaptation as auxiliary cruisers.

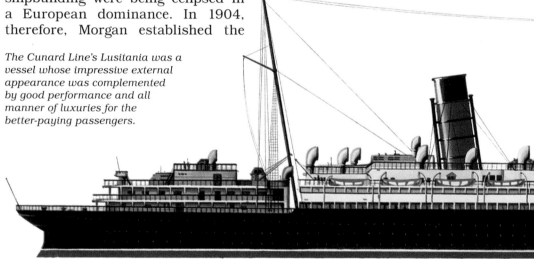

International Mercantile Marine not just to redress balance between U.S. and European interests but, he hoped, establish an effective U.S. monopoly on the mercantile routes across the North Atlantic. Morgan quickly bought controlling interests in a number of major shipping companies including the Hamburg-Amerika Linie and Norddeutscher Lloyd of Germany, and the White Star Line of the UK.

Concerned not just with the shorter-term impact this would have

The initial result was the *Mauretania* and *Lusitania*, the latter built by John Brown & Co. Ltd. of Clydebank in western Scotland and named for the Roman province of what is now Portugal. These two sister ships were the largest, fastest and most comfortably (if not luxuriously) appointed transatlantic liners of their day. The *Lusitania* was laid down on June 16, 1904, and launched on June 7, 1906, and steamed from Liverpool on her maiden voyage to

New York and back on September 7, 1907. During the following month, the speed capability of the new liner was confirmed by her record-breaking westward passage between Daunt's Rock and Sandy Hook at 23.9 kt, and similarly record-breaking eastbound passage of 23.6 kt. The ship's fastest crossing was westbound at 25.7 kt in 4 days, 16 hours and 40 minutes on 8/12 August 1909. The *Lusitania's* only rival in the speed stakes was her sister ship *Mauretania*, which was marginally faster.

The UK sought to maintain a maritime blockade of Germany after the start of World War I in August 1914, but a close blockade proved not to be feasible and therefore on November

by a submarine, even if they were only passengers on a British ship, might draw down the wrath of the U.S. and precipitate an American entry in the war on the Allied side.

After the sinking of *Falaba* in March 1915, embassy the Germans in the U.S. promulgated a warning that "Travellers intending to embark on the Atlantic voyage are reminded that a state of war exists between Germany and...Great Britain...; that the zone of war includes the waters adjacent to the British Isles; that, in accordance with formal notice given by the Imperial German Government, vessels flying the flag of Great Britain...are liable to destruction in those waters and that travellers sailing in the war zone on the ships of Great Britain...do so at their own risk."

3, 1914, the UK declared a naval interdiction area in the North Sea and all the waters bounded by Iceland, Norway and Scotland. Knowing this to be contrary to international law, Germany issued an equally illegal declaration of an "area of war" around the British Isles and Ireland, advising all in general, and the U.S. in particular, that the sinking of neutral ships in this area might be unavoidable. The German authorities appreciated that the deaths of U.S. citizens in an attack

This notice appeared for the first time on May 1, 1915, the day on which the *Lusitania*, commanded by Captain William Turner, sailed from New York with 1,965 passengers and crew. Five days later the ship entered the German-declared war zone. Although the British were fully aware of the presence of German submarines off southern Ireland (a U-20 had sunk three ships on May 6), but provided the *Lusitania* with no escort in the belief that the ship's best defense was

her speed. Turner had been issued explicit orders to plot a zigzag course, and to stay in mid-channel, well clear of headlands and ports.

By the afternoon of May 7, the *Lusitania* was maintaining a speed of between 15 and 18 kt along a straight course, only 12 miles 19 km) south of the Old Head of Kinsale near Queenstown (now Cork), and thus some way north of the mid-channel course he had been told to follow. The ship was spotted at 1:20 p.m. by Kapitänleutnant Walter Schwieger of the U-20. Some 20 minutes later, at a range of just 765 yards (700 m), the U-20 fired one torpedo. This struck the starboard side of the *Lusitania*'s steel hull aft the bridge, and within seconds the ship had listed 15°. Only 18 minutes separated the torpedo hit and the moment the Lusitania slid into 315 ft (96 m) of water.

Only six of the *Lusitania*'s total of 48 lifeboats survived the sinking,

many of the boats being dropped from a height and crushing the passengers for whom they were intended. Thus, only 764 persons survived the sinking, and the death toll was 1,201 passengers and crew. The latter total included no fewer than 128 neutral Americans who lost their lives in the disaster.

Many of the survivors claimed that there was a second explosion, and some said that they had seen the wake of a second torpedo. Schwieger in fact launched just the single weapon, and wrote in his log that "the explosion of the torpedo must have been followed by a second one (boiler or coal powder)." There have since been claims that any second explosion must have involved the munitions which the *Lusitania* was carrying: the ship's cargo manifest listed 51 tons of fragmentation shells and 10 tons of rifle ammunition. It is almost certain, however, that any and

all later explosions were occasioned by the rupturing of the ship's boilers and high-pressure steam lines. Such ruptures were responsible for the eventual loss of many ships (most of them in 10 minutes or less) during World War I even though their initial torpedo damage appeared to be only slight or moderate.

A great deal, much of it notably ill-informed or even polemical, has been written about the career of the *Lusitania* in World War I. At one extreme, there are some who claim that the British in general, and First Lord of the Admiralty Winston S. Churchill in particular, deliberately sent the *Lusitania* into a known danger zone in the hope that deaths among the American passengers would be instrumental in dragging a still strongly isolationist U.S. into

the war on the side of the Allies. The other end of the spectrum of opinion is occupied by the claim that the sinking of the *Lusitania* was just another in a long list of deliberate German atrocities. As it was, the Germans quickly appreciated that the sinking of the *Lusitania* was helping to turn the tide of American opinion against the German cause, and the German authorities therefore quickly checked the extent and severity of their submarine campaign. The U.S. did not in fact enter World War I until April 1917 after the Germans had, in February of that year, resumed an unrestricted submarine campaign.

The reality of this catastrophe is therefore that the *Lusitania*'s dead were probably the inevitable "collateral" casualties of war.

Lusitania

Type:	transatlantic liner
Tonnage:	31,550 gross registered tons
Dimensions:	length 787 ft (239.9 m); beam 87 ft 6 in (26.7 m); draft not available
Propulsion:	four Parsons geared steam turbines delivering 76,000 shp (56666 kW) to four propellers for 25 kt
Complement:	552 first-, 460 second- and 1,186 third-class passengers plus 850 crew

San Isidoro (1915)

The Eagle Oil and Shipping Co. was established in the UK to ship oil from the oil fields of Mexico to Europe. The company's ships were involved in merchant convoys during both world wars. The company owned *San Demetrio*, reboarded by her crew and saved after being set on fire by a German surface attack in 1940, and was also the manager of the *Ohio* (owned by the Texas Oil Company) in a classic relief convoy to Malta in

28, 1940 as one of convoy H.X.84's 38 ships escorted by the armed merchant cruiser HMS *Jervis Bay*. On November 5 the German pocket battleship *Admiral Scheer* attacked the convoy. The *San Demetrio* was hit several times, the shells setting the upper deck on fire and destroying the bridge and poop deck. The captain thought that the fire would probably set off the aviation fuel and ordered the crew to abandon ship. The two lifeboats

1942. The firm was merged into the Shell International Petroleum Co. in 1959 and disappeared.

The 8,073-ton *San Demetrio* had loaded 12,000 tons of aviation fuel in Galveston, Texas, and was bound for Avonmouth in the UK when she left Halifax, Nova Scotia, on October

became separated in the night, one with the captain and 25 other men being found and the survivors being taken to Newfoundland. The 16 men in the other lifeboat drifted for 24 hours and then sighted the still-burning *San Demetrio*. The men opted to remain in their lifeboat, but after a second freezing night decided to reboard the tanker. They put out the fire, jury-rigged a steering system in the absence of navigation equipment, "guesstimated" a course from glimpses of the sun, and reached the Clyde on November 16.

At the time of her construction, *Ohio* was the largest oil tanker in the world. She was the most important survivor of Operation "Pedestal". During the operation, she was hit by a torpedo, several bombs and one crashing airplane. With her engine room wrecked and nearly broken in half, she was abandoned and reboarded twice before being towed into Grand Harbor, and lashed between two destroyers, on August 14 with most of her cargo of 12,500 tons of fuel for the beleaguered island before finally breaking in two.

Completed in 1914 by Sir W. G. Armstrong Whitworth & Co. Ltd. at Elswick, Newcastle-upon-Tyne, the *San Isidoro* of 15,700 deadweight tons was one of an unprecedented class of 10 very large tankers built for Eagle in 1913-15. The lead unit, the *San Fraterno*, was the largest tanker in the world on delivery in May 1913. At the start of World War I, the *San Isidoro* was sold to France as a naval oiler, and was renamed as the *Dordogne*. She was scuttled in Brest Roads in June 1940 to prevent her falling into German hands in World War II.

San Fabian (class of six similar to the San Isidoro)

Type:	oil tanker
Tonnage:	13,000 gross registered tons
Dimensions:	548 ft (167.0 m); beam 68 ft (20.7 m); draft 32 ft 4 in (9.9 m)
Propulsion:	three geared steam turbines driving one propeller for 10 kt
Complement:	48

River Clyde (1905)

The *River Clyde* was a collier built by Russell & Co. of Port Glasgow in 1905 for the River Clyde S.S. Co. Ltd. There was nothing remarkable about this workaday vessel, which nonetheless acquired fame from April 25, 1915, for her part in the amphibious landing at Cape Helles during the Gallipoli campaign against Turkey in World War I. Carrying some 2,000 troops, mainly of the 1st Battalion Royal Munster Fusiliers, the vessel was beached at "V" Beach beneath the Sedd el Bahr castle on Cape Helles, right at the tip of the Gallipoli peninsula. However, the plan failed and the *River Clyde*, lying under the guns of the Turkish defenders, became a death trap.

For this episode the *River Clyde* was under the command of Commander Edward Unwin, who was a former merchant seaman and Royal Navy officer who had returned from retirement at the start of the war to command a torpedo gunboat, HMS *Hussar*, in the Mediterranean. As revised for the Gallipoli operation, the *River Clyde* had 11 0.303-in (7.7-mm)

in the sides of the hull as ports from which the troops could attack onto a pair of lowered gangways, and thence advance over a bridge of smaller boats linking the ship to the beach. The hull was painted a sandy yellow as camouflage, but the work was incomplete by the time of the landing.

Three attempts were made by the infantry companies of the Munster Regiment

machine guns, provided by the Royal Naval Air Service, installed over the bow behind a breastwork of boiler plate and sandbags. This battery was intended to allow the suppression of Turkish fire as the ship approached the peninsula and then after she had beached herself. Holes had been cut

and also the Hampshire Regiment to get themselves onto the beach, but all ended in bloody failure. Further attempts to land were then abandoned and the surviving soldiers waited until nightfall before trying again. The sailors, who sought with immense bravery to maintain the bridge from the ship to the beach, and to recover the wounded, were awarded six Victoria Crosses, one of them posthumous.

After the Helles beach-head had been established, "V" Beach became the base for the French contingent, and the *River Clyde* remained as a dock and breakwater. Her condensers were used to provide fresh water for the parched men ashore, and a field dressing station was set up in her steel hull. The vessel remained a constant target for Turkish gunners on the Asian shore, south across the narrows of the Dardanelles.

World War I ended in November 1918, and in the following year the *River Clyde* was refloated and repaired in Malta. The vessel was then operated as a tramp steamer in the Mediterranean by Spanish shipping companies for the following half-century. During this time the vessel sailed under a number of names, the last of them being *Maruja y Aurora*. In 1965 there was a British attempt to purchase the vessel for preservation, but in 1966 she was sold for scrap instead and broken up.

River Clyde

Type:	cargo vessel
Tonnage:	3,913 gross registered tons
Dimensions:	344 ft 2 in (104.9 m); beam 49 ft 8 in (15.1 m); draft 19 ft 9 in (5.4 m)
Propulsion:	one triple-expansion steam engine driving one propeller
Complement:	not available

Hedwig von Wissman (1897)

Before World War I, Lake Tanganyika was the border between German East Africa and the Belgian Congo. The Germans planned a flotilla based at Kigoma, its first vessel being the *Hedwig von Wissman*, built in Germany during 1895 by Schiffswerft & Maschinerie of Hamburg. Originally based at Dar-es-Salaam on the coast, she was dismantled and sent by rail to Kigoma, where she was reassembled and relaunched on August 12, 1914. Two days later, she damaged the Belgian *Alexandre Delcommune*. During November, the launch *Kingani* arrived in sections and was soon in service. With the incapacitation of the *Delcommune* and two smaller vessels, the Germans controlled the lake. Two 40-ft (12.2-m) motor boats, named *Mimi* and *Toutou*, were shipped from London to Cape Town and then forwarded by rail, traction engine and river to reach the lake. On December 22, 1915, the first boat was launched at Kalemie. Four days later, the *Kingani* was captured after a short fight, and became the *Fifi*. The British waited for the Germans to investigate, and on February 9 the *Wissman* appeared and was chased by the *Mimi* and *Fifi*. The faster *Mimi* approached the German vessel and engaged her with 12-pdr fire. A shell detonated in the engine room, and the *Wissmann* slowed and sank.

Hedwig van Wissman

Type:	general-purpose steamer
Tonnage:	60 tons
Dimensions:	65 ft (19.8 m); beam 10 ft (3.1 m); draft not available
Propulsion:	one compound steam engine driving one propeller
Complement:	not available
Armament:	one 47-mm gun and one 37-mm gun

Kingani (1894)

The *Kingani* and *Wami* were a pair of customs launches built in Germany by J. L. Meyer of Papenberg in 1894, shipped to German East Africa, and named after rivers in that colony. The two boats were based in at the island of Zanzibar until 1913, when they were transferred to Dar-es-Salaam on the east coast of Africa. In the absence of vessels suitable for service on Lake Tanganyika at the start of World War I, the Germans disassembled the *Kingani* and transported her components by rail to Kigoma, where they arrived on November 10, 1914. Reassembled, she and the *Hedwig von Wissman* maintained a German supremacy on the lake until completion of the larger steamer *Götzen* in June 1915. On December 26, 1915, the *Kingani* was patrolling the lake's Belgian coast when she was attacked by the two British motor boats *Mimi* and *Toutou*. The *Kingani* was captured after a direct hit had damaged her gun and the steam line to the engine, and also killed five of her crew. The vessel was towed to Kalemie, where she was repaired for British service as the *Fifi*, and later took part in the destruction of the *Wissman*. With a shortage of lake vessels after the war, the *Fifi* became the mail steamer along the Tanganyika shore until declared obsolete and scuttled late in 1924.

Kingani

Type:	steam launch
Tonnage:	45 tons
Dimensions:	52 ft (15.85 m); beam 11 ft (3.35 m); draft not available
Propulsion:	one compound steam engine driving one propeller
Complement:	not available
Armament:	one 37-mm gun

British Standard Ships (1917)

Mercantile shipping was the lifeblood of the British economy before World War I, but suffered heavy losses in the first part of the war. Safeguarding the remaining mercantile fleet was clearly a matter of the highest priority, and was in fact not solved until 1917 and the introduction of the convoy system. Also vital was the construction of new shipping by yards whose services were not needed by the Royal Navy. The first meeting of the Merchant Shipbuilding Advisory Committee in December 1916 accepted the notion of building standard ships as a means of maximising building capacity. It was obviously desirable that the number of accepted types should be limited, and the capabilities of the various yards were taken into account in the decision to adopt several lengths. Designs were requested from builders with experience of the type of vessel needed, and the ships were to be cargo vessels with maximum cargo space and minimum use of materials and labour. Experience mandated changes to most of the plans, two major revisions being the relocation of crew accommodation from the forecastle to the poop, and features to lower the silhouette,

The "A" and "B" types were the first and most numerous of types of cargo vessel, the two being one- and two-deck vessels, respectively. The first of the standard vessels was the

"A" type *War Shamrock,* completed in Belfast by Harland & Wolff during August 1917. This company was the major builder of the "A" and "B" types. During 1918, the company completed 33 ships (15, 13 and five in Belfast, Glasgow and Greenock, respectively),

and of this total 26, totalling 136,287 gross registered tons, were standard vessels. This was a greater number of standard type vessels than built by any other British yard. Harland & Wolff excelled not only in numbers of ships, but in the speed with which they were completed: in August 1918, for example, the company completed a ship laid down only 24 weeks earlier.

Note the low profile of British standard ships.

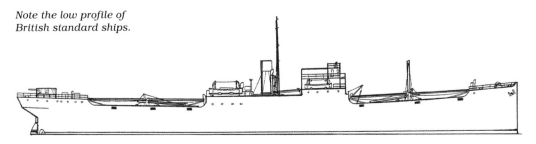

The "A" and "B" types were followed by "C" type with a length of 331 ft (100.9 m) and a deadweight tonnage of 5,050. This was a scaled-down version of its predecessors and built largely for the carriage of coal and/or iron ore. The "D" type had a length of 285 ft (86.9 m) and a deadweight tonnage of 2,980, and these vessels were laid down on shorter slipways

the "C" and "D" types had less power.

There followed the slightly larger the "F" and "F1" shelter-deck types, the latter with between decks included in the cargo space. But the best and largest ships were those of the "G" type. They were also the fastest, being designed for 13 kt with either one or two propellers. The type was designed for fast carriage of frozen

Dazzling camouflage distorted the size, speed and most importantly, the actual course of the vessel, especially through a submarine periscope.

as these became free. A fifth type, the two-deck "E" type, with a length of 376 ft (114.6 m) and a deadweight tonnage of 7,020, was built on slipways not needed for the "A", "B" and "C" types. Only two standard engine sets were used in these five types. The "A", "B" and "E" types were given a unit developing 2,500 hp (1864 kW) while

meat from South America, Australia and New Zealand. In this capacity, when sold to private owners, they were outfitted with different volumes of refrigerated space. Most of the ships were incomplete at the end of the war in November 1918, but were completed to different lines' specific requirements.

"A" type

Type:	cargo ship
Tonnage:	5,030 gross registered tons
Dimensions:	length 412 ft (125.6 m); beam 52 ft (15.85 m); draft not available
Propulsion:	one triple-expansion steam engine delivering 2,500 hp (18634 kW) to one propeller for 11 kt
Complement:	not available

"Z" type (1917)

Given the fact that coal was produced in vast quantities in the UK during World War I, when the use of oil as a fuel was still at a comparatively young and therefore limited stage, it is not surprising that the British construction of dry cargo vessels during this conflict considerably exceeded its building of oil tankers for the mercantile marine.

The first standard tankers built in World War I were the "AO" and "BO" developments of the "A" and "B" type cargo vessels, but there soon followed a dedicated and therefore more fully optimized design, the "Z"' type created specifically for the transport of heavy fuel oil. The design was still based on that of the "A" and "B" types, retaining the same basic dimensions and the same triple-expansion steam machinery, but the gross registered tonnage was increased to about 5,560 tons and the corresponding deadweight tonnage to some 8,460.

1918 the signature of the Armistice was followed by the cancellation of six contracts.

So far as the appearance of the types was concerned, the primary external difference was the addition of an expansion trunk centrally on the weather deck of the "Z" type, the customary side tanks being omitted and creating a low deck on either side of the trunk. Internally the cargo holds were fitted with centerline and tank bulkheads, while the double bottom of the "A" and "B" type cargo ships was replaced by a single hull, characteristic of current tankers, under the cargo spaces.

Of the six vessels cancelled at the end of World War I, two were completed as dry cargo ships by Russell & Co. of Port Glasgow. These were two of the trio with the usual "Z" type names (*War* followed by the name of a warrior race) completed by this yard as 385-ft (117.3-m) between

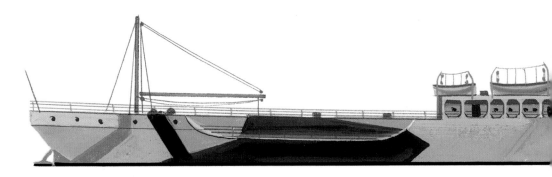

A total of 40 "Z" type tankers was ordered, but despite the urgency attached to the type's design and building as a result of steadily rising demand for oil, the development of the type was slow. Only some six of the tankers had been completed by the end of World War I, and in November

deckers. The third vessel was the *War Peshwa* completed as the tanker *Maudie*, which was specially outfitted for the transport of whale oils and the like.

Many of 34 "Z" type tankers eventually completed were akin to the "AO" and "BO" type tankers in

Dazzle-painted camouflage makes it hard to tell the ship's direction.

being used early in their careers as fleet oilers. Most of these were then sold out of the service in the early 1920s to mercantile operators. Many of the vessels were bought by the Anglo-Saxon company as part of its "C" class. At the same time, other vessels were transferred to the Admiralty as fleet oilers, these then totalling 15 in all.

A significant post-war change in profile was effected in many of the vessels by the replacement of the wartime single-pole mast with pairs of orthodox masts as there was no longer any reduce to reduce the vessel's silhouettes.

Vessels were fitted with a telescopic mast to reduce profile height.

"Z" type

Type:	oil tanker
Tonnage:	5,571 gross registered tons
Dimensions:	412 ft (125.6 m); beam 52 ft (15.85 m); draft not available
Propulsion:	one triple-expansion steam engine delivering 2,500 hp (1864 kW) to one propeller for 11 kt
Complement:	not available

Imo (1889)

The *Runic* was built by Harland & Wolff of Belfast in 1889 as a White Star Line cargo liner and livestock carrier, and in 1912 was sold for conversion as the Norwegian *Imo* for support of whaling operations. On December 6, 1917, the vessel was involved in a collision which led to the world's most powerful man-made explosion before the detonation of the first atomic device in July 1945. The explosion is believed to have been in the order of 3 kilotons, killed an estimated 2,000 people, injured more than 9,000 others, and caused both a tsunami-type wave in the harbor and a pressure wave of air that snapped trees, bent iron rails, demolished buildings, grounded vessels, and carried fragments of the French transport ship *Mont-Blanc* over quite a considerable distance.

On December 1 the 3,121-ton *Mont-Blanc* had departed New York City to join a convoy assembling in the Bedford Basin of Halifax, Nova Scotia. In order to reduce the chance of an attack by German submarines, the vessel was not flying warning flags for its dangerous cargo, which comprised some 2,611 tons of sundry explosives. The ship reached Halifax on December 5, too late for entry as the anti-submarine booms had been closed for the night. At the same time the *Imo* was closed into the harbor as its coal supply had arrived late.

At 8:45 on the morning of the following day, the two vessels should have passed each other in the harbor mouth, but after a flurry of late signals collided, the French ship caught fire, her crew abandoned ship and the vessel drifted onto Pier 6, and at 9:04

The Imo was involved in the collision resulting in the worst explosion in maritime history.

The abandoned Guvernuren (ex-Imo) off the Falkland Islands.

a.m. her cargo exploded. The *Mont-Blanc* was instantly destroyed in a huge fireball that rose more than 5,250 ft (1600 m) into the air and spread into a great mushroom cloud. Shards of hot metal rained down across Halifax and nearby Dartmouth. The force of the blast created a wave some 60 ft (18.5 m) high, and this crashed into Halifax's water front and inland, dragging back and drowning many persons as it receded. The shock-wave through the air knocked over stoves, lamps, and furnaces, and the resulting fire spread throughout the devastation, particularly in Halifax's North End. Firefighters, troops and other volunteers finally had most of the fires contained by the evening. Some 325 acres (841.75 hectares)

of Halifax had been destroyed, leaving everything within a 1-mile (1.6-km) radius of the blast centre uninhabitable. Damage was caused to a radius of 10 miles (16 km), and the explosion was felt to a radius of 225 miles (362 km). Some 1,630 homes were completely destroyed in the explosion and following fires, with 12,000 more houses damaged. The dockyard and industrial sector was destroyed, and many workers were among the casualties.

Six of the *Imo*'s 39-man crew were killed, but the vessel survived and was repaired for use as a whale oil tanker as the *Guvernuren*. The vessel ran aground on rocks off the Falkland Islands on November 30, 1921 and was abandoned.

Imo

Type:	cargo and livestock vessel
Tonnage:	5,043 gross registered tons
Dimensions:	length 430 ft 7 in (131.25 m); beam 45 ft 2 in (13.75 m); draft not available
Propulsion:	one triple-expansion steam engine delivering 424 hp (316 kW) to one propeller
Complement:	not available

König (1896)

After the July 1890 ratification of the Treaty of Berlin by the British and German governments, in which the holdings of the Sultan of Zanzibar on the mainland of East Africa were divided between Germany and the UK, the former started to give serious thought to the development and exploitation of German East Africa (now Tanzania). The German parliament voted to provide a subsidy

received its first purpose-built ships, the *Herzog* and *König*. Each of these was able to carry 65 first-class as well as 50 second- and third-class passengers. Built by the Reiherstiegwerft of Hamburg, the *König* was switched to the route linking Zanzibar and Bombay during 1911, and remained on this route until July 30, 1914, when she reached Dar es Salaam on the eve of World War I's outbreak.

for a mail steamship line to the new colony, and the Deutsche Ost Afrika Linie was established in Hamburg during this same year. The new line's vessels operated via the Mediterranean and the Suez Canal to Zanzibar, Dar es Salaam and finally Durban.

The DOAL's first ships carried few passengers, but in 1896 the line

On October 21, one month after the sinking of the 1897-vintage light cruiser HMS *Pegasus* at Zanzibar by the more modern light cruiser SMS *Königsberg*, the modern light cruiser HMS *Chatham* anchored off the port in search of the raider. The British look-outs could see masts of the *König*, *Feldmarschall* and *Tabora* over the coastal tree line, and the British warship opened fire at the ships in the belief that the masts were those of the *Königsberg*. The Germans hoisted a number of white flags and the firing ceased after the *Feldmarschall* had suffered two men wounded. After identifying the three ships, the *Chatham* departed.

Some five weeks later, the Royal Navy returned on November 28 to disable the vessels. A raiding party consisting of the tug *Helmuth* and two steam cutters set off to investigate

the ships under the terms of a ceasefire agreement. Then the *König*'s engine was rendered inoperative by a demolition charge, and the British party soon had to retire, under fire, to the reassuring bulk of the pre-dreadnought battleship HMS *Goliath*, which was lying at anchor just offshore. The battleship responded to the latest turn of events by shelling the town and destroying the governor's residence. Just a few days later, the *König* was towed to the harbor entrance, where she was to be scuttled as a blockship. The ship swung just before settling on the bottom, however, and ended in the shallows on one side of the harbor entrance rather than in its deeper central channel.

With German East Africa now the British-mandated territory of Tanganyika after World War I, Dar es Salaam started to grow considerably in commercial as well as political importance, and the erstwhile commander of the *Pegasus* was contracted to clear its harbor of wrecks. The *König* was the first of the ships to be refloated, during 1921, and was moved to the upper reaches of the harbor, well clear of the working parts of the port and its approach channel. Three years later she was sold for £500 to a local company, Jiwanji Brothers, for eventual scrapping.

König

Type:	passenger and freight vessel
Tonnage:	4,825 tons displacement
Dimensions:	403 ft (122.8 m); beam 47 ft (14.3 m); draft not available
Propulsion:	two triple-expansion steam engines delivering 2,500 ihp (1864 kW) to two propellers
Complement:	not available

"C1" type Standard Coaster (1918)

Only at a stage late in World War I did the British add coasters to the list of mercantile shipping which should be built in standard types for ease and speed of construction. Thus, only a few such vessels had been completed before the war's end in November 1918. As with the larger standard types, extensive consultation was undertaken with operators and builders before any plans were finalized. There emerged types suited to a number of specialized applications such as coal transport, short-sea transport and, perhaps most importantly of all, the coastal coal and general cargo roles along the east coast of the UK, which were vital but also very vulnerable.

the two-mast *War Arun* and *War Medway* with all aft.

There were also variations in size and designation, for whilst those of the "C6" type were usually 235 ft (71.6 m) long with a deadweight tonnage of 2,040, those of the "C5" type were longer and had a deadweight tonnage of 2,400. Though many of the coaster types were ordered during the war, from more than 20 yards, many were cancelled at the time of the Armistice and some were completed by yards in an effort to capitalize on the anticipated revitalisation of the coastal trade after the war. It should not be imagined, though, that all of the late-war coasters were built to government-sanctioned "new" specifications, for many of the types accepted as standard were in fact successful pre-war designs whose construction continued

The "CS" (Coaster, Standard) type comprised seven sub-types designated between "C1" and "C7" with deadweight tonnages between 400 and more than 3,000 respectively. Despite all efforts to create as small a number of standard types as possible, there could be large numbers of variants within any one sub-type. The "C1" type, for example, included the three-mast *War Irwell* and *War Kennet* with their machinery aft, bridge midships and a raised quarter-deck, and also

in parallel with that of "standard types" both during and after the war.

Typical of this last type was one by H. & C. Grayson Ltd., which had also built four for private owners and was then accepted as a standard shelter-deck type of which the nine were ordered. Two were completed as the War Mersey and War Yare, and in 1919 three more were completed MacAndrews & Co. Ltd., with more in 1920-21 for this and other companies.

Right:
Rough weather made dazzle camouflage even more effective.

Below:
The neat, uncluttered profile of the coasters is obvious even with dazzle paint.

Another example of coasters to standard dimensions extending from the pre- to the post-war years was a series of "three-island" colliers, whose officially ordered units in the war were the *War Thames* and *War Wandle*. These followed the similar private *Lesto* delivered in April 1918, and were themselves followed by more units for private owners, including the *Vae Vectis* delivered in July 1920 and the *Lightfoot* delivered July 1922.

Of the many coasters which were constructed under the war "standard type" effort, many survived for more than 30 years, some including a number of the smallest type for more than 40 years, and a few for more than 50 years. The longest-lived of the vessels were primarily the colliers intended for the British coastal trade and were maintained both well and regularly. One such vessel, the *Jetblack* built by Dublin Dockyard, had by 1949 completed 1,259 coal-carrying voyages between the ports of north-eastern England and London, and then served another five years in the general trade before being scrapped.

After the end of World War I, the arrangement adopted for the disposal of ocean-going "standard type" ships was extended to the smaller "standard type" vessels in an effort to help "rebuild" the British merchant marine after the ravages it had suffered in World War I.

"C1" class *(War Medway)*

Type:	coasting vessel
Tonnage:	366 gross registered tons
Dimensions:	length 143 ft (43.6 m); beam 23 ft 6 in (7.2 m); draft 10 ft 4 in (3.15 m)
Propulsion:	one two-cylinder steam engine driving one propeller
Complement:	not available

Q Ships (1915)

The Q-ship was generally a merchant vessel carrying concealed armament, or, alternatively, an armed vessel designed along mercantile lines. The type was created by the British in World War I in an effort to tackle the German submarine arm, whose boats often surfaced to sink small targets with their guns rather than expend considerably more expensive torpedoes. In the UK the vessels selected for this role were codenamed Q-ships by the Admiralty, but were also known as "decoy vessels," "special service vessels" and "mystery ships." The Germans had similar but larger ships which operated in the merchant raider task against Allied surface shipping. The Q-ship was technically a violation of the Hague Conventions and international law.

In the 1st Battle of the Atlantic, by 1915, the UK had an acute need for a countermeasure against the submarines slashing her maritime lines of communication. The concept of the escorted convoy was initially rejected by both merchant skipper and the Admiralty, the latter citing a lack of the resources required. There was no effective means of establishing the position and depth of a submerged submarine, so the depth charge, though effective in itself, could not be used to any real purpose. Thus the only realistic methods left to sink a submarine were gunfire or ramming. The problem was luring the U-boat to the surface.

The solution to this problem was, it was hoped, the Q-ship. This was apparently an easy target, but at the crucial moment would unmask its armament, which was heavier than that of the submarine, and sink the boat. The Q-ship was typically an old

tramp steamer calmly sailing alone close to an area in which a submarine had been reported. By giving the impression of being an easy target for the submarine's deck gun, the Q-ship lured the submarine to the surface for a gun rather than torpedo attack. The Q-ship's cargo was usually wood in one form of another, so that even if torpedoed by a submerged boat it would remain afloat, thus encouraging the submarine to surface and finishing off the target with its gun. The Q-ship's crew could even stage an "abandon ship" routine.

Once the submarine was in a suitable position and fully surfaced (the diving times of the period were relatively lengthy), the Q-ship underwent a transformation: false panels being dropped to reveal

previously hidden guns, which immediately opened fire. At the same time, the mercantile red ensign was replaced by the naval white ensign. Exploiting the element of surprise and heavier firepower, the Q-ship quickly sank the submarine. This was the theory.

The first Q-ship success was recorded on July 24, 1915, when the *Prince Charles* sank the *U-36*. In August of the same year, an even smaller vessel, a converted fishing trawler named *Inverlyon*, sank the *UB-4* near Great Yarmouth. The *Inverlyon* was an unpowered sailing vessel armed with a 47-mm gun.

On August 19, 1915, the *Baralong* sank *UB-27*, which had been preparing to sink a transport ship in the same area. About a dozen of the sailors escaped the sinking submarine, and the *Baralong*'s skipper, fearing the Germans would scuttle the merchant ship, instructed his men to shoot the German sailors as they swam towards the transport, and then sent a boarding party aboard the ship prevent any attempt to sink it. This episode became known as the "Baralong Incident."

Despite some spectacular actions and a great deal of propaganda, the Q-ships was not very successful in overall terms. In the course of 150 engagements, Q-ships sank only 14 submarines and damaged another 60, at a cost of 27 out of 200 Q-ships lost. The Q-ship was responsible for only about 10% of all submarines destroyed, ranking it considerably below the humble mine field in overall effectiveness.

Her crew having apparently abandoned ship, a Q-ship drops the disguising shields over her armament and opens fire on a surfaced German submarine.

Clyde puffer (1904)

The Clyde puffer was the type of small steam coaster which was the vital supply link around the west coast and Hebridean islands of Scotland (and also around the coasts of Ireland) in succession to sailing schooners and barges. The typical puffer was characterized by great sturdiness, an initial length of about 66 ft (20 m) as dictated by the lock size on the Forth & Clyde Canal, the ability to carry about 100 tons of cargo, and gear to load and unload in the absence of shore facilities.

The puffer had triangular crew's quarters with a table, cooking stove, a folding table, benches and bunk beds in the forecastle, single mast with derrick forward of the large hold, funnel and wheel above the engine room, and captain's small cabin in the stern. When Neil Munro's stories of the puffer *Vital Spark* and her skipper, Para Handy, began to appear in 1905, the wheel was still in the open but a wheelhouse was then added aft the funnel. The puffer also had a flat bottom, allowing the vessel to beach and unload at low tide, a capability essential for the supply of remote communities without a pier.

The puffer developed out of the gabbert, a small single-masted sailing barge of the Scottish coastal trade in the days before steam. The first puffer was the *Thomas*, an iron canal boat of 1856, powered by a simple steam engine without a condenser so that it "puffed" with every piston stroke. Such canal puffers drew their water from the canal, so there was no need to economize on water use. By the 1870s, similar boats were being adapted for use beyond the canal in salt water, and were therefore fitted with steam condensers so that the water could be recycled. Despite the fact that such vessels no longer puffed, the name stuck. Another addition of this period was the derrick on the single mast.

There were three puffer variants. The "inside boat" continued to serve on the Forth & Clyde Canal. The "shorehead boat" reached as far

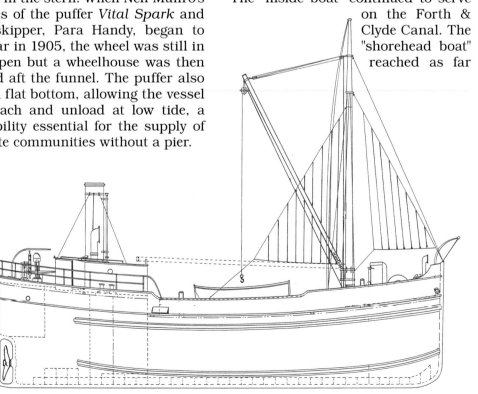

to the east as the Firth of Forth and west as far west as the Isle of Bute and the top of Loch Fyne. Both types had a three-man crew. The third type was the "outside boat" created for the rougher sea routes to the Hebrides with a crew of four and the length increased to 88 ft (26.8 m). This length was determined by the lock size of the Crinan Canal, whose use allowed puffers to avoid the long passage round the Kintyre Peninsula. There were more than 20 builders in Scotland, mainly on the Forth & Clyde Canal at Kirkintilloch and Maryhill, Glasgow. During World War I, the payload and ready availability of the puffer suggested its use in the everyday task of servicing warships, and puffers saw service as far north as Scapa Flow in the Orkney Islands. In World War II the Admiralty placed a 1939 order for generally similar vessels, mostly built in England, with the class name of VIC (victualling). After the end of this war, several VICs came into the coasting trade.

The *Innisgara* was revised with an internal combustion engine in 1912, and though the puffer was still powered by steam for the most part, after World War II new vessels were sometimes completed with a diesel engine and a number of VICs were converted to diesel power. The coasting trade was operated by the Glenlight Shipping Co. until 1993.

A later puffer preserved in Scotland.
Note the wheelhouse behind the funnel.
Photos: John Batchelor.

Sealight (1930)

Type:	"outside boat" puffer
Tonnage:	154 gross registered tons
Dimensions:	length 85 ft 6 in (26.1 m); beam 19 ft 8 in (6.0 m); draft 9 ft 3 in (2.8 m)
Propulsion:	one two-cylinder compound steam engine delivering 50 hp (37 kW) to one propeller
Complement:	4

Oorama (1921)

The Adelaide Steamship Co. Ltd. was established in South Australia during 1875 to operate steamship services linking Adelaide with Melbourne farther to the south-east in Victoria, and subsequently with Australian ports steadily farther afield. For the first 100 years of its life, the company limited its primary activities to conventional mercantile shipping operations along the coasts of Australia for the movement of raw materials, consumer goods and passengers. The extent of the company's activities spread steadily to encircle the whole of Australia including the region round the north coast between northern Western Australia and northern Queensland. The shipping operations were supported by a substantial network of agency offices located in nearly every Australian port of any economic significance. Thus the Adelaide Steamship Co. was, with the Australasian Steam Navigation Co., Huddart Parker, Howard Smith and McIlwraith McEarcharn, one of the pioneers of Australian coastal shipping.

During World War I, the company's passenger and cargo ships saw extensive service as hospital and freight vessels, respectively. The ships also saw extensive military and quasi-military use in World War II.

Though its activities were marked by a number of notable milestones, the company's activities were confined to the Australian coast and as a result the company was known in the international shipping community. Among these milestones, however, two are especially notable. In the 1930s, the company joined with other shipping companies to merge their fledgling airline subsidiaries. These

other shipping companies included Holyman, P & O and Union, and the resulting airline was Australian National Airlines (ANA), which later merged with Reg Ansett's operation to become Ansett ANA, later Ansett Airlines. Perhaps still more significant was the design and development, with McIlwraiths, of the world's first purpose-built container ships. The

Kooringa entered service on the route linking Melbourne and Fremantle in Western Australia during 1964. The vessel was, in effect, a model for the Overseas Container Line and Associated Container Transportation companies, which each sent teams to examine the new concept.

A relatively minor sideline, launched in the 1890s, was tug operations. These operations were gradually extended to a steadily larger number of ports, but until the middle of the twentieth century they remained the poor relation of the financially more-important coastal shipping operations. As the significance of coastal shipping declined, however, towage became more important to the company. Thus, by the 1960s, towage and its associated operations represented a significant part of the company's activities. This continued, even during the 1970s and 1980s when the Adelaide Steamship

Now known as Adsteam Marine Ltd., the company doubled its size in May 2001 when it acquired the towage interests of Howard Smith, its partner in many towage ventures.

Typical of the ships used by the company after World War I was the *Oorama* steam ship of 1,051 gross registered tons. This vessel was completed in 1921 at Paisley on the Clyde as Australia had no yards able to handle the construction of vessels of this size. This was a

Company became the foundation for one of the country's major conglomerate organizations before a stock market crash led to a major fall on share values, halted only by a major disposal of assets.

Towage started to reassert itself as an important element of the company at this time and, after considerable strengthening by merger, the company became a valuable asset disposal candidate in 1997.

two-masted vessel with derricks, holds fore and aft of the central bridge, accommodation structure with access by four hatches, and the engine spaces and further accommodation aft. In 1949 her original owner sold the vessel to the Wallarah Coal Co. Ltd., which operated the vessel for some years as a collier on the route to Sydney in New South Wales.

Princess Louise (1921)

On January 12, 1901, the Canadian Pacific Railway assumed control of the Canadian Pacific Navigation Co., which was revised as the British Columbia Coast Service and resumed operations on May 15, 1903, to provide coastal shipping and ferry services. Through most of its history, the organization included "Princess" in its vessels' names, starting with the 932-ton side wheeler *Princess Louise* of 1869. The organization finally became Coastal Marine, and on November 17, 1998, this and its last ships, the *Carrier Princess* and *Superior Princess*, were sold to the Washington Group of the U.S., ending CPR's 95-year link with Canadian west coast shipping.

With the 1918 loss of one of its newest vessels, the 2,320-ton *Princess Sophia* completed in 1911, the CPR needed a replacement. This presented problems as construction in World War I, which ended in November 1918, had occupied the shipbuilding capability of the British yards from which the CPR had traditionally ordered its ships. Moreover, it would be some years before these yards' order backlogs could be cleared. So the CPR contracted the Wallace Shipbuilding & Drydock Co. of North Vancouver, for a steamer to operate the CPR's route between Vancouver and Alaska. This was the second *Princess Louise*, which was launched on August 29, 1921 as a vessel of almost wholly Canadian construction. Local yards hoped that the completion of this fine steamship would demonstrate that the CPR's later ships should be ordered from Canadian yards. When

launched, the *Princess Louise* was the "Princess" fleet's largest ship.

Built for passenger and cargo operations, the *Princess Louise* was a very reliable and seaworthy vessel right through almost 40 years of continuous service. Her passenger accommodation was originally 133 first-class staterooms and 26 single berths, but because of their small size some of her staterooms were enlarged, reducing the passenger number to 126. She was withdrawn from service in 1964, and in 1966 bought by

the Princess Louise Corporation and towed to Long Beach, California, for use as a restaurant. During a refit, she sank, but was refloated and, while being towed toward Santa Catalina Island to be sunk as a fishing reef, sank once more, this time in the deep water of the San Pedro Channel, in June 1990.

Princess Louise

Type:	coastal passenger and cargo steamer
Tonnage:	4,032 gross registered tons
Dimensions:	length 317 ft 3 in (96.7 m); beam 48 ft 1 in (14.65 m); draft not available
Propulsion:	one triple-expansion steam engine driving one propeller
Complement:	not available

Kungsholm (1928)

With the technical and operational success of the diesel-powered motorship for the transatlantic passenger trade proved by the Gripsholm and completed in 1925, the Svenska Amerika Linien (Swedish America Line) ordered another, but somewhat larger, motorship. Named *Kungsholm*, it was built in Germany by the Blohm und Voss yard of Hamburg for completion in 1928. The ship was specially strengthened for safe navigation through ice, had a displacement of 26,400 tons, and was powered by two Burmeister & Wain four-stroke eight-cylinder direct-acting diesel engines, which burned 75 tons of fuel per day; the maximum fuel capacity was 2,212 tons.

With two masts and two pairs of derrick masts, located equally fore and aft of the central superstructure block, which was surmounted by the pair of funnels containing the diesel engines' exhausts, this nicely conceived motorship operated on the line's route linking Gothenberg and New York right through the 1930s. In this initial phase of her life, the vessel carried up to 1,500 passengers as well as some 294,000 cu ft (8325 m³) of cargo. On the outbreak of World War II in September 1939, the vessel was in New York at the end of the outbound leg of her round-trip service, and at this time the Svenska Amerika Linien redeployed the vessel to the Caribbean cruise trade from American ports.

In December 1941, when Japan precipitated the U.S.'s entrance into World War II with its air attack on Pearl Harbor, the U.S. authorities took over the ship, then released her after

The Kungsholm was the pride of the Swedish merchant marine.
Her funnels were dummies as the ship was powered by diesel engines.

The ship built as the Swedish-flagged Kungsholm later became the U.S.-flagged John Ericsson and Italian-flagged Italia before ending her career as a floating hotel.

a flurry of diplomatic anger from Sweden. Finally in January 1942, the U.S. War Shipping Administration formally bought the *Kungsholm* and renamed her as the *John Ericsson* in honour of the great Swedish-born engineer who had proven so important in the development of U.S. engineering during the middle of the nineteenth century.

The *John Ericsson* was operated as a troopship under the management of the United States Lines. In this capacity the vessel performed very useful service, and after the war she was returned to mercantile service, plying the route between New York and Southampton, via Cobh (near Cork) in Ireland and Le Havre in France, until she suffered severe damage in a fire in New York during March 1947. The vessel was bought back by the Svenska Amerika Linien during July and then sold to the Panamanian-flagged Home Lines in December. Renamed as the *Italia*, the vessel re-emerged from a major refit at Genoa with revised accommodation for totals of 226 first-, 296 cabin- and 800 tourist-class passengers.

The *Italia* made her first voyage from Genoa to South America in 1948, but the emigrant trade for which she had been bought declined rapidly as Europe began to stabilize economically after the end of World War II, and the vessel returned to the service across the North Atlantic, in this instance between New York and ports in the Mediterranean. From 1952 the Hamburg Amerika Linie operated the vessel between Germany, the U.S. (New York) and Canada, and between 1960 and 1964 she worked as a cruise ship from New York, sailing to the Bahamas and the Mediterranean.

Sold to Freeport Bahama Enterprises in 1964, the vessel was moored as the floating hotel *Imperial Bahama*. In 1965 the now elderly vessel was retired and sold to the breaker for scrapping at Bilbao in northern Spain.

John Ericsson

Type:	passenger liner
Tonnage:	20,200 gross registered tons
Dimensions:	595 ft (181.35 m); beam 78 ft (23.8 m); draft 29 ft 3 in (8.9 m)
Propulsion:	two diesel engines delivering 14,000 bhp (10438 kW) to two propellers for 18.5 kt
Complement:	1,500 passengers and 340 crew

Iroquois and *Navahoe* (1907)

Increasing demand for oil at the end of the nineteenth century meant a rapid and major increase in both the number and size of the world's oil tanker fleet. The increase in size was attractive from the owner's point of view, for it allowed the transport of a large volume of oil in a single hull with only one set of machinery, but raised problems for the naval architect. He had long appreciated the need to keep larger tankers, it proved necessary to build tankers with their machinery midships rather than in the after end. This removed the tendency of the vessel to trim by the stern, but was almost inevitably attended by a number of other problems almost always related in one way or another to the tanker's safety. The number of cofferdams isolating the cargo spaces had to be doubled from two to four,

the tanker's payload spaces as tightly grouped as possible. Unfortunately, however, as the oil tanker started to increase in size in the latter part of the nineteenth century, the methods of ship construction at the same time did not allow the concentration of the payload. With the tanker in light condition, the concentration of the machinery at the after end resulted in a large trim by the stern, with the bow possibly lifting out of the water. The result was hull stresses too great for the normal design practices of the day. So when economic factors demanded the design and construction of still but worst of all was the necessity of taking the shaft tunnel through the cargo spaces. Given the fact that the ships of the type were of riveted not welded construction, there was inevitably a measure of working along the seams, and this meant that the shaft tunnel was never gas-free.

Technical solutions to these and other problems were gradually found and implemented, but the desirability of reducing operational costs was a constant concern to the owners of tankers. Faced with the task of transporting large quantities oil across the North Atlantic, the U.S.

parent (Esso) of the Anglo-American Oil Co. Ltd. was, at the start of the twentieth century, making progress with a novel concept, that of tankers towing large tank barges, both along the east and west coasts of the U.S. and also from the West Coast to Hawaii. Anglo-American ordered a larger version of the same concept for transatlantic service, and the result was delivered by Harland & Wolff of Belfast in northern Ireland during 1907-08 as the 9,200 ton tanker *Iroquois*, which was also the world's

towing winch, and winches at each mast for hoisting sails. The thickened fore mast enclosed the funnel for the boiler which supplied the steam for all these auxiliary purposes. With a favourable wind the sails were set to ease the tow load, and the sails could also allow the *Navahoe* to reach port if the tow cable parted and she lost touch with the *Iroquois*.

Between 1908 and 1917, this pair of fascinating vessels made 148 North Atlantic crossings in tandem, averaging a speed of 9 kt. This routing

first tanker of any size to be powered by twin propellers, and the 7,720-ton "barge" *Navahoe*, which was in fact a six-masted sail-assisted schooner.

This combination, which almost inevitably became known as the "horse and cart," had a combined deadweight capacity of more than 18,000 tons of oil. The Iroquois's poop housing accommodated a winch with 1,000 yards (915 m) of 7-in (178-mm) towing wire. The winch was fitted with a steam valve which eased a taut wire and then picked up slack as required. The *Navahoe* was also fitted with engines for heating and pumping, a

was suspended in 1917 as not suitable for the convoy system which had been newly introduced in an effort to reduce losses to German submarines in World War I, and the two vessels were transferred to the route between Texas and Halifax, Nova Scotia. They returned to the U.S.-to-London (usually Thameshaven) route in 1918 and continued on it until 1930. In that year the *Navahoe* became a storage hulk in Venezuela. The *Iroquois* remained in service as a tanker to 1946, when she was scrapped at Dalmuir.

Empress of Britain (1930)

The *Empress of Britain* was an ocean liner of the Canadian Pacific Steamship Company, and in her time the largest, fastest and most luxurious liner operating between the UK and Canada. Built by John Brown & Co. Ltd. on Clydebank, the *Empress of Britain* was launched on June 11, 1930, and departed on her maiden voyage on May 27, 1931. The *Empress of Britain* was designed for cruising as well as liner service, and, in the former, two of her four turbines were shut down and their propellers removed.

On her maiden voyage from Southampton to Quebec, the *Empress of Britain* captured the Canadian Blue Riband by steaming between Cherbourg and Father Point in 4 days, 18 hours and 26 minutes. The ship steadily lowered the time between Europe and Canada in the course of her first six voyages, and in 1934 she recorded an eastbound crossing of 4 days, 6 hours and 58 minutes.

At the start of World War II, (1939-45) the ship was used for trooping between the UK and Egypt via the Cape of Good Hope. At about 9:20 a.m. on October 26, 1940, off the north-western coast of Ireland with 647 persons on board, the *Empress of Britain* was spotted by a Focke-Wulf Fw 200 bomber, which made three attacks and hit the ship twice. The detonations began a fire which quickly raged out of control and began to spread throughout the hapless ship, and by 9:50 a.m. the captain had given the order to abandon ship. Later in the day, the British destroyers HMS *Echo* and HMS *Empress* arrived on the scene, but by then the ship had been evacuated. Now virtually out, the fire had left the ship incapable of moving under her own power, even though she was in no immediate danger of sinking. At 9:30 a.m. on the following day a boarding party readied the ship to be towed by the

Designed and built for the route linking the UK and the east coast of Canada, the Empress of Britain was a fine and capable liner.

Seen here in happier times, the Empress of Britain had the unfortunate distinction of becoming the largest liner to be sunk by enemy action in World War II.

Polish destroyer *Burza*. Hearing of the crippled liner by radio, the submarine *U-32* intercepted the ships later in the same day and followed for some time. At about 2:00 a.m. on October 28, the U-32 fired three torpedoes, one of which hit the *Empress of Britain*, which sank nine minutes later. The ship was the largest vessel sunk by a German submarine, and also the largest liner lost, in World War II.

Many believed that the *Empress of Britain* had been carrying bullion when she sank, for at this time the UK was shipping gold to North America to improve its credit, and had called at Cape Town in South Africa, a major gold producer. Most South African gold went from Cape Town to Sydney in Australia and thence to the U.S., but at the time there were not enough ships suitable for this task, and gold was proceeding no farther than Sydney. Some believed, therefore, that the Empress of Britain might have been used to take gold from South Africa to the UK for shipment to North America.

In 1995 a salvage group found the *Empress of Britain* lying upside-down at a depth of 500 ft (150 m). Divers entered the wreck and found that the fire had destroyed most of the decks, leaving little more than an empty shell on the bottom. The bullion room was intact, however, but contained only a skeleton, though why this should be the case had yet to be explained.

Empress of Britain

Type:	transatlantic liner
Tonnage:	42,348 gross registered tons
Dimensions:	length 790 ft (240.8 m); beam 97 ft 4 in (29.7 m); draft not available
Propulsion:	four geared steam turbines delivering 66,500 shp to four propellers for 26.5 kt
Complement:	465 first-, 260 tourist- and 470 third-class passenger, and 740 crew

Vienna (1929)

When the Great Eastern Railway was merged with two other British railway companies to form the London & North Eastern Railway in 1923, the steamship services previously operated by the GER continued under the LNER name. Ordered as the first of three ships intended as replacements for earlier ships, the *Archangel, St Denis* and *St George,* the *Vienna* was ordered in 1928 from John Brown & Co. Ltd. of Clydebank, and launched at which the cross-Channel service was growing that even though the design offered considerably more payload space and volume than had been provided by the predecessor type, there was need for greater space by the early 1930s. In 1932, therefore, the ship was taken in hand to have her promenade deck extended aft to the main mast to generate additional saloon space. In June of the same year, the ship was committed to a

on April 10 of the following year. The *Vienna* and her two sister ships were scheduled for service on the night service between Harwich in eastern England and Hoek van Holland in the Netherlands. The ships were the largest yet ordered for cross-Channel services.

The *Vienna* entered service on July 15, 1929, and such was the pace program of summer cruises to ports along the coast of continental Europe. This summer-time career lasted to 1939, when the threat of war ended all thought of continuing the program in the near future.

In July 1935 the *Vienna* was present, with guests, at the Spithead silver jubilee naval review of King George V. The ship continued on her cross-Channel service until March 1940, when the Hoek van Holland was closed as a result of the threat of German invasion. The ship was immediately reallocated to the trooping role, ferrying British soldiers from Southampton to across the English Channel to ports in northern France. In 1941 the *Vienna* was bought by the Ministry of War Transport, and was converted as a depot ship for motor torpedo boats operating in the Mediterranean, and in November 1942 was moved to Algiers after the Allied invasion of French northwest Africa. The ship continued initially as a repair ship for MTBs, but was later adapted as an accommodation ship and fitted with a number of anti-aircraft guns so that she could contribute to the defence of the port against Axis air attack.

The *Vienna* remained in the Mediterranean for some time, at Bari in southeastern Italy from a time late in 1943, before finally being returned to the UK. In 1945 the ship was operated by LNER management once more, although under the supervision of the Ministry of War Transport, as a troopship between Harwich and the Hook of Holland. With World War II over, the ship was refitted as a 1,048-berth leave ship for the British occupation forces in Germany (later the British Army of the Rhine), still under LNER management. In this capacity, the ship operated between Harwich and the Hook of Holland and between Tilbury and Ostend.

On February 11, 1952, the *Vienna* was badly damaged in an explosion and fire, which killed two persons, while berthed at Harwich. The engine room suffered damage which required many weeks of repair. The ship returned to service after this, and maintained its cross-Channel operations until being retired in July 1960. On September 4 of the same year, the vessel arrived in Ghent and was scrapped by Van Heyghen Frères.

In her day the Vienna and her two sister ships were the largest ferries operating on the routes across the English Channel and southern end of the North Sea.

Vienna

Type:	short-sea ferry
Tonnage:	4,227 gross registered tons
Dimensions:	length 350 ft 8 in (109.9 m); beam 50 ft 1 in (15.25 m); draft 26 ft (7.9 m)
Propulsion:	two Brown-Curtis geared steam turbines driving two propellers for 21 kt
Complement:	444 first- and 104 second-class passengers, cars and freight, and crew

President Hoover (1930)

Scottish-born Robert Dollar emigrated to Canada in 1857 at the age of 13. In 1893 he bought a sawmill on the U.S.'s Pacific coast, and soon had a flourishing timber business. In 1893 or 1895, Dollar bought his first vessel, a 120-ft (36.6-m) steam schooner named *Newsboy,* from a bankrupt sawmill, to move his lumber to markets down the west coast of the U.S.. In the process, Dollar established the Dollar Steamship Co., which soon built up a modest fleet. In 1902 the company entered the international market, initially using a chartered vessel, for services to Yokohama in Japan and to Filipino ports.

In 1923 Dollar bought seven "502 President" ships from the U.S. Shipping Board, which had built them in World War I. In March 1925 Dollar took over an additional eight "535 President" ships from the Shipping Board but managed by Pacific Mail Steamship Company for services across the Pacific. Dollar's all-cash offer was lower than Pacific Mail's cash and stock offer, so for an outlay of U.S. $5.625 million, therefore, the company secured ships worth US$30 million, and was now able to start a westbound round-the-world service in addition to its standard routes across the Pacific. In 1925 Dollar took over Pacific Mail, and also bought the bankrupt Admiral Oriental Line.

The Dollar Line was now one of the world's most profitable shipping companies. In 1929 the company was renamed the Dollar Steamship Line Inc., bought two more ships for its round-the-world route, and decided on a major transpacific expansion with six new ships. The line received a loan of more than US$5 million from

the U.S. government on condition that the vessels carried the U.S. mail.

In the event, only two of the six vessels were built, as the sister ships *President Hoover* and *President Coolidge,* by the Newport News Shipbuilding & Drydock Co. of Newport News, Virginia. The first was launched on December 6, 1930 by Mrs Herbert Hoover, and the second on February 21, 1931 by Mrs Grace Coolidge, widow of President Calvin

The President Hoover was an attempt to buck the economic decline of the period, but could nor do so.

Coolidge. When the *President Coolidge* was delivered on October 1, 1931, the Dollar Line had the two largest passenger ships built in the U.S. up to that time. The two ships were stunning by the standards of the day, and the luxurious accommodations and Art Deco furnishings of the ships rivalled those of the best hotels of the period. Each ship boasted outdoor swimming pools, a gymnasium, and a telephone system linking every stateroom and passenger cabin. The two ships' levels of luxury and elegance contrasted starkly with the grim nature of this time in the middle of the Great Depression, which lasted in diminishing form until the outbreak of World War II in 1939. The design of the two ships included a number of innovative features, some of them notably advanced. One of these was a turbo-electric propulsion arrangement with steam turbines powering electric motors, and the layout proved very economical.

By the late 1930s, the threat of another world war was having an adverse effect on passenger traffic and thus the line's profitability, and the ships were at times laid up. On December 12, 1937, while on passage from Kobe to Manila, the *President Hoover* ran aground off Formosa. Many efforts were made to salvage the vessel before she was declared a loss. The line became bankrupt in the same year, but was bought by the U.S. government as "American President Lines."

President Hoover

Type:	passenger liner
Tonnage:	21,936 gross registered tons
Dimensions:	length 654 ft (199.3 m); beam 81 ft (24.7 m); draft not available
Propulsion:	two geared steam turbines powering two electric motors driving two propellers for 20 kt
Complement:	307 first-, 133 tourist-, 170 third- and 378 steerage-class passengers, and 324 crew

Great Lakes ships

Steamers were introduced on the eastern Great Lakes in 1816, and first appeared on Lake Superior in 1845. These were side-wheelers, and there is no evidence of stern-wheelers on Lake Superior, and the first propeller-driven steamers were introduced in 1840. The steamers were generally laid out with two or more decks, with holds for cargo below decks. Accommodation was provided in cabins on deck, and steamers lacking such passenger cabins were known as package freighters. They had two boilers midships. Most early side-wheelers also carried one to three masts. Propeller-driven steamers had one or two propellers, and their machinery was located aft. Some propeller steamers carried masts into the closing stages of the nineteenth century. Propeller steamers were the most important type on Lake Superior, the most western of the lakes, and were used for passengers and freight. The vessels increased in size throughout the nineteenth century, and came to have iron

With the pilot house forward and machinery aft, the Great Lakes bulk carriers had the whole of the central portion free for bulk cargo.

decks and side-loading gangways. Specialized types of steamers were developed after 1850, but the basic types continued into the twentieth century.

Side-wheel steamers had two large paddle wheels with their engines and or, later, steel hulls. The steamers worked in conjunction with railways until the early part of the twentieth century, but then the demand for waterborne freight decreased as rail capability increased. The same then came to apply to passengers as the railways were supplemented and then largely replaced by the car, bus and airplane. The last of the large passenger steamers ended their lives as excursion vessels.

Bulk freight steamers were generally of the propeller-driven type for the movement of cargoes such as coal, grain, iron ore and stone. Such vessels included steamers, steam barges and more specialised types such as whalebacks. The propeller-driven vessels generally had two decks and a small raised forecastle, and nineteenth-century bulk freight steamers generally carried three or four masts. The first bulk freighters were built around 1865 to carry timber, but the basic design was adapted for "coarse freight" in 1869, creating a unique hybrid type.

Steam barges were small, single-decked propeller steamers with powerful engines and small cabins at the stern, and also had raised poop decks. The pilot house was located aft on the early steam barges, but from 1880 was placed on a raised forecastle with a well-deck between bow and stern. Most carried up to three masts. Steam barges carried a modest cargo and towed two or more barges.

Lady Elgin (1851)

Type:	passenger steamer
Tonnage:	819 tons displacement
Dimensions:	252 ft (76.8 m); beam 33 ft 9 in (10.3 m); draft 14 ft 4 in (4.4 m)
Propulsion:	one steam engine driving two side paddle wheels
Complement:	200 cabin and 100 deck passengers, 800 tons of freight and 43 crew

Europa & Liberté (1929)

Built by the Blohm & Voss yard of Hamburg in north Germany, the *Europa* and her sister ship *Bremen*, built by A. G. Weser of Bremen, were oceanic liners built in the late 1920s for the NDL (Norddeutscher Lloyd) line, which wanted advanced and very comfortable liners for passenger service on its prestigious transatlantic route. Both very handsome, with two low but long-chord funnels, the ships were very similar but not in fact identical, the *Bremen* being slightly larger, among other differences. The ships were designed for a cruising speed of 27.5 kt, which made feasible a North Atlantic crossing of five days. This made it possible for NDL to operate a regular weekly crossing schedule with two ships, a feat which otherwise required three ships.

It had been intended that the two ships should be completed at the same time, but the *Europa* was damaged by a severe fire as she was being fitted out, and sank to the bottom, although only in shallow water. The vessel was repaired and refloated, but there was an inevitable delay of several months before she could enter service with accommodation for 687 first-, 524 second-, 306 tourist- and 507 third-class passengers. Thus it was March 19, 1930 before the *Europa* departed on her maiden voyage and captured the Blue Riband from the *Bremen* in the course of this run, recording an average of 27.9 kt between Cherbourg and the Ambrose Light. The *Bremen* regained the Blue Riband after modifications to her machinery in June 1933, and held it until the Italian liner *Rex* took it in August 1933.

In August 1939 the *Europa* was about to enter the Atlantic when her captain received an order to return to Bremerhaven, blacked out and in radio silence. At Bremerhaven the ship's passengers disembarked, and a few days later World War II began. The ship was painted grey and was used as a stationary accommodation ship for the German navy. In 1940 she was moved to Hamburg, as was the case with the *Bremen*, for conversion as a troopship to be used in the planned German invasion of the UK. The plan was later abandoned but the Europa returned to Bremerhaven, some thought then being given to the ship's conversion as an aircraft carrier. The *Europa* survived World War II, and was seized by the advancing U.S. forces on May 8, 1945. The vessel was then pressed into service as a troopship until it was discovered

The Liberté was notable for her very handsome appearance, little altered from the German original, but the inside had been completely "Gallicized" with Art Deco public rooms.

Left: A French publicity poster for the Liberté.

that years of wartime neglect had exercised a malign effect on her hull and wiring.

In 1946 the *Europa* was allocated to France as war reparation, and there began a four-year refit program. While being refitted at Le Havre, the ship snapped her moorings in a storm, ran into the wreck of the pre-war liner *Paris,* and sank. She was raised and moved to St Nazaire for the completion of her refit, and in August 1950 she made her maiden voyage under her new name, *Liberté* (originally to have been *Lorraine*), to New York. Working in concert with the *Ile de France* and *Flandres,* the *Liberté* was the mainstay of the French transatlantic passenger capability for the next 10 years. The ship was withdrawn from service in 1961, and in the following year was broken up at La Spezia.

Liberté

Type:	transatlantic liner
Tonnage:	51,839 gross registered tons
Dimensions:	length 936 ft (285.3 m); beam 102 ft (31.1 m); draft 34 ft (10.4 m)
Propulsion:	four geared steam turbines delivering 105,000 shp (78288 kW) to four propellers for 27.5 kt
Complement:	569 first-, 562 cabin- and 382 tourist-class passengers, and about 965 crew

Knight of Malta (1929)

The *Knight of Malta* was the single most important ship of her type built for Maltese owners. It has been suggested that her nice profile and owned by Blands of Gibraltar, operated services between Gibraltar and both Tangier and Casablanca.

Built and engined by Swan, Hunter

indicates at least some knowledge by the designer of a pair of 1,800-ton P & O ships, the *Isis* and *Osiris*. Before World War I, these two had operated an express service delivering mail from Brindisi in southern Italy across the Mediterranean to Suez in Egypt, where the mail was passed on to the P & O's larger oceanic mail ships sailing to the east. A slightly more probable link is provided by the fact that during the early 1920s the Isis, now renamed as the *Gibel Sarsar*

& Wigham Richardson Co. Ltd. of Newcastle-upon-Tyne in northeast England, the *Knight of Malta* was not as fast as the two P & O "fliers." The ship resulted from a contract placed by the Casser Co. Ltd. of Valetta on Malta for a vessel to serve in the passenger and mail role between Malta and Syracuse in Sicily, and also between Malta and other Mediterranean destinations.

The vessel could carry more than 2,000 tons of payload, and her machinery was based on one triple-expansion steam engine provided with steam by three single-ended, multi-tubular boilers. The *Knight of Malta* had two decks and two holds, the latter served by two 3-ton derricks and steam winches. The hull was double-bottomed and carried water ballast, but nonetheless acquired a reputation for rolling. Midships on the bridge and upper decks, there was accommodation for 63 first-class passengers in one- and two-berth cabins, and the ship's public rooms included an entrance hall/music room, smoking room, and dining saloon; there was also a sheltered observation area at the forward end of the promenade deck. Aft there were four-berth cabins and some public rooms for about 30 second-class passengers, while forward there was steerage-class accommodation for 16 emigrants.

The *Knight of Malta* was launched from Neptune Yard at Walker-on-Tyne on October 2, 1929, and carried out successful trials in December of the same year, recording a speed of more than 15.5 kt. In her initial period of service the ship black-topped white funnels, but these were later repainted red to avoid the possibility of confusion with the ships of the Tirrenia Line, which also operated in this part of the Mediterranean.

At the outbreak of World War II in September 1939, the *Knight of Malta* was impressed by the Ministry of War Transport, for which it was managed by Harris & Dixon Ltd. of London. After being used in turn as an armed boarding vessel and naval store carrier, the ship was lost to enemy action in March 1941.

There was nothing remarkable about the Knight of Malta, which nonetheless gave good service in the tasks and on the routes for which she was designed.

Knight of Malta

Type:	passenger and cargo vessel
Tonnage:	1,555 gross registered tons
Dimensions:	length 270 ft (82.3 m); beam 47 ft (11.3 m); draft 15 ft 8 in (4.8 m)
Propulsion:	one triple-expansion steam engine driving one propeller for 15.5 kt
Complement:	63 first-, 30 second- and 16 steerage-class passengers, cargo, and crew

Llangibby Castle (1929)

The Union-Castle Line operated a substantial fleet of passenger liners and freighters between Europe and Africa between 1900 and 1977. The company came into being on March 8, 1900 as the Union-Castle Mail Steamship Co. Ltd. through the merger of the Union Line and the Castle Shipping Line, the latter taking over the fleet. Union-Castle named all of its ocean-going ships with the first word "Castle" in their names, and became celebrated for its lavender-hulled liners with black and red funnels. In May 1919 the company bought Bullard, King's Direct Line, and in October resumed the weekly mail service to the Cape of Good Hope and the service round Africa, both of which had been interrupted by World War I.

The *Llangibby Castle* was built by Harland & Wolff at Govan near Glasgow and launched on July 4,

1929. After completion, the vessel was delivered as the first motor ship (diesel-engined vessel) for service on the route round Africa. In 1934 the third-class accommodation was upgraded to tourist-class, and "Round Africa" cruises were introduced at fares of £105 first- and £40 tourist-class respectively.

In July 1940, after the vessel had arrived in Falmouth from Cape Town, she was requisitioned for service as a dedicated troopship as her accommodation was ideal for the transport of one battalion, and she initially carried troops from the UK to South Africa and East Africa. On December 21-22, 1940, she was one of 11 ships damaged in a German air raid on Liverpool. En route from the Clyde to Singapore on January 16, 1942, the ship was torpedoed north of the Azores by the U-402, losing her stern and after gun but retaining

Llangibby Castle in its unique color scheme.

her propellers. The ship was carrying 1,400 troops as well as her crew, but only 26 men were killed in this episode, and the ship managed to reach Horta at 9 kt, beating off attacks by German long-range bombers as she did so. The Portuguese authorities allowed only 14 days for emergency repairs, and on February 2 the *Llangibby Castle* steamed to Gibraltar under escort, still with the troops on board and lacking her stern and rudder. On the following day, the group of ships encountered and fought off the attack of a U-boat pack. A tug took the *Llangibby Castle* in tow to assist in course keeping, and on February 8, the ship reached Gibraltar, where the troops were landed. After 57 days the ship left Gibraltar on April 6, still lacking her rudder and still with an escort, for the trip back to the UK, which she reached on April 13 using only her engines for steering.

On November 9, 1942 the *Llangibby Castle* was part of the assault force involved in the Allied landing in French North-West Africa. In 1943 the vessel returned once more to the UK for repair to her bow, which had been damaged at Gibraltar as preparations were being made for the Allied assault on Italy. The opportunity was taken to convert the ship into an LSI (Landing Ship Infantry) with 18 landing craft. After working up in her revised role in Loch Fyne, the vessel served in the Mediterranean for six months as a troop transport.

In 1944 she was allotted to the assault force for the landing on Juno beach in Operation Overlord. In this undertaking, implemented on June 6, 1944, she was to deliver 1,590 troops embarked at Southampton. On D-Day she landed the first wave of 750 Canadian troops at Courseulles, but as they returned from the beach 10 of her landing craft were swamped. The second wave of 750 men was nonetheless landed by the remaining landing craft in two lifts. The *Llangibby Castle* remained off Juno breach for nine hours, and later, during the invasion, landed men on the Omaha and Utah beaches, and finally at Le Havre. During this phase of her life, the *Llangibby Castle* recorded more than 70 Channel crossings and carried more than 100,000 men.

When the European campaign of World War II ended in May 1945, the *Llangibby Castle* moved to the Far East, where she carried out more trooping duties. In January 1946 she made three voyages repatriating some 6,000 troops.

The *Llangibby Castle* was restored to the Union-Castle Line in January 1947, after a period in military service in which she had carried 156,134 troops. A refit was essential, and in 1949 she had to cancel one such voyage after a fire in one of her holds. On June 29, 1954, the ship steamed from Tilbury to Newport in Wales for breaking.

Llangibby Castle

Type:	passenger and cargo liner
Tonnage:	11,951 gross registered tons
Dimensions:	length 485 ft 7 in (148.0 m); beam 66 ft 2 in (20.2 m); draft not available
Propulsion:	two Burmeister & Wain eight-cylinder diesel engines delivering 1,300 hp (969 kW) to two propellers for 14.5 kt
Complement:	not available

Chulmleigh (1938)

At the outbreak of World War I (1914-18), the Tatem Steam Navigation Co. Ltd. was one of the most significant shipping companies based in south Wales, and had a fleet of 16 modern steamers. Only eight of the ships tramping role, and offered passenger accommodation on none of its ships. The company's tramp steamers were generally in the order of 5,000 tons. Typical of the breed during the 1930s was the 5,445-ton *Chulmleigh*,

survived World War I, and were then sold off as the company decided to buy six modern ships. The company continued to expand during the 1920s and 1930s despite the poor economic situation which affected many of the shipping companies of the time. The company relocated to London in the 1960s as a result of the steady decline of the south Wales coal industry. The company sold its last vessel, the *Exning*, in 1973 and then turned to other interests.

The Tatem shipping company operated its vessels in the world-wide which was registered in London and had been built in 1938 by William Pickersgill of Sunderland in northeast England. In external appearance the *Chulmleigh* was a typical but attractive South Wales tramp with masts and derricks for the holds fore and aft of the central superstructure, and a raised bridge and central funnel for the standard steam machinery. Internally, however, the *Chulmleigh* was quite radically different from most of her contemporaries, which might charitably be described as offering spartan rather than opulent accommodation. Tatem was an entirely self-made man and had developed a taste for the better things in life. This penchant was evident in the type of crew accommodation on which he insisted for his ships. Thus the *Chumleigh*'s cabins, for the crew as well as the officers of the 58-man complement, were both spacious and

well furnished, the dining saloon was panelled with polished mahogany, and the quarters of the captain were in no way significantly inferior to those offered by many first-class hotels. The same level of concern was also evident in the first-class nature of the vessel's construction and maintenance, and in the machinery. This last was accommodated in an engine room of notable cleanliness, and was based on a triple-expansion steam engine made by Richardsons, Westgarth & Co. Ltd. of Hartlepool, also in the north-west of England.

The machinery was not powerful, as speed was not required for tramping service, but it was solid, reliable and economical.

In the autumn of 1942, while awaiting clearance to depart from Philadelphia, Pennsylvania with a 5,000-ton cargo of war matériel, the ship was ordered to proceed to Halifax, Nova Scotia, for further orders. These informed the *Chumleigh*'s captain that his was to be one of 10 vessels tasked with running independently to a port in the northern USSR, braving weather which was likely to be appalling, and German attack which was likely to be intense.

The ship was some 20 miles (32 km) north of her intended course as she passed to the south of Spitsbergen, however, and ran onto a reef late on November 5. The crew could not get the vessel off and abandoned ship just before she was attacked by German bombers as she lay stranded. There followed a period in which the British sailors needed great endurance as they sought to reach Spitsbergen in open boats and then survive on this barren Arctic island. The men managed to find a deserted hut, and survived in diminishing numbers to January 2, 1943, when they were found by a Norwegian patrol. Taken to Barentsburg, the nine survivors were nursed back to health over a period of two months, and then two months after that were collected by a British warship.

The *Chumleigh* had not been allowed any respite as her crew fought to remain alive. Eleven days after she ran aground, the wrecked vessel was torpedoed by U-625 and again bombed. Her rusting hulk still rests off the southern point of Spitzbergen, a monument to the 51 members of her crew who died.

Tugs

An essential element of all types of maritime operations, the tug was and still is a relatively small but notably sturdy vessel with a high power/weight ratio. The ocean-going tug is used for the towage of ships at sea, and the harbor tug has its metier in maneuvering and assisting ships in confined spaces, especially when berthing. Such vessels were first known as tug-boats. The tug appeared, of course, only with the advent of steam power, and the first steam vessels adopted by the Royal Navy, in 1822, were the tugs *Comet* and *Monkey*.

Harbor tugs are usually fitted with a single propeller (originally two side paddles) or two propellers if they have to operate outside a harbor, and with a displacement of 250 tons to 2,500 hp (1864 kW). Ocean-going tugs are larger, with a displacement of up to 2,000 tons and upwards of 15,000 hp (11184 kW) available. Ocean-going tugs also have greater endurance, and are operated either for salvage of ships disabled at sea, or for the towage of ships, floating docks and the like to distant destinations. A basic design of all tugs is the very pronounced overhang of their counters to ensure that the towing hawser, should it part or fall slack into the water, does not foul the tug's propeller(s).

The first tug was the *Charlotte Dundas*, which revealed the

Above:
HMS Rollcall was built in World War I as an ocean-going rescue tug, and was sold after the war to become the tender tug Romsey in the Solent.

Right:
The Danny nicely represents the unglamorous but totally necessary nature and function of the harbor tug.

tug's basic capabilities. These early vessels were general-purpose paddle steamers which were operated as ferries and tugs. Towing ships was more profitable than the carriage of passengers, though, and ferry timetables were often disrupted so that a vessel could undertake a towage job. Steam towage had developed as a single-role task on the Tyne and the Clyde by 1830, on the Thames by 1833 and on the Mersey by 1836.

Early tugs were propelled by side paddles powered by low-pressure boilers supplying steam to side-lever engines. From the middle of the nineteenth century, many paddle tugs had a pair of engines side by side to drive the paddle wheels separately and to offer greater agility. Experiments with propeller-driven tugs started in 1836, but some paddle tugs remained in service until the 1960s. As it was always buried in the water, the propeller produced more power than paddle wheels, but lacked the latter's manoeuvrability.

The first propeller tug was the *Francis B. Ogden*, designed by John Ericsson. Its trials on the Thames were moderately successful, but propeller propulsion was not adopted for tugs until the 1870s, after the advent of high-pressure boilers, compound engines and more effective propeller designs.

From the mid-nineteenth century, the tug escalated steadily in size, power and versatility, and in the last part of the century the tug became more specialized. The harbor tug was and indeed remains the most common type. Such a tug has to maneuver large vessels with little steerage way of their own in confined spaces without damaging other ships and dock installations. Before radio allowed vessels to arrange to be met by a tug, some of the larger harbor tugs cruised at sea in the hope of securing the custom of a sailing vessel which might not otherwise be able to reach port conveniently. Another option for a tug on the look-out for trade in open water was the chance of coming across a sailing vessel in danger on a lee shore, saving her and claiming salvage.

The introduction of the propeller and the compound engine were important developments in the 1880s. The propeller offered more power at a time when ever-larger ships were being built, and the compound engine provided more power and lower fuel consumption than the traditional side-lever engine. The tow-rope is also a key component of tug gear, and has to be strong but at the same

A tug in a Greek port. Note the long after deck and overhanging counter to ensure the safe working of the tow-rope.
Photo: John Bathelor.

Tugs *continued*

Tugs at work.

time elastic to cope with the sudden shocks it can receive. The minimum-size tow-rope was about 7 in (173 mm) in circumference, and the tow-rope was made from manila, sisal or coir. Man-made fibres are common today.

A length of one of these materials is usually attached to steel wire rope for the required combination of strength and elasticity. The tow-rope is attached amidships to a swivelling towing hook, though to keep the tug stable it is sometimes lashed down in a central position while the boat is at work in dock or sheltered waters. The towing hook has a quick-release mechanism so that the tow can be slipped if the tug is being pulled over by its charge, and an iron frame or frames on the stern deck keep the rope clear of the deck.

Left: The Abeille No. 12 harbor tug in Le Havre.

Below: A typical harbor tug in a graving dock.

The definitive harbor tug form had appeared by 1900. The vessel was about 100 ft (30.5 m) long with the steering position forward, a tall funnel to provide plenty of draft for the large single boiler below, a long clear after deck over the engines and crew quarters (right over the noisy propeller shaft), and the towing hook almost amidships for maximum stability.

The size of tugs steadily increased and additional features, such as a wheel-house, were added. Some owners introduced diesel-engined tugs from the late 1940s, but most remained loyal to steam power for its reliability and easy maintenance. Steam-powered tugs were built into the late 1950s with oil- rather than coal-fired boilers and a Kort nozzle (shrouded propeller) for great power and, in its swivelling form, enhanced agility.

Large vessels may need more than one tug, including one at the bow to steer the ship, one at the stern to check the ship and prevent its stern from swinging, and one or two to push the ship sideways into its berth. All tugs are fitted with a heavy bow fender for this work. Large liners may need as many as six harbor tugs. Since the late 1960s there has been something of a change, characterized by larger and more powerful tugs. The modern tug is diesel-engined with more than double the power and bollard pull of earlier tugs.

The end of the line for hard-working but elderly British harbor tugs moored as they await their turn in an American east-coast breaker's yard in the late 1970s.

"YTB" class (1961)

Type:	large harbor tug
Tonnage:	400 tons full load
Dimensions:	length 109 ft (33.2 m); beam 30 ft 6 in (9.3 m); draft 13 ft 6 in (4.1 m)
Propulsion:	two diesel engines delivering 2,000 bhp (1491 kW) to two propellers for 12.5 kt
Complement:	12 crew

Arcturus (1937)

The Argo Line was set up in Bremen during 1896 by a local ship owner, Heinrich Friedrich Bisschoff, and other local interests as the Dampfschifffahrtsgesellschaft Argo with five Bisschoff ships, and began with services east into the Baltic Sea and to Russia, and west to the West Indies and to New Orleans in the southern U.S. In July 1897 Argo took over the North Sea routes of Norddeutscher Lloyd, together with the seven vessels which NDL had used for these routes. The company's growth was rapid, and by 1901 it had 26 ships and had begun a new liner service to Italy. By 1902 Argo had gained control of the Hanseatischen Dampfschifffahrtsgesellschaft undertaking services in the Baltic Sea, and complete ownership during 1906. After poor results, the service to New Orleans had been terminated in 1904, and the ships which served this route were initially chartered to other shipping companies and then sold to the Woermann Linie. In 1905 Argo and NDL established the Dampferlinie Atlas to operate services into the eastern end of the Mediterranean. Three years later, Atlas merged with the Deutsche Levante Linie, and in this same year ended services from Bremen to Italy.

In 1914 Argo had 30 ships, of which 12 were lost in World War I. In 1918 the company had eight ships on order or under construction, but in 1919-21 was compelled to hand over nine to France and the UK as war reparations; four were later sold back to the company. In 1922 Otto Wölff gained control of the company, but later in the same year sold his holding to the Roland Linie, after which Argo was merged into Roland.

At the end of 1923 a new company, the Dampfschifffahrtsgesellschaft Argo, was established to take over Roland's European services. The NDL took over Roland at the end of 1925 and the Argo funnel markings and house flag disappeared from 1926. Then in 1933 the NDL created Argo Reederei through the merger of two other NDL lines, namely the Hanseatischen

The Arcturus was typical of the type of freighter built in the later part of the 1930s.

Dampf-schifffahrtsgesellschaft and Reederei Aktien Gesellschafft von 1896.

In 1936 the Argo Reederei became the Argo Reederei Richard Adler & Co. Two ships which entered service soon after this were two half-sister freighters, the 2,500-ton diesel-powered motor ship *Antares* of 1937 and the 2,600-ton *Arcturus* of 1938 with double-compound steam engines delivering 1,750 (1305 kW). The two vessels were readily distinguishable from the rest of the line's fleet by their small, short funnels. The company's fleet at the start of World War II was 44 ships, reduced to just four at the time of the war's end: 18 had been lost in the war and 22 were seized by the Allies in May 1945. In the two years immediately following the end of the war, the Allies allowed German shipping to undertake only coastal services, but in 1947 Argo was allowed to resume oceanic Nah Ost Linie to undertake services to the Levant, and in the same year the parent company was renamed as Richard Adler & Söhne. By 1960 the revised company owned 35 ships. Five years later, the company terminated its service to London and later either sold of scrapped the ships which had been used on it. By 1974, the line had been trimmed to just nine ships. Two years later, it terminated its service between Rotterdam and Ipswich. In 1986 the

services with two ships. In 1948 a passenger service to Finland was inaugurated in collaboration with the Finska Angfartygs, and in 1949 there followed a service linking Bremen and London. In the same year the company built its own shipbuilding yard, the Adler Werft in Bremen.

The company's first vessel built after World War II was the motor ship *Adler*, which entered service in 1950. In 1952 the company launched the company sold the Nah Ost Linie to the Hamburg Südamerikanische Dampfschifffahrts Gesellschaft. By 1990, the company's ships had been reduced to five in number, and two years later, five ships; in 1992 the service to Finland was terminated. The last service operated by the company with its own ship was that of 1999 to Harwich and Felixstowe using the Ro/Ro ship *Arneb*.

Queen Mary (1936)

Before they merged in 1934 as Cunard White Star Line, the Cunard and White Star Lines had each planned the construction of a single very large liner. Cunard ordered an 80,000-ton steam ship from John Brown of Clydebank, while White Star considered the *Oceanic* as a 60,000-ton motor ship from Harland & Wolff of Belfast, but then abandoned the idea because of its parlous financial situation. Cunard's ship, whose name was selected as late as possible and then kept a closely guarded secret, was *Queen Mary* after the wife of King George V. The ship, ordered on April 3, 1929 and laid down on December 1, 1930, was designed as the first of two ships for Cunard's planned weekly express service between Southampton and New York as the company's response to the threat to its transatlantic superiority

posed by a pair of German "super-liners," the *Bremen* and *Europa*, with the French *Normandie* still to come.

The John Brown & Co. Ltd. yard at Clydebank started work on the ship in December 1930, but construction was suspended one year later because of economic depression. Cunard requested a loan from the British government to complete the new ship, and in fact received sufficient funding both to complete the ship already under construction and built the second new vessel which Cunard wanted, which emerged as the *Queen Elizabeth*. The government insisted, however, that the receipt of the loan was dependent on a merger between Cunard and the White Star Line, Cunard's primary British rival. With the merger agreed and completed in March 1934, work on the *Queen Mary* was resumed, and the ship

The Queen Mary and her attendant flock of tugs.

was launched by Queen Mary on September 26, 1934.

As there was already a *Queen Mary*, a Clyde turbine steamer, Cunard reached agreement with the owner that its vessel would be renamed *Queen Mary II*.

When she sailed on her maiden voyage from Southampton on May 27, 1936, the *Queen Mary* measured 79,500 gross registered tons. The *Queen Mary*'s greatest rival, the

recaptured the record back during 1937, but in 1938 *Queen Mary* resumed her pre-eminent position with average speeds of 30.99 kt westbound and 31.69 kt eastbound, records which stood until lost to the *United States* in 1952.

Late in August 1939, the *Queen Mary* was on passage from New York to Southampton as the outbreak of World War II seemed imminent, and was shadowed home by the battle-cruiser HMS *Hood*. The liner departed for New York again on September 1, and by the time she reached her American destination the

The spacious bridge of the Queen May, third largest and sole surviving example of the classic transatlantic liner.

preceding year's *Normandie* of 78,027 gross registered tons, had just been modified to increase her gross size, and was thus still the world's largest liner. The *Normandie* was also of more modern appearance with her public rooms completed in the latest style. The *Queen Mary*, on the other hand, drew her appeal from the undeniable stateliness of her external appearance and the greater modesty of her interior, which was nonetheless very luxurious. In terms of speed, however, the *Queen Mary* proved to be superior. In August 1936, she captured from the *Normandie* the Blue Riband for transatlantic crossings in each direction, with an average speed of 30.14 kt westbound and 30.63 kt eastbound. The *Normandie*

UK was again at war. Her captain was instructed to keep the *Queen Mary* in New York, where the *Normandie* was also remaining, and in 1940 these two great ships were joined by the *Queen Elizabeth*. There was clearly little point in keeping these great ships merely out of harm's way, so it was decided that they should be used as troopships. The *Queen Mary* therefore departed New York for Sydney in Australia, where she became one of several liners adapted as a troopship to deliver Australian and New Zealand troops to the UK. Eventually joined by the *Queen Elizabeth*, the two Cunard liners were the largest and fastest troopships of World War II, and often carried 15,000 men on each voyage.

Queen Mary continued

Because of their speed, they often sailed independently and without escort, relying on their great sustained speed for protection, which could be matched by no major warship. Painted a war-time grey, during this part of their lives the two ships were known as the "Grey Ghosts."

The size and high propaganda value of the ships apparently that German agents had reported her last refuelling stop and that a submarine was lurking on her course, The ship's captain was alerted, and changed his ship's course.

The most unfortunate incident of the *Queen Mary* occurred on October 2, 1942, when the ship accidentally sank one of her escorts. The light cruiser HMS *Curacao* tried to cross

persuaded the Germans to offer a decoration and possibly also a cash reward for the captain of any submarine which sank either of them. The ships' high speeds meant that it was almost impossible for any submarine to intercept them except by chance. Only once did the Germans approach success: when the *Queen Mary* was in South American waters, an intercepted radio signal suggested ahead of the liner, but misjudged the *Queen Mary*'s speed and was hit amidships, sliced in two and went down with the loss of 338 men. With the inevitable threat of German submarines in the offing, the *Queen Mary* could neither halt nor even slow to search for survivors.

After the end of World War II in 1945, the *Queen Mary* re-entered mercantile service on May 31, 1947, and she and the *Queen Elizabeth* were without doubt the pre-eminent liners of the North Atlantic passenger business. But despite modernization with features such as fin stabilizers, the position of the liner in the transatlantic role was already being threatened by developments in air transport, largely as a result of the great stimulus to the creation of large but reliable long-range aircraft in World War II. In 1958 the launch of transatlantic air services by jet-powered airliners marked the start of the final phase of commercial viability for the transatlantic liner. In these closing stages of an era, the *Queen Mary* not infrequently reached port, especially in the winter months, with a crew numbering more than the passengers. In an effort to buck the worst of the trend, the *Queen Mary* was used for cruises during the winter months from 1963, but Cunard's profits on the transatlantic route continued sink and, in 1965, disappeared. The company was then in the throes of building a new ship, the *Queen Elizabeth 2,* and, in an effort to secure additional financial resources, mortgaged the whole of its current fleet, including the *Queen Mary.*

Then, hit by a combination of the ship's age, lack of a realistic market, the steady growth of high-speed air travel, and the effects of a major seamen's strike, Cunard decided to sell the *Queen Mary.* The company received many offers for the celebrated ship, but ultimately it was that of Long Beach, California, which was preferred to that of a Japanese breaker's yard. The *Queen Mary* completed her last passenger-carrying voyage on December 11, 1967 and was then withdrawn from service.

After steaming to Long Beach, the ship was completed as a permanently moored museum and hotel, which she remains to this day as a very popular attraction for local residents and visitors alike.

The Queen Mary under way in the striking livery of the Cunard Line.

Queen Mary

Type:	transatlantic liner
Tonnage:	81,237 gross registered tons
Dimensions:	length 1,019 ft 5 in (310.7 m); beam 118 ft 6 in (36.1 m); draft 39 ft (11.9 m)
Propulsion:	four Parsons geared steam turbines delivering 200,000 shp (149120 kW) to four propellers for 32.5 kt
Complement:	776 first-, 784 tourist- and 579 third-class passengers, and 1,101 crew

Marwarri (1935)

Founded in 1801 at Whitehaven in the northwestern English county of Cumberland, Thos. & Jno. Brocklebank Ltd. could claim, at the time of its disappearance in 1983, the longest continuous existence of any shipping line in the world. The mercantile connection extended still farther back, however, for in 1770 the founding brothers' father, Daniel Brocklebank, had set himself up as a shipbuilder and merchant in New York, but returned to Britain in 1775 on the eve of the American War of Independence, and in 1788 established a British shipbuilding yard.

Later known as the Brocklebank Line, the company began life with just a single sailing vessel, and initially concentrated its efforts on the coal trade. In 1813 the Honourable East India Company's monopoly on British trade with India was terminated, and the Brocklebanks decided to try their hand in the India trade. This soon became the growing company's most important and lucrative endeavour, but the Brocklebanks also traded across

London and the British treaty ports in China Treaty during 1858, but two years later terminated its schedule of regular services to Brazil.

A major change in the nature of the trade to India and the Far East was heralded by the opening of the Suez Canal in 1869, but the Brocklebank Line remained faithful to the traditional route around the Cape of Good Hope for another 30 years, for the first two-thirds of this period with sailing vessels. It was only in 1889 that the Brocklebank Line bought its first steam ship, but it was 1901 before the line disposed of its last sailing vessels. In 1906 the Brocklebank Line bought an interest in the Shire Line (David Jenkins & Co. Ltd.) and transferred five of its own ships to this company, which

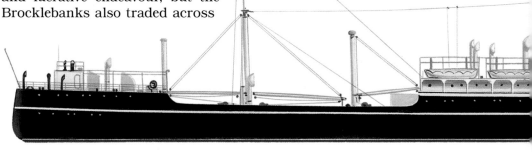

the Atlantic Ocean with North and South America and the West Indies, and also with the East Indies. In 1819, the company was relocated to the rapidly growing shipping city of Liverpool, which became its base of operations. The Brocklebank Line inaugurated a service between

operated services to Japan. The part of the Shire Line not own by the Brocklebank Line was bought in 1907 by the Royal Mail Steam Packet Co. Ltd., which in 1911 also bought the Brocklebank Line's interest in the Shire Line.

This was part of a major

reorganization, for in the same year the company organized the sale of its sharers to the directors of the Cunard Line, which also bought the Anchor Line at much the same time. The two Cunard subsidiaries were then reconstituted as Anchor-Brocklebank Ltd. In 1916 the company took over Tyzack & Branfoot's Well Line of Sunderland.

In the 1920s and 1930s, the company operated some of the finest merchant ships afloat, and in 1938 added a pair of first-class vessels in the form of the *Marcharda* and *Marwarri*, both built by William Richardson. Like the other vessels of the Brocklebank Line, these had no passenger provisions. The ships each had six hatches accessing their holds, and freight was handled with the aid of six 5-ton, nine 10-ton and three 20-ton derricks. Engined by David Rowan & Co. Ltd., each of the ships

had four boilers fired by 675 tons of coal and 1,074 tons of oil.

During World War II the company lost many ships, and emerged from the war in 1945 with only 11 ships. This severely curtailed the extent to which the company could re-establish itself on the world stage, and the situation was further worsened in 1947 by the granting of independence to India, which was then partitioned into India and Pakistan. The two new countries introduced stringent new trading regulations. The situation was then worsened by the closure of the Suez Canal between June 1967 and January 1971, entailing a 5,000-mile (8045-km) lengthening of the route to India and the Far East round the Cape of Good Hope. Cunard-Brocklebank Ltd. was formed in 1968, the two partner companies pooling their ships, but financial losses continued; the last two Brocklebank-liveried ships were sold in 1983 and the company went out of business.

The Marwarri is depicted in the livery of the Brocklebank Line, which included blue and white funnel strips.

Marwarri

Type:	freighter
Tonnage:	8,100 gross registered tons
Dimensions:	length 472 ft (143.9 m); beam 63 ft (19.2 m); draft 27 ft 10 in (8.5 m)
Propulsion:	three geared steam turbines delivering 5,200 shp (3877 kW) to one shaft for 14 kt
Complement:	90 crew

Nordcoke (1936)

In the 1920s and 1930s, coal was still the lifeblood of European industry. This was especially true of German heavy industry in regions such as the Ruhr, where the combination of large coal and iron ore deposits, together with the ready availability of vast volumes of water, had been a catalyst for of the German industrial revolution.

and locomotives, and also invested in new steelmaking techniques and in mining. The company began to make steel artillery in the 1840s, and by the late 1880s armament manufacture represented around 50% of Krupp's total output. When Alfred started with the company, it had five employees but at his death in 1887, 20,000 persons

There were many great industrial empires in the Ruhr, but none greater than the Friedrich Krupp A.G. of Essen. Friedrich Krupp had launched the family's fortune by building a small steel foundry in Essen in 1811. His son Alfred invested heavily in new technology to become a significant manufacturer of railway materials

were employed by Krupp, which was then the world's largest industrial company. The company continued to grow to and though World War I and, after a slump following World War I, again rose to prominence in the heavy industrials and armaments roles.

Coal products were at the heart of Krupp's activities in the period between the world wars, and it ordered several vessels to support its need for coal. One of this was the *Nordcoke*, which was operated for Krupp by the Norddeutscher Kohlen und Kokes-Werke of Hamburg. The vessel was built for European service, including the Baltic Sea, and was strengthened for ice navigation. She could carry coal in two holds accessed by four hatches and with four 5-ton and one 3-ton derricks, and could also carry ore or timber.

The vessel was taken over in 1940 for military service in World War II with the name *Nordlicht*, and was seized by the Allies in 1945. In British service for the Ministry of War Transport, she was the *Empire Conwear*, then passed to the USSR in 1946 as the *Armavir*, and finally to Poland in 1947 as the *Kolno*. She was scrapped in 1971.

The Nordcoke was a thoroughly utilitarian bulk freighter of the mid-1930s, and eventually served under four flags.

Nordcoke

Type:	coal, ore and timber freighter
Tonnage:	2,487 gross registered tons
Dimensions:	length 297 ft (90.5 m); beam 44 ft (13.4 m); draft not available
Propulsion:	one steam engine driving one propeller
Complement:	not available

Bremen (1928)

Built by A. G. Weser of Bremen and launched on August 16, 1928, the *Bremen* was, with the *Europa*, one of two half-sister liners built for the NDL (Norddeutscher Lloyd) line for transatlantic passenger service. The so permitting NDL to operate a weekly service with two rather than three ships. It was claimed that the *Bremen* reached 32 kt on her trials.

Though it was planned that the two ships would enter service

Bremen was characterized by a low, almost streamlined profile. The construction of the two ships in the late 1920s kicked off the race among European nations for prestigious high-speed liners in the 1930s. The *Bremen* and *Europa* were created for a cruising speed of 27.5 kt, which opened the way to a transatlantic crossing in five days, simultaneously, the completion of the *Europa* was delayed by fire, and the *Bremen* made a solo maiden voyage, leaving Bremerhaven for New York on July 16, 1929, and arriving four days, 17 hours and 42 minutes later, in the process capturing the 20-year old westbound Blue Riband from the

Mauretania with an average speed of 27.83 kt. On her next voyage she took the eastbound Blue Riband at an average of 27.91 kt in a time of 4 day 14 hours and 30 minutes.

The *Bremen* lost the westbound record to the *Europa* in 1930, and the eastbound record to the *Normandie* in 1935.

On August 26, 1939, the German naval high command, knowing that Germany's invasion of Poland was scheduled for September 1, ordered all German shipping to make for German ports without delay. The *Bremen* was westbound at the time, two days out from New York, and her captain decided to continue to New York to disembark her 1,770 passengers. The ship departed New York on August 30 without taking on any passengers, and exploited adverse weather and her high speed to avoid British warships reaching the northern Soviet port of Murmansk on September 6. On December 10 the *Bremen* made a high-speed run to Bremerhaven, which she reached on December 13.

The ship was then used as an accommodation vessel and nothing came of plans to adapt her as a transport in the planned German invasion of the UK. In 1941 the *Bremen* was completely gutted after a crew man started a fire, a long investigation then establishing that the event had been sparked by a grudge against the ship's owners rather than as an act of sabotage. The hulk was broken up in 1946.

The Bremen in the livery of NDL. Like the Europa, the Bremen carried a small floatplane on a catapult between her two funnels. This was launched when the ship was still some 36 hours from docking, allowing air mail to reach its destination one day earlier than would otherwise have been the case.

Bremen

Type:	transatlantic liner
Tonnage:	51,656 gross registered tons
Dimensions:	length 939 ft 1 in (286.3 m); beam 101 ft 9 in (31.1 m); draft not available
Propulsion:	four geared steam turbines driving four propellers for 27 kt
Complement:	800 first-, 500 second-, 300 tourist- and 600 third-class passengers, and 990 crew

Regent Panther (1937)

The company which became C. T. Bowring & Co. was established in the 1820s in the port city of St John's, Newfoundland, by an English immigrant to Canada, Benjamin Bowring. Bowring was heavily involved in the sealing trade, and by 1823 owned a fleet of small sailing vessels which traded across the North Atlantic. By the 1840s Charles Tricks Bowring, son of Benjamin Bowring, had become the driving

going steamships, and in 1888 formed a new company, the English & American Shipping Co. Ltd., as its subsidiary for the operation of passenger and cargo services, most particularly across the North Atlantic between Liverpool in England and St John's and New York in North America. From the early 1880s C. T. Bowring & Co. also operated the Red Cross Line (more formally the New York, Newfoundland & Halifax Steam

force behind the company, which had expanded both its size and the scope of its operations and shifted its headquarters to Liverpool in the north-west of England. During the 1860s the company embarked on a program of rapid development, in the course of which its inaugurated services to India, Australia, New Zealand and the west coast of the U.S. From 1880 the company built up a considerable fleet of ocean-

Ship Co.) to undertake passenger and freight services along the Atlantic seaboard of North America to and from New York, and later expanded into the cruising business out of New York.

C. T. Bowring & Co. suffered the loss of many of its ships in World War I, when the late introduction of the convoy system meant that the North Atlantic was peppered with independently routed merchant ships which were located and sunk in increasing numbers by the boats of a steadily more capable German submarine arm. The company also had to sell the Red Cross Line, the ships being transferred to Furness, Withy & Co.'s Bermuda & West Indies Steam Ship Co. during 1929 at the height of the Great Depression.

The English & American Shipping Co. had been liquidated in 1919 and a new company was established as the Bowring Steamship Co. The company abandoned the passenger aspect of its operation at about this time and

The house flag and funnel marking of C. T. Bowring & Co., as seen on the Regent Panther, was a red cross of St Andrew on a white ground.

Bowring now concentrated on the oil tanker, iron ore and freight aspects of its business.

Two of the vessels which entered service with C. T. Bowring & Co. in 1937-38 were the sister ships *Regent Lion* and *Regent Panther*, built by Swan Hunter & Wigham Richardson Ltd, of Tyneside in north-east England, as dedicated tankers with a diesel-engined propulsion arrangement based on a four-cylinder horizontally opposed Swan Hunter-Doxford diesel engine drawing its fuel from a capacity of 1,344 tons. There was also a small steam plant for the operation of auxiliary items.

Each of the ships was able to carry payload in the form of oil and cargo. The oil was accommodated in eight tanks fore and aft of the central superstructure, and there was also a small cargo hold forward of the of the fore mast. The oil was handled with the aid of four pumps, which could discharge the load at the rate of 280 tons per hour, and the ship also had one 5-ton derrick on the for mast, and one 7-ton derrick on the main mast. The officers had single cabins, and the accommodation for the crew was based on two-berth cabins.

Both of the ships were heavily involved in the British effort in World War II. The *Regent Lion* was torpedoes and sunk, to the south-west of Gibraltar, on February 17, 1945. The *Regent Panther* survived the war and remained in service to 1959, when she was retired and sold to a breaker's yard for scrapping.

Regent Panther

Type:	motor tanker
Tonnage:	9,600 gross registered tons
Dimensions:	length 490 ft (149.4 m); beam 67 ft (20.4 m); draft 28 ft 10.5 in (8.8 m)
Propulsion:	one four-cylinder diesel-engine driving one propeller for 11.5 kt
Complement:	not available

Imperial Star (1934)

Based in London, the Blue Star Line was established and wholly owned by Vestey Brothers, whose main commercial interest was the Union Cold Storage Co., which imported frozen meat from South America and Australasia. While it had hitherto chartered refrigerated ships to meet its requirements, in 1909 the Union Cold Storage Co. decided that advantages would accrue from the purchase and operation of its own ships. In 1911 the Blue Star Line was established under the Union Cold Storage Co.

The new line concentrated its initial efforts on the Vestey Brothers' core interest. It was only in 1926, the year in which it went public, that the company started to offer accommodation to small numbers of first-class passengers on some of its most modern ships. This facility was first offered on the South American route, and was extended to ships plying to and from Australia and New Zealand during 1933.

coincidence by the adoption of a basic name followed by "Star" as a separate word, as in *Imperial Star.*

Built by Harland & Wolff of Belfast for launch on October 9, 1934, the first *Imperial Star* was completed in January of the following year with seven bulkheads containing six refrigerated holds served by no fewer than 22 7- and 10-ton derricks as well as one special 50-ton derrick on the single pole mast. Propulsion was based on two 10-cylinder Burmeister & Wain diesel engines.

In 1941 the ship was transferred to Frederick Leyland & Company, and on March 12, 1941 was damaged in Liverpool's Brocklebank Dock in a German bombing raid. On September 27, 1941, while making for Malta from Liverpool with 8,000 tons of supplies, the ship was torpedoed and badly damaged by Italian aircraft northeast of Tunis. The ship was taken in tow by the destroyer HMS *Oribi,* but the tow was not successful and the

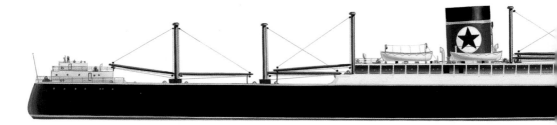

The Blue Star Line's vessels were initially given names with "star" appended straight onto the end of the basic name; for example, *Empirestar.* When the line's "A" class vessels were introduced, offering passenger accommodation as well as refrigerated freight volume, the ships had no "star" anywhere in their names. Finally the two systems were brought into

Imperial Star was slipped early on September 28. Depth charges were placed on board the ship as scuttling charges, and the ship sank. There were no casualties.

In 1935 the Blue Star Line bought the goodwill and services, but not the ships, of Frederick Leyland & Company, thereupon transferring the registration of some of its existing

The house flag and colors of the Blue Star Line were a five-pointed blue star on a white circle, as seen here on the funnel of the Imperial Star.

vessels to the Leyland company, which was now treated as a subsidiary of the Blue Star Line. A similar process was adopted during 1944 when the Blue Star Line bought the Lamport & Holt Line, and purchased the Booth Line during 1946. There followed a considerable number of ship registration transfers between the three companies.

Further development came in 1952, when the Austasia Line was established for the specific purpose of operating services between Singapore, Indonesia, Malaysia and Australia. The Blue Star Line bought the North American and Pacific coast services from the Donaldson Line in 1954, and during 1957 went into partnership with the New Zealand Shipping Company, Port Line, and Shaw, Savill & Albion to create the Crusader Shipping Company. Another offshoot, Calmeda S.p.A di Navigazione Cagliari, was formed by the Blue Star Line and Italian shippers in 1965. The Blue Star Line terminated all passenger services on its South American routes during 1972, but continued with cargo and container services. The rapidly and radically changing face and nature of shipping in the last stages of the twentieth century were finally reflected in the sale of the Blue Star Line to P & O Nedlloyd for £60 million.

A handsome and useful motor ship, the Imperial Star was lost in the course of a stores convoy to the beleaguered island bastion of Malta during September 1941.

Imperial Star

Type:	refrigerated cargo motor ship
Tonnage:	12,427 gross registered tons
Dimensions:	length 424 ft (73.75 m); beam 70 ft 4 in (21.4 m); draft 32 ft 4 in (9.85 m)
Propulsion:	two diesel engines driving two propellers
Complement:	first-class passengers, and crew

British Fidelity (1939)

In May 1901 William Knox D'Arcy was granted a concession by the Shah of Persia (from 1935 Iran) to search for oil, which he found in May 1908. On April 14, 1909, the Anglo-Persian Oil Company was set up to develop and exploit this find. The company grew slowly until the outbreak of World War I in 1914, when the strategic importance of its operations in Persia persuaded the British government to acquire controlling interest in the company.

After the end of the war in November 1918, the company moved to secure outlets in Europe and elsewhere. However, its main interest was still oil production in Persia, and following the signature of the Anglo-Persian Agreement of 1919, the company continued to trade profitably in that country. In the 1920s, however, there emerged a growing Persian dissatisfaction with the politically imperialist and economically unfair position occupied by the Anglo-Persian Oil Company. In 1932 the Shah ended the company's concession, and this spurred negotiations leading to the agreement of a new agreement within a year, this covering a reduced area with an increase in the Persian government's share of profits. When Persia became Iran, the Anglo-Persian Oil Company became the Anglo-Iranian Oil Company.

Right:
Waves crashing over the bow of the Fidelity.
Photo: Bill Batchelor.

Left:
The British Fidelity at sea. This tanker had provision for the carriage of up to eight passengers.

In 1915, the growing volume and importance of the oil being shipped from Persia to the UK led to the Anglo-Persian Oil Company's establishment of the British Tanker Co. Ltd to handle its sea transport requirements and thereby achieve a contained and fully integrated oil company. The British Tanker Co. Ltd. never operated anything but tankers, initially under a house flag which was red with a horizontal white band (expanded in its center into a circle) with the black letters "BTC," the "T" larger than the "B" and "C". In 1926 the livery was changed to incorporate a Persian element. The new flag was the cross of St George (red on a white field) with a diamond in green (the Persian national colour) in its center and carrying a golden lion. In 1955 the company name changed to BP Tanker Co. Ltd. and at that point the lion was changed to rampant and its color to red. In 1968 there came further alteration, the flag being changed to white with a green border and carrying in its center the green BP shield with the letter "BP" in its centre.

Typical of the tankers used by the British Tanker Company, and all bearing the a name prefixed by the word "British," was the *British Fidelity*. This 8,465-ton motor tanker was built by Harland & Wolff of Belfast in 1938 with the machinery aft and two groups of oil tanks separated by a central superstructure block. The vessel was powered by one Burmeister & Wain six-cylinder four-stroke diesel engine for a speed of 11.5 kt. The ship saw extensive use in World War II, which she survived to continue in service up to 1958, when she was retired and scrapped.

British coastal colliers (1914-2000)

Designed for the carriage of a bulk load of coal, the collier had a long history, but was changed radically by the advent of steam propulsion. This allowed the creation of the steam collier, offering the possibility of greater reliability and punctuality on coastal services, and also opened the need for ocean-going colliers carrying up to 6,000 tons of coal to stock and then to restock overseas coaling stations for mercantile and naval vessels alike. The type of cargo carried by the collier also diversified somewhat as the twentieth century loomed, the price of steamers fell and so promoted more construction; and the improvement of roads (triggered by

World War I caused freight rates to rise rapidly. The cost of building a new coastal collier tripled or even quadrupled, but such was the need for colliers and the return on their capital cost that orders for such vessels continued to rise. In the later part of the war owners generally anticipated a good market for their vessels as post-war reconstruction became important, and therefore ordered larger colliers in expectation of increased demand from merchants and also from the electrical power stations that were increasing in number and size. There was indeed a short-term boom, but there followed

The British coastal collier Norrix, a vessel typical of this unsung but vital type.

the appearance of motor vehicles) increased the demand for road stone, which could often be quarried on the coast for transport in adapted colliers. Ultimately, of course, it was road and rail transport which killed the collier.

the Great Depression of the mid-1920s onward. Owners who had contracted for ships at high prices and taken delivery were faced with the insoluble problem of making increased mortgage payments from reduced freight rates. Inevitably, many

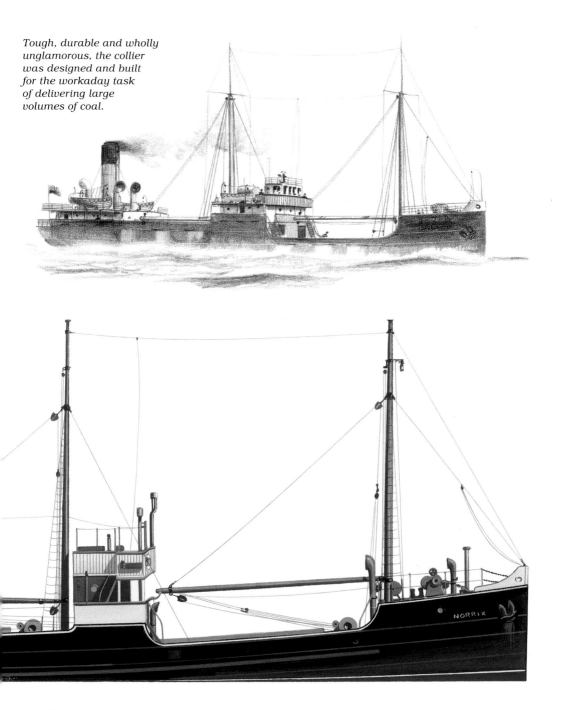

Tough, durable and wholly unglamorous, the collier was designed and built for the workaday task of delivering large volumes of coal.

Norrix

Type:	steam collier
Tonnage:	576 gross registered tons
Dimensions:	length 165 ft (50.3 m); beam 27 ft (8.2 m); draft 11 ft (3.35 m)
Propulsion:	one steam engine driving one propeller
Complement:	not available

British coastal colliers *continued*

companies failed or were compelled to trim their fleets. Used colliers were now very cheap, favoring those owners who had decided not to try to capitalize on the boom market and could now buy almost new vessels for about 25% of the building cost.

Freight rates continued to be low into the mid-1930s, but toward the end of the 1920s more careful owners found that work-strapped yards were offering to build colliers for about 33% of the price they had demanded in 1919. By 1930s, however, the Depression had become so acute that many owners and yards went out of business.

The steam coasters were well built for the most part, and had long lives. The vessels in question were anything between 66 and 270 ft (20 and 122.5 m) in length, but the average was something slightly less than 190 ft (57.9 m), and while many fleets were consolidated and the less economical vessels mothballed, most of these latter never saw further use.

Another factor which further complicated the trade was the advent in the 1930s of Dutch motor coasters, whose capabilities were a strong incentive for more far-sighted British owners to start considering the use of diesel power. This was now reliable, compact to install, economical to run and of good power/weight ratio (allowing the carriage of a greater payload on a reduced draft), and also allowed a useful trimming of manpower requirements.

The small motor collier soon proved itself a match for the small steam coaster in many trades round the Irish Sea, and did not finally disappear until the 1950s. They offered no competition to the larger coaster, but by the 1930s

there were higher-powered diesel engines for larger vessels, and it was the Dutch who first exploited their capabilities. British owners began to adopt diesel power in the 1930s as freight rates improved slightly, and the larger type of collier with aft-mounted machinery also appeared on the east coast; experience soon showed that it was much more efficient than the mid-engined vessels it supplanted.

At the outbreak of World War II in 1939, all the remaining laid-up coasters were pressed back into service, and freight rates were fixed by the government at a little above pre-war levels. In World War II the losses of the coaster fleet were somewhat greater than those in World War I, but this was offset to a limited extent by the building of a series of standard vessels of various types. By the end of the war, the colliers which had worked through the conflict were in dire need of major overhaul, but this was difficult as drydock space was at a premium at a time when all vessels needed such maintenance.

The decline of the steam coaster, which had started in the 1930s, therefore continued even though the coal trade of northeastern England remained committed to the steam collier. Even so, adverse factors which now intervened were the nationalization

The design of the motor collier was initially derived from that of the steam collier, but by the late 1950s the bridge had been relocated aft, so reducing cost by eliminating the need for two separate central heating systems, reducing cable runs, and shortening the piping associated with the individual washing facilities which were becoming general in the officers' accommodation. The change also opened up the deck and so eased the task of working the cargo. The one adverse effect was a worsening of the

The Cordene was another of the large numbers of British coastal colliers.

of the coal-mining industry and the virtual cessation of coal exports. The nationalized gas and electricity organizations built up comparatively large fleets to support their own requirements, but the management of these fleets was left largely in the hands of Stephenson Clarke. Even so, however, motor colliers steadily eroded the position of the steam collier in this, its last stronghold.

fields of vision over the bow. Another change was the conversion of many steamers to burn oil rather than coal but the demand for coal was declining as power stations were converted to burn oil or gas.

By the 1960s, the steam collier had all but vanished from the waters around the Irish Sea, and remained in smaller numbers for just a few more years of the east coast of England.

Queen Elizabeth (1938)

During the 1930s, when there was great rivalry among major shipping lines (predominantly those of France, Germany and the UK) to secure an undisputed mastery of the passenger trade across the North Atlantic, the Cunard Line of the UK believed that the route to success lay in the provision of a weekly service. Cunard decided that economic success in this task could be provided by a service linking Southampton and New York using very large but notably fast ships, which would permit it to operate with just two rather than three ships. This would provide significant savings, not just in the reduced capital expenditure associated with the manufacture of just two vessels, but also in the reduced operating costs resulting from smaller manpower requirements etc.

The first of Cunard's "superliners" was the three-funnelled *Queen Mary*, which was launched in 1934 and entered service in 1936. The *Queen Mary* was rivalled only by the French *Normandie* in terms of size and speed, and the two ships vied strongly for possession of the Blue Riband title associated with the fast west- and east-bound crossings of the North Atlantic. To provide the other arrow in its quiver of two "superliners," the Cunard Line planned the *Queen Elizabeth*. Like the *Queen Mary*, the two-funnelled *Queen Elizabeth* was ordered from the Clydebank yard of John Brown & Co. Ltd. near Glasgow, laid down during 1936, and launched on September 27, 1938, by Queen Elizabeth, the wife of King George VI. Benefiting from a carefully consideration of the strengths and weaknesses of the *Queen Mary* and other Cunard liners, and effectively clandestine assessments of the liners operated by rival companies, Cunard and the ship's designers were able to create an excellent ship whose fitting

The excellent Queen Elizabeth at full cruising speed.

out was undertaken as a matter of very high priority until the yard's capabilities were increasingly diverted to the demands of the Admiralty during 1939 as the threat of war became ever more obvious.

In the opening months of World War II, there was great worry about the vulnerability of the incomplete *Queen Elizabeth* to the attentions of German bombing. In February 1940, therefore, it was announced that the ship would proceed to Southampton for the completion of her fitting out. It was hoped the attention of the Germans would thereby be drawn to the south of England. On March 3 the *Queen Elizabeth* sailed, but when he opened his sealed orders, Captain Towney found that he was to take the *Queen Elizabeth* to New York. At the time she was due in Southampton, the German air force bombed the city. On arrival in New York on March 7, 1940, the *Queen Elizabeth* was berthed alongside her running mate, *Queen Mary,* and the *Normandie*. This was the only occasion when all three of the world's greatest liners were moored and seen together.

Features of the great new vessel's design were her two rather than three funnels as noted above, a more clean bridge face, a bow anchor of the type not fitted on the *Queen Mary*, no well deck, and degaussing cables around her main deck to defeat German magnetically fused mines. Work on completing the vessel continued in New York until November 1940, when the *Queen Elizabeth* steamed to Singapore, and then to Sydney in Australia, for the completion of her fitting out not as a liner, however, but as a troopship, after thought had been given to her adaptation as an aircraft carrier.

As a troopship, the *Queen Elizabeth* initially operated on the vital routes across the Indian Ocean linking Australia, India and Egypt. During 1942 the ship returned to New York, and here her troop capacity was increased from 5,600 to 15,000 troops so that she could operate in the vast program to deliver U.S. ground forces

As a troopship in World War II, the Queen Elizabeth could deliver virtually a full division of troops across the Atlantic in a single voyage.

Queen Elizabeth *continued*

from the east coast of the U.S. to the UK in preparation for the great Allied invasion of Europe that was now being planned after the U.S. had been precipitated into World War II by the Japanese attack on Pearl Harbor in December 1941. Although the *Queen Elizabeth* was never as fast as her older companion, the *Queen Mary*, her speed was nonetheless the ship's greatest defense as only chance could have put a German submarine, with a surface speed of little more than 20 kt in the best of conditions and considerably less under the water, in the position of intercepting her with a spread of torpedoes. Thus the *Queen Elizabeth* was able to work independently in the submarine-infested waters of the Atlantic Ocean

After the end of World War II in 1945, the *Queen Elizabeth* could finally be outfitted for service in the mercantile passenger role for which she had been designed. The refitted ship made her first civilian passenger voyage, between Southampton and New York via Cherbourg in 1946. The *Queen Elizabeth* and *Queen Mary*, which were the two largest passenger liners to have survived World War II, became the most profitable pair of ships ever put in service, even after the commissioning of the world's fastest ocean liner, *United States* of the United States Lines, during 1952, and some 10 years later, the *France* of the Compagnie Générale Transatlantique, otherwise the French Line.

But by the 1950s airliners were

The Queen Elizabeth edges toward her berth with the aid of a tug.

offering much shorter journey times across the North Atlantic, and all the more so from 1958 as jet-powered airliners came into service for this premier route. Despite its attractions in terms of luxury, the transatlantic passenger liner trade had heard its death knell, and its importance feel swiftly into a steep decline. Thus in the period between 1957 and 1965, the fare-paying passenger numbers on the North Atlantic route dropped from as all-time high of more than 1 million passengers to

without escort for the rest of the war. During her "naval" career, the *Queen Elizabeth* carried more than 750,000 troops and sailed some 500,000 miles (804550 km) without undue incident, and thereby was a major contribution to the Allied war effort and thus the Allied victory over Germany in World War II.

650,000, while the number of passengers carried by airliners quadrupled to 4 million. In the short term, and as a result of their enormous prestige, the *Queen Mary* and *Queen Elizabeth* were able just to hold their own against the assault from the sky even as most other passenger liners were withdrawn from transatlantic service.

There could be no denial of the fact that profits had been hit, and hit hard, so while the *Queen Elizabeth* remained on the transatlantic route during the summer months, during the winter months the ship was operated from New York as a cruise liner to destinations such as Nassau in the sun-soaked Bahamas Islands. So successful was she in this revised role that in 1965 Cunard was persuaded to offer something of a reprieve to the *Queen Elizabeth*, which was reconditioned and fitted out with a lido deck with outdoor swimming pool and air conditioning.

This could only slow an inevitable process, however, and in the end the viability of the great ship could not longer be claimed. In 1968, the *Queen Elizabeth* was withdrawn from service, sold to an American company called Queen, Inc., and laid up in Port Everglades, Florida, as a tourist

An ignoble end: the Seawise University on fire and heading toward the bottom of Hong Kong harbor.

attraction. Two years later, she was auctioned off to a Taiwanese shipping magnate. C. Y. Tung, renamed Seawise University (a pun on Tung's first two initials), and sailed for Hong Kong to be converted as an ocean-going university. After the ship had been cycled through a U.S. $6 million refit, a fire of suspicious origin broke out and the Seawise University then capsized in Hong Kong Harbor on January 9, 1972. Salvage proved impossible, and the ship was scrapped where she lay.

Queen Elizabeth

Type:	transatlantic passenger liner
Tonnage:	83,673 gross registered tons
Dimensions:	length 1,031 ft (314.25 m); beam 118 ft (36.0 m); draft 39 ft (11.9 m)
Propulsion:	four geared steam turbines driving four propellers for 29 kt
Complement:	823 first-, 662 cabin- and 798 tourist-class passengers, and 1,318 crew

Nissin Maru (1936)

The most modern phase of the whaling industry can be found between 1865 and the end of the nineteenth century in the creation of the harpoon gun by the Norwegian Sven Foyn and the introduction of steam-powered whale catchers. For the first half of the twentieth century the whaling industry was concentrated in Antarctic waters, and a major development came in the 1920s with the development of winches and stern ramp up which the whale was hauled aboard for processing with the aid of other powered machinery.

The whale factory ship of the 1920s and 1930 were typically of some 20,000 tons displacement. When one of the attendant whale catchers killed a whale, its crew inflated the carcass with compressed air to that it remained afloat, and marked it with a

The whale factory ship Nissin Maru at sea.

the whale factory ships operating on the high seas and independent of licensed shore bases. The availability of the factory ship for the processing of whales also provided a base for smaller whale catchers and allowed the whole whaling process to remain at sea far longer than would otherwise have been the case.

The whale factory ship was characterized by its power-operated small flag on a short pole driven into the carcass. This allowed the whale factory ship to work its way round its whale catchers' operating area to recover and process the carcasses. When retrieved, the carcass was hauled up the stern ramp onto the flensing deck. Here the flensing irons were used to cut the blubber loose for removal by tackles and subsequent movement for rendering into whale oil. The carcass was then stripped of its meat, and the usable bone was then removed and cleaned with steam hoses for transport back to port. The whole process of extracting the oil, preserving the meat, cleaning the bone, etc., was carried out on board the whale factory ship, which also carried the stores, equipment and accommodation both to maintain its little fleet of catchers and to remain at sea on the selected whaling ground or grounds for the whole of the whaling season.

Though comparatively late entrants into the field of oceanic whaling, the Japanese soon became a major force in the first part of the twentieth century. Typical of the type of whaling factory ships used by the Japanese in the last years before the outbreak of the Pacific war of World War II in 1939 were the two *Nissin Maru* (*Nisshin Maru* up to 1938) vessels. These were built by Kawasaki for the Taiyo Hogei K. K., a Tokyo-based subsidiary of the Shimonoseki-based Hayashikane Shoten K. K. This mercantile group also operated a large fleet of whale catchers to work with the two whale factory ships, and also a substantial fishing fleet. The deadweight of each of the two vessels was in the order of 20,200 tons of whale products.

The company's ships had black hulls and funnels, the latter were marked with a Japanese symbol or emblem inside a white circle. Both the *Nissin Maru* and *Nissin Maru No. 2* saw extensive whaling service in the late 1930s and early 1940s, The ships were pressed into military service during the Pacific war, and on May 6, 1944 the *Nissin Maru* was torpedoed and sunk by the U.S. Navy's "Balao" class fleet submarine USS *Crevalle*, which took the *Nissin Maru* for an oiler. Operating from a base in Australia, this boat was undertaking her third war patrol, and sank the Japanese vessel in the South China Sea.

Nissin Maru

Type:	whale factory ship
Tonnage:	16,764 gross registered tons
Dimensions:	length 550 ft (167.6 m); beam 74 ft (22.6 m); draft 13 ft (4.0 m)
Propulsion:	two steam engines driving two propellers
Complement:	not available

Rex (1938)

The Navigazione Generale Italiana dominated Italian shipping between 1881 and Italy's entry to World War II in 1940, and was the first Italian shipping company to order vessels of more than 20,000 tons. The first of these were the transatlantic liners *Giulio Cesare* and *Duilio* of 1921-22, and these were followed by the *Roma* of 32,583 tons and the *Augustus* of 32,650 tons.

The line's most important market before the outbreak of World War I in 1914 was emigrants to the Americas, but after the end of this war in 1918, the migrant trade declined but was balanced by a steady increase in affluent passengers willing to pay well for more comfortable travel. In this period the NGI and a rival, Lloyd Sabaudo, ordered the two largest passenger liners ever to have sailed under the Italian flag. These were the *Rex* of 51,062 gross registered tons, which was launched by Ansaldo & Co. at Sestri Ponente on August 1, 1931 for the NGI, and the *Conte di Savoia* of 48,502 gross registered tons, which was launched by the Cantieri Riuniti dell' Adriatico at Monfalcone, near Trieste, on October 28 of the same year for Lloyd Sabaudo. The ships were to rival the current Atlantic champions, the German *Europa* and *Bremen*.

Almost immediately after this, under pressure from the Italian government, which wished to create a major shipping company able to challenge British, French and German interests, NGI of Genoa, Lloyd Sabaudo of Turin, and Cosulich of Trieste merged to create Italia Flotte Riunite, which became known as the Italian Line. It was hoped that the advent of the two new liners in 1932 would mark the opening of a new level of capability for the Italian merchant marine.

At the time of her debut, the *Rex* was the fourth largest liner in the world in tonnage terms. The *Rex* completed successful running trials, and there seemed to be the clear promise of a record-breaking maiden voyage from Genoa to New York via Naples. All went well at first, but then engine problems forced the ship into Gibraltar for three days. The *Rex*'s engine problems were soon diagnosed and rectified, and once again Italy looked forward to great things.

In July 1933 the *Europa* broke her own record for the second time, but in the following month the *Rex* improved on the *Europa*'s Blue Riband speed by a full knot, steaming from Gibraltar to the Ambrose Light at 28.92 kt in a time of 4 days, 13 hours and 58 minutes, recording a maximum speed of 29.61 kt on August 15. The ship never succeeded in establishing and eastbound record, but together with *Conte di Savoia* did much to make popular the notion of first-class travel to the Mediterranean.

At the end of 1936, there was a reorganization of the companies and the routes deemed by the Italian government to be of national importance. The Italian Line then absorbed all the companies and routes connected with the Americas; Lloyd Triestino (at the time called the Linee Triestine per l'Oriente) and all those connected with Asia, Africa and Australia; Adriatica of Venice and all the traffic for the eastern Mediterranean and the Black Sea; and Tirrema of Naples and all the traffic for the central and western Mediterranean plus a route to western

The Rex was one of the two most important liners in Italian service between the two world wars.

Europe. The four companies all came under the aegis of the Società Finanziana Marittima based in Rome.

At the beginning of World War II, the Italian Line had 37 ships with a gross tonnage of 456,442. In this total were the two major transatlantic liners *Rex* and *Conte di Savoia*, worthily supported by two liners of more than 30,000 tons (the *Roma* and *Augustus*), three of more than 20,000 tons (the *Vulcania, Saturnia* and *Conte Grande*), and two of 19,500 tons (the *Oceania* and *Neptunia*). The *Rex* remained in service in the opening months of World War II,

sailing between Genoa and New York until May 1940. Italy declared war on France and the UK in June 1940, and the *Rex* was laid up at Pola, in what is now Slovenia, where she remained until 1944. In the summer of that year, the Germans decided to scuttle the ship at Trieste to impede the Allied advance. As she was being moved into position on September 9, 1944, she was sunk by British bombers off Cape d'Istria just south of Trieste. After the war, the Italian Line briefly considered raising and refitting the ship, but she lay in what were now Yugoslav waters, and the wreck was scrapped by the Yugoslavs

Rex

Type:	transatlantic liner
Tonnage:	51,062 gross registered tons
Dimensions:	length 879 ft 9 in (268.2 m); beam 97 ft (29.6 m); draft not available
Propulsion:	four geared steam turbines driving four propellers for 28 kt
Complement:	640 first-, 378 special-, 410 tourist- and 866 third-class passengers, and 810 crew

Ile de France (1927)

Built by the Chantiers de l'Atlantique (Penhoët) of St Nazaire, the *Ile de France* from the outset marked a major change in the design approach to large liners. The first large liner built after the end of World War I in 1918, the *Ile de France* was orthodox in engineering terms but broke completely with the established

A sales poster for the Ile de France in her second and much revised form after World War II.

traditions of passenger liner concepts in her Art Deco interior. This was the first taste of the design stream which would reach its culmination in the *Normandie*. Thus the *Ile de France* was the first in the innovative period of the Compagnie Generale Transatlantique, or the French Line.

By an agreement of 1912 between the French government and the French Line, four passenger and mail ships were to be built for transatlantic service. The first was be the *Paris* of 1921 and the second the *Ile de France*. Launched on March 14, 1926, the *Ile de France* had become a source of great French pride and popularity even before she took to the water. After the launch there followed a 14-month fitting-out period before the new liner embarked on her sea trials on May 29, 1927. The new liner then steamed to her home port of Le Havre on June 5. On June 22 of the same year the *Ile de France* departed on her maiden voyage to New York, where there was a buzz of excitement as great as that which had attended her first days in France. In 1928 a catapult was installed so that a mail-carrying seaplane could be launched while the ship was still offshore, but this capability was removed in 1930. Two years later the accommodation was revised to 670 first-, 408 tourist- and 508 third-class passengers. This enlargement of the first-class accommodation at the expense of the other classes reflected the ship's enormous popularity among the wealthy, and by 1935 the *Ile de France* had carried more first-class passengers than any other liner plying the transatlantic route.

At the outbreak of World War II in September 1939, the *Ile de France* was laid up at Pier 88 in New York harbor, just opposite the *Normandie*. In 1940 the ship was despatched to Saigon with war matériel, but then diverted to Singapore. Here she was taken over by the British, and after making several supply runs for the British was converted as a troopship in 1941, serving under the British and Free French flags. The British returned the ship to French

The Ile de France is depicted in her final two-funnelled form.

ownership in September 1945 after the end of World War II.

In 1947 the *Ile de France* was handed over to her builder for a refit and modernization in a two-year program which changed many of the liner's characteristics, both interior and exterior. The most obvious change was the replacement of the three slightly raked original funnels, one of them a dummy, by two longer-chord funnels, giving the vessel a more streamlined appearance. Now of 44,356 gross registered tons, the ship had accommodation for 541 first-, 577 cabin- and 227 tourist-class passengers.

From the start of her post-war maiden passenger voyage in 1949, the *Ile de France* enjoyed a prosperous decade of service, wealthy passengers still flocking to the ship, as the French Line was renowned for the quality of its service. The *Ile de France* brushed with notoriety on several occasions during her post-war career. In July 1956, she helped in the rescue of survivors from the sinking of the Italian liner *Andrea Doria* after the had been struck by the Swedish liner *Stockholm*. By 1958 the start of the era of jet-powered air transport spelled the end for the ocean liner. The French Line sold the *Ile de France* to a Japanese breaker, and the ship departed Le Havre on February 16, 1959, with the revised name *Furansu* (France) *Maru*. The ship's last appearance was as the central, half-sunk prop in the disaster film *The Last Voyage*. Filming complete, the ship was towed to the breaker's yard.

Ile de France (1927)

Type:	transatlantic liner
Tonnage:	43,153 gross registered tons
Dimensions:	length 791 ft (241.1 m); beam 92 ft (28.0 m) m); draft not available
Propulsion:	four geared steam turbines driving four propellers for 24 kt
Complement:	670 first-, 408 cabin- and 508 third-class passengers, and 800 crew

Dredgers

Dredging is the excavation of bottom material, mostly below the surface of the water, undertaken in shallow salt or fresh water areas. The object of dredging is to gather bottom sediments so that these can be removed and dumped elsewhere. The most important reasons for dredging include increasing or maintaining the depth of water in a navigation channel; point excavation before the start of work on major waterfront construction (bridges, piers or dock foundations); harvesting sand for use in the production of concrete or in beach restoration; and waterway management and maintenance for the purpose of flood and erosion control.

The device to scrape or suck the bottom is called a dredge, and a dredger is a vessel equipped with a dredge, though in U.S. terms any vessel with dredging equipment is called a dredge.

There are many forms of dredging depending on role and equipment, but three of these are the most important. Capital dredging is used to create a new harbor, berth or waterway, or to deepen existing facilities, and is normally effected with a cutter-suction dredge. Maintenance dredging is the deepening of navigable waterways which have become silted, and is often effected by means of a trailing suction hopper dredge. Most dredging is for this purpose. Beach repair is largely dependent on the mining of sand offshore and placing on a beach to replace sand eroded by storms or wave action, and is typically the task of a cutter-suction dredge or trailing suction hopper dredge.

Suction dredging uses a long tube through which the dredged material is drawn, and a plain suction dredger has no tool at the end of the suction pipe to disturb the material. A trailing suction hopper dredger trails its suction pipe when working, and loads the dredge spoil into one or more hoppers in the vessel. When the

A typical bucket dredger with a pair of tugs and a lighter standing by to receive the soil from the sea bottom.

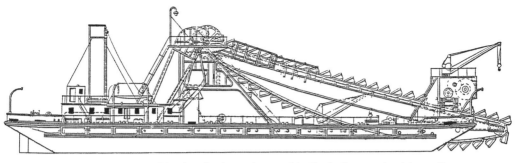

The power-operated bucket dredge is lowered to the bottom and set in motion when the dredger is working.

hoppers have been filled, the trailing suction hopper dredger moves to the allotted disposal area and either dumps the material through doors in the hull or pumps the material out of the hoppers.

A cutter suction dredger's suction tube is characterized by the cutter head at the suction inlet, to loosen the earth (or harder materials such as rock or gravel) and transport it to the suction mouth. The dredged material is normally drawn up by a wear-resistant centrifugal pump and discharged through a pipe line or to a barge.

There is also an augur suction type of dredging, which operates like a cutter suction dredger, but its cutting tool works on the Archimedean screw principle and is installed at right angles to the suction pipe.

Jet-lift suction exploits the venturi effect of a concentrated high-speed stream of water to draw nearby water, together with bottom material, into a pipe. The air lift type of dredge is akin to a small suction dredge. While it is sometimes used in the same manner as other dredges, at other times the air lift dredge is hand-held by a diver. It works by blowing air into the pipe, and dragging water with it.

A bucket dredge picks up bottom material by mechanical means, often with many buckets attached to a wheel or chain. Some bucket dredgers and grab dredgers are powerful enough to work through coral reefs to make a shipping channel.

A grab dredge collects bottom material with a clam shell grab, which hangs from an onboard crane, or is carried by a hydraulic arm, or is mounted like on a dragline. This technique is often used in excavation of bay mud.

A backhoe, or otherwise dipper, dredge has a backhoe of the type sometimes found on land excavators. A usable but not very efficient backhoe dredger can be made by mounting a land backhoe excavator on a pontoon.

Delver (built in Scotland during 1912)

Type:	bow well bucket dredger
Tonnage:	217 gross registered tons
Dimensions:	length 128 ft (39.0 m); beam 25 ft 2 in (7.7 m); draft not available
Propulsion:	one steam engine driving one propeller
Complement:	not available

Baron Cawdor (1935)

The term "tramp steamer" denotes a cargo-carrying merchant vessel which does not operate a regular route or schedule, but carries general cargo to any destination as required, and may be diverted to any port to pick up available cargo. In overall terms, therefore, the tramp steamer can be regarded as the modern counterpart of the older merchant adventurer who would take on a cargo of goods which he would attempt to sell at his various ports of call, usually buying other goods at those ports to sell at home at the end of the voyage. However, it must be noted that the latter-day tramp steamer did not buy and sell, but instead limited herself to the collection of other people's cargoes for delivery at their relevant destinations. When empty, she steamed in ballast to another port for the collection of a cargo, or part cargo, awaiting transhipment.

The last coal-burning tramp steamer to serve under the Red Ensign of the British mercantile marine, the *Baron Cawdor* was one of three sister vessels built for H. Hogarth & sons Ltd. of Glasgow by the yard of D. & W. Henderson Ltd. in the same city. The builder also engined the vessel, which was launched on December 10, 1934, and completed in 1935. The vessel was of typical tramp steamer concept with the machinery space, superstructure and bridge amidships with the slender ventilators and single funnel towering over them, and pairs of holds fore and aft of the central section with a single pole mast and four derricks between each pair of holds.

A notable episode in the vessel's otherwise humdrum existence occurred in 1957. The ship was working the east coast of Africa, and on August 24 called at Mombasa's Kilindini Harbor, in southern Kenya, to discharge a cargo of coal into lighters before sailing for Lourenço Marques in Portuguese East Africa (now Mozambique). Two days later, the ship returned and made a signal to the lighthouse for a pair of stowaways to be taken off. Only one day after this a boiler valve gasket blew and

the captain ordered both boilers to be shut down so that repairs could be effected. As this was being attempted, the ship drifted north out of control. The boiler fires were then relit, but almost immediately developed steam leaks in their back ends and the fires had to be doused once again on August 27. In the afternoon of this day the captain requested assistance, and reported the position of his ship as 12 miles (19 km) off Kilifi.

The tug *Simba* was dispatched and that night located the ship off Malindi with the international "not under command" signal (two vertical red lights) at her masthead. A towline was connected and the Simba towed the *Baron Cawdor* to Mombasa, the main port of Kenya.

On the morning of August 29, the two vessels entered Kilindini Harbor, where the tugs *Tiddler* and *Toroka* assisted in the mooring of the *Baron Cawdor* on the designated buoys. New boiler tubes were fitted and the necessary repairs were completed on September 19, and the tramp steamer then steamed south to Portuguese East Africa.

Three years later, the *Baron Cawdor* was sold to a Japanese breaker's yard, and arrived at Hirao on March 16, 1960.

Baron Cawdor

Type:	tramp steamer
Tonnage:	3,638 gross registered tons
Dimensions:	length 401 ft (122.2 m); beam 53 ft (16.15 m); draft 22 ft 5 in (6.8 m)
Propulsion:	one triple-expansion steam engine delivering 3,400 ihp (2535 kW) to one propeller for 11.5 kt

Normandie (1935)

The *Normandie* was a French transatlantic liner built in the Penhoët yard of the Chantiers et Ateliers de St Nazaire, on the west coast of France, for the Compagnie Générale Transatlantique. The vessel was laid down on January 26, 1931, and, when launched on October 29 of the following year, was the largest. Trials revealed that she was also the fastest liner in the world. The *Normandie* retains the cachet of having been the most powerful steam-driven liner ever built with turbo-electric machinery. Her novel design features and extraordinarily luxurious, even luxuriant, interiors persuaded many that she was the greatest of all the oceanic liners. Even so, the ship was not a success in commercial terms, and her operation was reliant on French government subsidies.

immigrants in the early 1920s, and the liner market responded with greater emphasis on middle-class passengers, This was the origin of a pair of "super-liners" planned by the British, and the German *Bremen* and *Europa*. The CGT, better known as the French Line, decided that it too must compete and started to plan its own super-liner able to compete with its rivals in terms of size and speed, but to exceed them in its French styling.

After initial consideration of a ship similar to current French Line

The *Normandie*'s origins can be traced to the period of excess in the mid-1920s, when shipping companies started to look for modern successors to the current fleets of transatlantic liners dating from the period before World War I. Although they offered magnificent accommodation for the wealthy, these ships had been designed to carry considerably larger numbers of steerage-class passengers emigrating to the U.S. This country reduced its intake of

ships, such as the *Ile de France*, the company responded to the overtures of Vladimir Yurkevich, who had been a ship architect in the Imperial Russian navy but emigrated to France after the Soviet revolution of 1917. Yurkevich's concept included a raked clipper bow with a bulbous forefoot beneath the waterline, a beamy hull tapering sharply at bow and stern, and fully enclosed deck machinery so that there was a clear field of vision right along the decks.

Work on the new vessel began in 1931. The French builder ran into financial difficulty during the Great Depression, and had to secure a government subsidy for the construction of what was an almost entirely French ship, for which the name *Normandie* was selected after national discussion.

The outfitting of the *Normandie* lasted to early in 1935, and the new vessel was ready for her trials in April of that year. The trials fully vindicated Yurkevich's hull form, for the *Normandie* created scarcely a ripple as she steamed at speeds up to 32.25 kt.

The *Normandie*'s interior spaces were marvellous confections of the Art Deco and *streamline moderne*

12 tall pillars of Lalique glass; along the walls stood 38 lighted columns. There were two chandeliers at each end of the room.

An especially popular space was the café leading into the grand salon, which was transformed into a night club during the evenings. The *Normandie* also had indoor and outdoor swimming pools (the second ship to have one after the Italian *Rex*), a chapel, and a theatre with stage and cinema functions. The elegance of the ship's interior was enhanced by the provision of long perspectives and spectacular features such as long, wide staircases.

In addition to her novel hull form, which provided great speed at comparatively modest and therefore

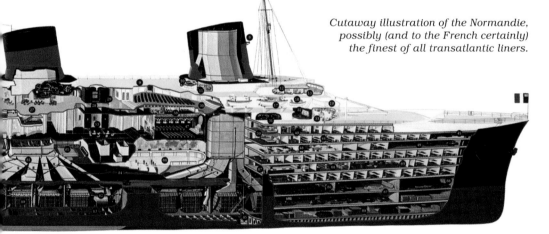

Cutaway illustration of the Normandie, possibly (and to the French certainly) the finest of all transatlantic liners.

styles, and contemporary artworks and photographs reveal a succession of huge public rooms of great elegance. The children's dining room was decorated by Jean de Brunhoff, who covered the walls with Babar the Elephant and his entourage. The dining room was 305 ft (93 m) long, 46 ft (14 m) wide and 28 ft (8.5 m) high, and could seat 700 diners at 150 tables. The ship's design prevented any natural lighting of the dining room, which was instead illuminated by

economical fuel power, the *Normandie* was a treasure house of modern technical features. Her turbo-electric propulsion system was notably fuel efficient, and also simplified control and maintenance. An early form of radar was fitted to detect icebergs and other ships.

The *Normandie*'s maiden voyage began on May 29, 1935, with all of France hopeful of a record crossing. The *Normandie* arrived in New York after just 4 days, 3 hours and 2

Normandie *continued*

minutes between Bishop Rock and the Ambrose Light, at an average of 29.98 kt, which took the Blue Riband from the Italian *Rex*. The return voyage was still faster, the average speed of 30.31 kt being the first crossing of the North Atlantic at a speed faster than 30 kt.

For 12 months the *Normandie* was unchallenged, but then in the summer of 1936 there appeared the Cunard Line's super-liner *Queen Mary*. Cunard had announced that the *Queen Mary* would be more than 80,000 tons, relegating the *Normandie* to the second largest liner in the world. The French Line thus decided to increase their flagship's size, primarily through the introduction of an enclosed tourist lounge on the aft boat deck. After the completion of this and some other alterations, the Normandie was re-measured at 83,423 gross tons, a figure which exceeded that of the *Queen Mary* by

some 2,000 tons. But in August 1936 the *Queen Mary* stole the Blue Riband from the *Normandie* with an average transatlantic speed of 30.14 kt. In July 1937 the *Normandie* regained the Blue Riband, only to lose it to the *Queen Mary* again in the following year.

At the outbreak of World War II in September 1939, the *Normandie* was in New York, and soon her rival *Queen Mary* and the new but incomplete *Queen Elizabeth* were berthed near her. The two *Queens* later left, and after the fall of France to the Germans in June 1940 the ship was left in limbo until after the U.S. had been drawn into World War II by the Japanese attack on Pearl Harbor in December 1941. It was clear that the U.S., facing a two-front war against the Japanese in the Pacific theatre and against the Germans and Italians in the European theatre, would need a huge expansion of her armed forces, and also in the

The Normandie was notable for the great efficiency of her passage through the water, with only a small bow wake even at high speeds, and a very limited wake, generally.

means to transport them to overseas theatres. The U.S. seized the *Normandie* in December 1941, and, after discussion of how best to use the great ship (as an aircraft carrier, as a troopship or as a hybrid carrier/troopship), decided to have the *Normandie* converted into a troopship carrying the name USS *Lafayette* in honour of the historical Franco-U.S. alliance of the War of Independence.

The ship was berthed at Pier 88 on Manhattan Island for the conversion, but on February 9, 1942 sparks from a welding torch ignited a great pile of life jackets filled with highly flammable kapok. The fire spread rapidly, as the hoses of the New York City fire department did not fit the ship's French inlets. As fire-fighters on shore and in fire boats deluged the blaze with water, the ship developed a dangerous list to port. At about 2:45 a.m. on February 10 the virtually gutted *Normandie* capsized, in the process crushing a fire boat.

The ship was finally righted during 1943 in the course of what was up to that time the world's most expensive salvage operation, but a year later she capsized yet again,

this time suffering severe damage to the hull and mechanical systems. Investigation then established that the cost of restoring the liner would be so great that the effort would not make economic sense, and might in fact take longer than the rest of the war.

After the U.S. Navy and the French Line had refused to consider the option, Yurkevich, the ship's designer, planned to cut the ship down and restore her as a mid-sized passenger liner, but this scheme also failed to attract the required financial backing. The shattered *Normandie* was then sold, for a mere US$161,680, to Lipsett Inc., a U.S. salvage company, and scrapped in October 1946. Many of the ship's interior features were sold to avid collectors and other purchasers.

Normandie

Type:	transatlantic liner
Tonnage:	79,280 gross registered tons
Dimensions:	length 1,029 ft 4 in (313.75 m); beam 119 ft 5 in (36.4 m); draft 36 ft 7 in (11.15 m)
Propulsion:	four turbo-electric engines delivering 200,000 shp (149120 kW) to four propellers for 32.25 kt
Complement:	58 de luxe-, 816 first-, 654 tourist- and 454 third-class passengers, and 1,345 crew

Orion (1934)

The *Orion* was one of the finest ships in the Australian immigrant business, and introduced a new standard in oceanic travel as the first British liner with air conditioning in all her public rooms. Built by Vickers-Armstrongs at Barrow-in-Furness, the ship was launched on December 7, 1934, and completed in August, 1935, for the Orient Steam Navigation Co. Ltd.

As completed, the *Orion* was Orient's largest liner and was built as a two-class ship, but by 1961 had been converted to a one-class liner. The ship's interiors made considerable use of use of chromium and bakelite, which set her apart from all previous Orient liners. After delivery to the Orient Line in August 1935, the *Orion* undertook several short cruises from London, and on September 28, left Tilbury on her maiden voyage to Australia. Until the outbreak of World War II in September 1939, the *Orion* operated to Australia with occasional cruises from the UK. During World War II, the ship was taken over by the British government for service as a troopship. On September 15, 1941, the *Orion* was part of a convoy to Singapore, and while following the battleship HMS *Revenge* in the South Atlantic, rammed the latter after the capital ship's steering gear had failed. Despite severe damage to her bow, the *Orion* made it safely to Cape Town for interim repairs before completing her voyage to Singapore, where a full repair was effected.

As Japanese forces overran Malaya in January 1942, the *Orion* embarked large numbers of civilians for evacuation to Australia. She continued as a troopship through the rest of the war, her troop capacity being increased from 5,000 to 7,000 men in 1943, though as Allied fortunes started to wax she generally embarked 5,000 men for every voyage. By the time she was restored to mercantile service, the *Orion* had carried more than 175,000 soldiers and civilians.

The *Orion* was returned to her builder on May 1, 1946, for a complete refit lasting almost one year,

A notable feature of the Orient Line's vessels, including the Orion depicted here, was the corn (light buff) colour of their hulls and funnels.

but this included a redesign of the accommodation for 546 first- and 706 tourist-class passengers. The ship departed from Tilbury on December 25, 1947, on her first post-war voyage to Australia. Besides her main line voyages, she also made three cruises to the west coast of America. In 1958 the ship was further changed to accommodate 342 cabin- and 722 tourist-class passengers. Six years later she became a one-class ship for 1,691 passengers. But at this time passenger numbers were falling away rapidly, and P & O, which had gained a controlling interest in the Orient Line in 1918, decided to retire the *Orion* in 1963.

The *Orion* left Tilbury on February 28, 1963 for her final voyage to Australia, sailing via the Suez Canal for Sydney. She departed Sydney with great fanfare on April 8 and reached Tilbury on May 15. She was chartered for four months as a floating hotel at the International Horticultural Exhibition in Hamburg, where she arrived on May 23 and provided accommodation for 1,150 guests. At the end of the exhibition on September 30, the *Orion* steamed to Antwerp, where she was broken up by the yard of Jos Boel et Fils.

Orion

Type:	oceanic liner
Tonnage:	23,371 gross registered tons
Dimensions:	length 665 ft (202.7 m); beam 82 ft (25.0 m); draft 30 ft (9.1 m)
Propulsion:	six Parsons geared steam turbines delivering 24,100 shp (17969 kW) to two propellers for 21 kt
Complement:	708 cabin- and 700 tourist-class passengers, and 466 (later 565) crew

Nieuw Amsterdam (1937)

Despite the Great Depression, there was a steady increase in the numbers and also in the quality of the passenger liners operated by the world's economically important nations throughout the 1930s. This could be attributed in considerable measure to the decision of many governments to subsidize the construction of ocean liners as a way of reducing unemployment and providing national icons that would, they hoped, show those at home and abroad that conditions would soon improve. In such circumstances appeared the sleek Holland-America liner *Nieuw Amsterdam*.

The new liner was built by the Rotterdam Drydock Co. and launched by Queen Wilhelmina in April 1937. The *Nieuw Amsterdam* was the largest liner ever built in the Netherlands. Modern in every way, the *Nieuw Amsterdam* reflected the Art Deco movement of the period in her exterior design and interior finishing. The interior spaces were characterized by fluorescent lighting, aluminium motifs and pastel paintwork to create a feeling of understated elegance, and this contributed in a major way to the liner becoming a favourite among seasoned transatlantic passengers.

The new liner departed on her maiden voyage on May 10, 1938, and there was widespread enthusiasm for the ship when she docked in New York at the end of this first voyage. Although she was not as large or as fast as many of her contemporaries plying the transatlantic route, the *Nieuw Amsterdam* became very popular. Her appearance, with an elegant hull and two slim but nicely proportioned funnels, gave her a striking profile, and her passenger numbers remained good despite the blandishments of larger and faster British and French liners such as the *Queen Mary* of the Cunard Line and the *Normandie* of the French Line. So, despite the fierce competition of these large ships, the *Nieuw Amsterdam* remained in service as one of the few genuinely profitable vessels of the day.

There were other threats looming over Europe and the great liners of its major powers, and in September

1939 the *Nieuw Amsterdam* was laid up at Hoboken, New Jersey, after the German invasion of Poland. At this time the ship had completed only 17 transatlantic voyages, but was idle for only one year before being requisitioned by the British Ministry of War Transport after the Netherlands

had fallen to German invasion in May 1940. Like so many other great liners at this time, the *Nieuw Amsterdam* was converted as a troop transport, and spent the rest of World War II carrying an eventual 350,000 troops and steaming 530,450 miles (853655 km).

After demobilisation in 1946, the *Nieuw Amsterdam* was taken in hand for a 14-month refit before resuming transatlantic service in October 1947. For the following 20 years, the *Nieuw Amsterdam* regained and maintained a loyal following and thus enjoyed sustained financial success. The ship underwent several refits during the 1950s to keep her accommodation up to the best possible standards, and the threat posed in the 1960s by mechanical problems was removed when her boilers were replaced. The commercial threat of jet-powered air travel could not be brushed aside, however, and the *Nieuw Amsterdam* was shifted to the Caribbean cruise market until 1974, when her owners bit the commercial bullet and sent the ship to the breaker's yard.

The Nieuw Amsterdam was nicely conceived and well built, and remained in useful service into the first part of the 1970s.

Nieuw Amsterdam

Type:	transatlantic liner
Tonnage:	36,667 gross registered tons
Dimensions:	length 758 ft 3.5 in (231.1 m); beam 88 ft (26.8 m); draft not available
Propulsion:	two geared steam turbines driving two propellers for 21.15 kt
Complement:	556 first-, 455 tourist- and 209 third-class passengers, and 700 crew

Willem Ruys (1947)

The origins of Rotterdamsche Lloyd N.V. (Rotterdam Lloyd) can be found in the 1844 decision of Willem Ruys to enter the shipping market to and from the Dutch East Indies. The company grew and expanded over the years, and despite losing several ships in World War I, in which the Netherlands were neutral, the company was well placed in the 1920s and 1930s. At this time both the Dutch Line and Rotterdam Lloyd operated on the route to the East Indies. The latter had ships such as the elegant 12,000-ton *Slamat*, *Indrapoera* and *Sibajak*. Despite their original elegance, these ships were now obsolescent as the Dutch Line had introduced a number of superior ships such as the *Johan van Oldenbarnevelt*, which began East Indian service in 1930 and was supplemented in 1939 by the thoroughly modern *Oranje*. This new vessel's first voyage was so successful that Rotterdam Lloyd concluded that it required a realistic competitor.

The new ship was laid down in January 1939 at the De Schelde yard in Vlissingen, but at the outbreak of World War II in September of the same year work was halted. After conquering the Netherlands, the Germans sought to complete the vessel, only to be stymied by Dutch resistance efforts.

After the end of the war against Germany in May 1945, the company (now prefixed "Royal") decided to complete the vessel, which was launched in July 1, 1946. The *Willem Ruys* was then completed, and departed on her first voyage to the Dutch East Indies (now Indonesia) on December 2, 1947. The *Willem Ruys* featured a superstructure very different from that of any other liner

yet built, and pioneered the carriage of aluminium alloy lifeboats low in the sides of the superstructure. By comparison with the *Oranje*, the *Willem Ruys* offered greater levels of luxury, and indeed set a new standard in comfort for all classes of passenger. The *Willem Ruys* quickly became the most popular liner plying to the Dutch East Indies until 1949,

when the islands became independent as Indonesia, and the traffic between the Netherlands and its former Far East empire disappeared virtually overnight.

The *Willem Ruys* was later placed in service across the Atlantic to the U.S. and Canada, and then between 1959 and 1964 on a round-the-world service via Australia and New Zealand. The refit for this service increased her tonnage to 23,114 with accommodation for 275-first and 770-second class passengers. The *Willem Ruys* embarked on her new career in March 1959, sailing eastward via the Panama Canal, while the *Johan van Oldenbarnevelt* and *Oranje* sailed westward via the Suez Canal. By 1964 passenger demand had fallen to the extent that the *Willem Ruys* and *Oranje* were both laid up and then sold to the Flotta Lauro Lines. In January 1965 the *Willem Ruys* thus became the Italian-flagged *Achille Lauro*.

After an eventful Italian career, which included onboard fires, collisions, a hijacking by terrorists and the bankruptcy of her owner, the *Achille Lauro* caught fire off the Horn of Africa on November 30, 1994 and sank on December 2.

The Willem Ruys pioneered several features which later became standard on cruise liners.

Willem Ruys

Type:	ocean liner
Tonnage:	21,119 gross registered tons
Dimensions:	length 631 ft 2 in (1932.4 m); beam 82 ft (25.0 m); draft 29 ft 2 in (8.9 m)
Propulsion:	eight Sulzer diesel engines delivering 27,000 shp (20131 kW) to two propellers for 21 kt
Complement:	344 first-, 301 second-and 255 third- and fourth-class passengers, and 400 crew

British trawlers (1900-1960)

The trawler is a type of fishing vessel designed specifically for the operation of a trawl net to gather bottom-lying fish. Before the introduction of power for propulsion and the working of the net, a sailing trawler could operate its trawl to a depth of 180 to 240 ft (55 to 75 m). Steam-powered trawlers steadily increased their working depth to 3,000 ft (915 m), and, as they increased in size, might steam long distances to reach the fishing grounds and then remain there for some time until its holds were full.

Steam was the great prime mover of the British trawler fleet before World War I's start in 1914, but a rival had already appeared in the form of the Gardner diesel engine perfected in Manchester during 1894. The first such engines were trialed on British fishing vessels early in the twentieth century. The power was first too low for a working vessel, but by 1908 the marine diesel engine was clearly a major threat to steam power in the UK's huge fishing industry.

Among the diesel pioneers were the Eyemouth-based Maggie Janes. This innovation was one in which Scotland (and especially Eyemouth) led the way. The Scots quickly appreciated the advantages of a power plant which did not have constantly to be fed with coal by a man thus unavailable for other duties; moreover, coal was cleaner, easier to handle and simpler to accommodate on board than coal and, perhaps most importantly of all, effected a major reduction in running costs.

Scotland had about 100 motor vessels by 1913, and European nations also emphasised diesel development rather than the expansion of their steam fleets. But for a somewhat longer time, the owners of English vessels remained adherents of steam power, and indeed it was 1926 before the Richards yard of Lowestoft laid down the *Veracity* as its first motor fishing vessel, having launched its last pair of steam fishing vessels, the *Forecast* and *Charter*, in the previous year.

World War I was a major stimulus to the penetration of motor power in the British fishing fleet. The reason for this was the fact that so many steam

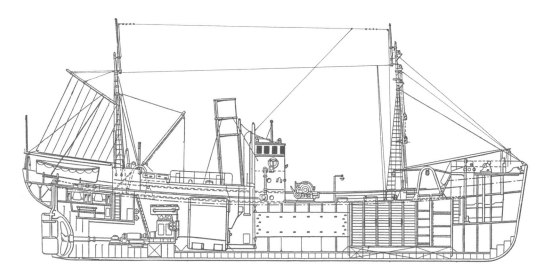

vessels were serving with the Royal Navy that catches of vital fish were declining. Thus the Board of Agriculture and Fisheries offered subsidies to the owners of hundreds of smaller inshore fishing craft, then wholly under sail, to allow them to fit auxiliary motors in order to keep fish supplies going.

When the steam fishing vessels were demobilised and returned to their home ports after the end of the war in 1918, their owners and crews no doubt hoped for a new "golden age" of fishing, especially of herring. There had been huge catches in 1913, but after the war, catches never matched those of this record season, and were indeed very variable right through the 1920s, with a peak in 1929, after which the herring industry went into a steep decline.

The problem caused by the lack of catches was only one of the difficulties faced by the British fishing industry in the aftermath of World War I, however, and often it proved impossible to sell the catches which were landed. The export trade was also only a shadow of its pre-war self: exports to Germany which had flourished up to World War I never became as strong again, nor did those to Russia, which had been the British fishing industry's second-largest export market before World War I, but the post-revolutionary USSR was a notably difficult market.

To make matters worse, there was a steep decline in the British domestic market as the British began to reject the cheap but highly nutritious herring in favour of cod, which became the core of the "fish and chip" dinner. By 1920 there were 25,000 fish and ships shops, which each year ordered some 150,000 tons of cod, a white fish of notably less nutritional value than the oil-rich herring. The demand for cod amounted to about 20% of the total fish landed in British ports.

The result was a disaster for the British herring fleets, in which an anticipated golden era rapidly turned into a major depression. Many thousands of men lost their work in the herring fleet, and many hundreds of steam herring drifters were broken up or alternatively left to rot. Nor, as the boom after World War I ended and the world slid toward a depression, was there money to replace exhausted ships and gear. During 1913, 1,500 steam drifters had earned £2,400 per vessel, but by 1933 there were only 1,000 such drifters and they brought in only some £1,100 each. The drifter owners of 1913 had a modern fleet which employed 25,000 men (half of the total for the 1880 sailing fleet) and brought in a record yearly total, but by 1933 the number of men employed had fallen to 15,000.

British Trawlers *continued*

During these dismal years, a development which further hit the herring industry was the invention in Germany of a trawl with a small third otter board located in the center to pull the trawl's mouth upward and so

After World War I, the trawler looked forward to a better future than the drifter, for during the war the types of fish caught by trawlers had swelled considerably in numbers, especially in the North Sea in which

allowing it to scoop in great quantities of fish, including herring, which fed at certain times of day nearer the bottom. Trawled rather than drift-netted herring were inferior and often included a high percentage of young fish, causing a decline in the stocks of maturing fish.

there appeared to be innumerable cod, haddock and plaice. The steam trawlers were landing well over twice the catches they had achieved before the war, but by 1922 overfishing had ended the North Sea boom and, before long, British trawlers were forced to operate as far away as the Atlantic off

Morocco and the Arctic between Bear Island and the Barents Sea.

The need to operate so far from home was one of the reasons for the demise of the steam trawler. The trawler of the 1920s was typically some 175 ft (53.3 m) long, powered by a triple-expansion engine supplied with 250 tons of coal, and holds able

to accommodate some 60 tons of fish. These vessels had been planned on the basis of six-day voyages no more than 100 miles (160 km) from their home ports, but by the 1930s most trawler voyages lasted between three and four weeks. Thus there was a considerable strengthening of economic case for a smaller number of larger vessels, and by this time the diesel engine offered major advantages over steam machinery for larger vessels. The death of steam power for trawler purposes was gradual but nonetheless inexorable, especially as the better steam engines of the period were very durable, and on the outbreak of World War II in 1939, the Admiralty could still requisition some 300 coal-burning drifters and trawlers.

The handful of sailing trawlers still working at that time then came to the end of their careers as harbor barrages. Many of the steam fishing vessels returned to work again after the war's end in 1945, but by 1950 they were dwindling fast and the last of the steam-powered fishing vessels survived their sailing counterparts by less than 30 years.

Unfortunately, little remains as a reminder of this important era of British maritime heritage. The only steam drifter to survive is the *Lydia Eve*, now owned by the National Maritime Trust. It seems that no steam trawler has been preserved.

Spleis (built in 1918)

Type:	trawler
Tonnage:	438 tons
Dimensions:	length 148 ft (45.1 m); beam 23 ft 6 in (7.2 m); draft 13 ft (4.0 m)
Propulsion:	one triple-expansion steam engine delivering 600 ihp (447 kW) to one propeller for 11 kt
Complement:	not available

Lurline (1931)

The Matson Navigation Co. subsidiary of Alexander & Baldwin is a privately owned ocean transport organization with its origins in the late nineteenth century. The company is credited with introducing mass tourism to Hawaii.

Although its stock in trade was oceanic cargo services, Matson decided to introduce a modest number of passenger liners as its means of capitalizing on the tourist trade, which became increasingly significant in economic terms from Pacific ports as well as Australia and New Zealand.

Two of the Matson Line's earlier combined passenger and cargo vessels, the *Maui* and *Wilhelmina*, were the first passenger ships with the engines located aft, and among other celebrated "white ships of Matson" were the *Lurline*, *Malolo*, *Mariposa*, *Matsonia* and *Monterey*. With the advent and steadily increasing domination of travel by routine and charter air travel between the

the late nineteenth century. Between the first years of the twentieth century and the 1970s, when it dropped out of a tourism market dominated by jet-powered aircraft, Matson liners operated from San Francisco and Los Angeles in California, on the western coast of the continental U.S., to destinations such as Honolulu in the Hawaiian Islands and also somewhat deeper into and across the Pacific Ocean, including a handful of South mainland and the Hawaiian Islands, Matson steadily trimmed its famous passenger service, and by the late 1970s the liners had been retired from Pacific services.

Matson is still the dominant cargo transport company in Hawaii; however, its main competitor in the U.S. domestic market is Horizon Lines.

Matson Lines started to operate between San Francisco and

destinations in Australia after its acquisition of the Oceanic Steamship Company, and steadily increased the number and size of its vessels. In 1928 the company decided to order a three-strong class of larger vessels for the Australia route. These were the "Mariposa" class ships. and the first of them was the *Mariposa*, which was launched on July 18, 1931, sold on 1954 to the Homes Line as the cruise ship *Homeric*, and scrapped during January 1974 in Japan after suffering a major fire. The second of the class was the *Monterey*, which was also launched in 1931 and in 1970 was

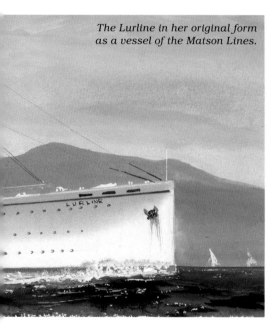

The Lurline in her original form as a vessel of the Matson Lines.

sold to the Chandris Line for service as the *Britanis* in the passenger and cruise liner roles. The ship was sold in 1998, to become the *Bolofin*, an unlucky vessel which sank on October 20, 2000, as she was being towed to the breaker's yard.

The third of the new vessels was the *Lurline*, which was built by the Bethlehem Shipyard of Quincy, Massachusetts, and launched on July 18, 1932. After completion, fitting out

and sea trials, the *Lurline* departed from San Francisco on December 27 of the same year on her maiden voyage to Sydney in eastern Australia, via a number of other Pacific ports. The *Lurline* returned to San Francisco on April 24, 1934. After her voyage across the Pacific and back, the *Lurline* and the older *Malolo* were placed in service of the very popular service linking San Francisco and Honolulu.

On December 7, 1941 the *Lurline* was about mid-way from Honolulu to San Francisco when Japanese carrierborne aircraft attacked the U.S. military installations in the Hawaiian Islands, in particular air bases and the naval base at Pearl Harbor. This drew the U.S. into World War II, which had started in Europe in 1939, and the country became a member of the Allied alliance. The *Lurline*'s captain ordered maximum speed for the rest of the voyage to San Francisco. Here, she and her sister ships loaded troops and vital war equipment and steamed in convoy back to Hawaii at a time that many in the U.S. believed would be marked by a Japanese landing on the islands.

For the rest of World War II, the *Lurline* and other Matson Line vessels worked in the unglamorous but wholly essential task of trooping to the islands of the Pacific and also to Australia, which was the base area where U.S. forces were built up for the campaign in New Guinea and eventual return to the Philippine Islands. On one occasion the *Lurline* carried John Curtin, the prime minister of Australia, to the U.S. for talks with President Franklin D. Roosevelt.

In the period following the surrender of Japan in August 1945, the *Lurline* continued in military service, largely for the repatriation of U.S. combat troops from the Pacific theatre. In the middle of 1946,

Lurline *continued*

however, the ship was returned to her owner, and after an initial survey was quickly committed to a major overhaul and refit at Alameda, California, in 1947-48 as a cost estimated at US$20 million. The *Lurline* re-entered mercantile service on April 15, 1948, on the service between San Francisco and Honolulu. The ship quickly regained her reputation as the best liner operating in the Pacific.

The success of the *Lurline* persuaded Matson in 1950 to undertake a similar refit of the *Monterey* to become the Matsonia. The two liners now provided a service, first-class only, between California and Hawaii, but on occasion cruises were also undertaken. Jet-powered airliners were now major competition, however, and in September 1962 the *Matsonia* was laid up. On February 3 of the following year, the *Lurline* reached Los Angeles with a major problem in her port turbine. The company decided to sell the ship, as the cost of repairs would be very high, and to recommission the *Matsonia* as a "new" *Lurline*.

The original *Lurline* was sold to the Chandris Lines on September 3, 1963, and, after her engines had been repaired in the U.S., the ship was refitted and modernised at North Shields in north-eastern England. While the ship's exterior was somewhat modernised, most of her Hawaiian decor and furniture was retained. The accommodation was also greatly increased, the passenger capacity now becoming 1,668 in a one-class arrangement.

Renamed as the *Ellinis*, the ship looked very attractive with her revised upperworks and in her new livery. The *Ellinis* departed on her maiden

Eugene Savage (1883-1978) was born in Covington, Indiana and was a highly accomplished muralist and sculptor. In 1940 he completed a two-year mural project for the Matson Co. to be used as menu covers. He produced a series of 4 x 8 foot murals that went

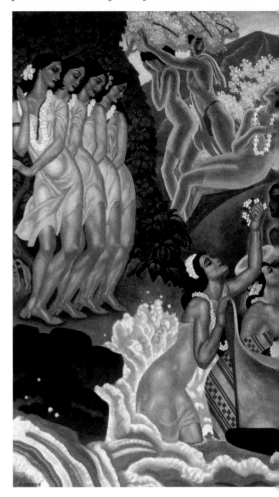

voyage from Piraeus, the port of Athens, to Sydney on December 30, 1963, and from 1964 every other homeward passage was routed via the Panama Canal to Southampton. For the next 10 years, the *Ellinis* made regular voyages to Australia and also served as a an occasional cruise liner. And for several years she operated an eastward round-the-world route.

In April 1974 the *Ellinis* again suffered engine problems, and her

194

straight into his basement and were never used in the buildings or on the ships. The menu covers were never used before World War II because the Matson ships were requisitioned as U.S. transport ships. The designs were finally used in 1948. Due to demand for them, they were also produced as a set of 6 which could be purchased from Matson Lines for a nominal fee. The American Institute of Graphic Arts honored the menu covers with its highest award in 1950. The original murals are now on permanent display at the Smithsonian Institute.

owner bought an engine from the *Homeric*, as the *Mariposa* now was, since she was about to be scrapped. The healthy engine was installed at Rotterdam, allowing the *Ellinis* to re-enter service in March 1975. In October 1981 the *Ellinis* was laid up in Greece, and in 1986 was sold to a Taiwanese breaker.

Lurline

Type:	ocean liner
Tonnage:	18,021 gross registered tons
Dimensions:	length 632 ft (192.6 m); beam 79 ft (24.1 m); draft not available
Propulsion:	geared steam turbines driving two propellers for 22 kt
Complement:	475 first- and 240 tourist-class passengers, and 350 crew

Delorleans & Crescent City (1940)

The "C3" type of standard mercantile hull was created in the late 1930s at the behest of the U.S. Maritime Commission specifically to ease the task of mass production at a time of rapidly worsening international relations, and production of this type of hull, in a number of variants with single- or twin-propeller propulsion, started in 1939 and lasted to 1947, with some 465 hulls being completed. The first of these were delivered to mercantile operators, but later ships were taken straight into naval service and many of the first vessels were adapted for military purposes in World War II.

Ordered by the Mississippi Shipping Co. Inc. (otherwise the Delta Line), the *Delorleans* was of the "C3-P Delta" subtype optimized for the freight role but with provision for a few passengers. The ship was built by the Bethlehem Steel Company at its Sparrows Point yard in Maryland, launched in February 17, 1940, and delivered to her owner on August 23, of the same year, mainly for services linking New Orleans and ports in Central and South America.

The Delta Line ordered the *Delorleans* and five sister ships specifically for high-speed mixed freight and passenger services to and from Argentina with up to 8,600 tons of freight and up to a maximum of 50 first- and 50 second-class passengers, although a more typical number of passengers was 67.

Only nine months after her debut in mercantile service, however, during June 1941, the *Delorleans* was taken over by the U.S. Navy and transferred to the Alabama Dry Dock Organization at Mobile, Alabama, for conversion as an AP (troop transport). In this capacity the vessel was renamed as the USS *Crescent City* (the nickname of New Orleans), and was later adapted as an APA (assault transport) for up to 1,400 troops landed with the aid of two LCM(3) medium landing craft and between 25 and 32 LCVP light vehicle/personnel craft. The *Crescent City* served in the former capacity during the Guadalcanal campaign of 1942-43, and in the latter capacity

during the Okinawa campaign of 1945, as well as on the U.S.'s east and Caribbean coasts.

In February 1945 the vessel was converted at Pearl Harbor into a temporary hospital ship, and after post-war service in the trooping role once more, the *Crescent City* was laid up at Suisun Bay, California, in the course of 1948.

Resting untouched until 1971, the ship was finally revived by the Vallejo-based California Maritime Academy as its second training ship, a role in which the vessel operated under the name *Golden Bear*. By this time most of the other 23 "C3-P" type ships, including her five sisters, had vanished, and the ex-*Delorleans* was now transformed for a major change in her career. With classrooms and dormitories built into her holds, she sailed for 24 years with a full company of cadets. In 1995, the *Golden Bear*

was finally retired and laid up once again at Suisun Bay.

The vessel rested between unemployed cargo vessels until August 1999, when she was brought out of reserve by the Artship Foundation, which intends to restore and revive the ship as a floating university of peace and as a cultural center. The vessel is presently berthed in Oakland, California as efforts continue to raise the sum of US$5 million required for the conversion.

The USS Crescent City is depicted in her troop transport form with the armament of one 5-in (127-mm), four 3-in (76-mm) and four 40-mm guns.

Delorleans

Type:	passenger and cargo ship
Tonnage:	7,922 gross registered tons
Dimensions:	length 491 ft (149.7 m); beam 65 ft 8 in (20.0 m); draft 25 ft 8 in (7.8 m)
Propulsion:	two geared steam turbines delivering 8,500 shp (6338 kW) to two propellers for 16.5 kt
Complement:	up to 100 passengers, and crew

America (1939)

The *America* was built for the United States Lines, but had many names in the 54 years between her completion in 1940 and her loss in 1994. She served as the *America* (in three different periods), USS *West Point*, *Australis*, *Italis*, *Noga*, *Alferdoss* and *American Star*. She served most notably in passenger service as the U.S.-flagged *America* and Greek-flagged *Australis* for the Chandris Line.

The *America* was laid down under a Maritime Commission contract on August 22, 1938, by the Newport News Shipbuilding & Drydock Co. of Virginia, was launched on August 31, 1939, and was the flagship of the United States Lines on August 22, 1940, when she departed on her maiden voyage.

Specifically designed for the prestigious North Atlantic passenger trade, in which the quality of accommodation and service was all important, the *America* succeeded the recently retired *Leviathan*. The clouds of war were already well up over the horizon before the *America* was laid down in 1938, and the ship was launched one day before the German invasion of Poland triggered the outbreak of World War II in Europe on September 1, 1939. In the somewhat dangerous circumstances typical of North Atlantic operations in 1940, the United States Lines decided not to commit their new flagship to the transatlantic passenger trade, but initially on cruises from New York to the Caribbean and California.

In May 1941 the ship was requisitioned into military service and later reached Newport News for conversion as a troop ship. The vessel was commissioned into the U.S. Navy as the USS *West Point* in June of the same year with accommodation for 8,750 troops and a defensive armament of four 5-in (127-mm), four 3-in (76-mm) and eight 0.5-in (12.7-mm) guns. In November 1941, the *West Point* sailed as part of a convoy of Canadian troops bound for Singapore via Cape Town, which she

The America is here depicted in war-time service after conversion from a liner into the troop ship USS West Point.

The officer who commanded the America was the most senior captain of the United States Lines.

reached two days after the Japanese attack on Pearl Harbor which drew the U.S. into World War II, and Bombay. The *West Point* was used to evacuate 1,276 people from Singapore two weeks before the fall of the port in February 1942. After this the ship was used for trooping between the Mediterranean and Australia and New Zealand, and later in the same task from the U.S. to the Pacific and Europe.

In 1946 the *West Point* was released from naval service and, following a US$6 million refit, at last embarked on the task for which she had been designed. The *America* departed from New York on November 10 for her first peacetime voyage to Europe. But as the transatlantic passenger trade passed steadily into the hands of jet-powered aircraft from the late 1950s, the *America* had to combine summer-month crossings of the North Atlantic with winter-month cruises to the Caribbean from the early 1960s. In 1964 the *America* was withdrawn from North Atlantic service, sold to Okeania S/A of the Chandris Group, and renamed *Australis* for use of the emigrant transport service from the UK to Australia. On each of these voyages, the *Australis* carried 2,258 one-class passengers, which was a total greater than that of any other passenger ship then in service, on a round-the-world route from and to Southampton.

From 1976 the fortunes of the ship changed frequently. First she was transferred from Panamanian to Greek registry, and made her last voyage from Southampton to New Zealand, after which she was laid up at Timaru. In 1978, she was sold to New York-based Venture Cruise Lines, which became bankrupt after two cruises of the vessel, now named once again as the *America*. The ship was bought for a second time by Chandris in 1978 and renamed as the *Italis*. The forward funnel, merely an aesthetic dummy, was removed, and the vessel re-entered service as a cruise ship from Barcelona. The ship was laid up for most of the 1980s before being renamed yet again, this time as the *American Star*, and bought by Thai interests for conversion to a floating hotel or prison. Under tow to Phuket in January 1994, the *American Star* was blown ashore by a hurricane on Fuertaventura in the Canary Islands and broke in two.

America

Type:	transatlantic liner
Tonnage:	33,961 gross registered tons
Dimensions:	length 723 ft (220.4 m); beam 94 ft (28.7 m); draft 32 ft (9.75 m)
Propulsion:	two geared steam turbines driving two propellers for 22.5 kt
Complement:	516 first-, 371 cabin- and 159 tourist-class passengers, and crew

USS *Platte* (1939)

The USS *Platte* was a "Cimarron" class fleet oiler of the U.S. Navy. The vessel was built by the Bethlehem Steel Company at its Sparrows Point yard near Baltimore, Maryland, launched on July 8, 1939 and commissioned on December 1, 1939. The vessel, absolutely vital for the prosecution of extended naval operations far from shore refuelling facilities, was fitted out in the Philadelphia Navy Yard and left on her first cruise on March 27, 1940, making two voyages to the oil docks of Houston, Texas, then supporting U.S. Navy units operating from the Panama Canal Zone, and providing support for a pair of tugs towing a great floating dock to Pearl Harbor in the Hawaiian Islands. The

forces patrolling the Coral Sea, and refuelled Australian and U.S. warships preparing to attack Salamaua and Lae, on New Guinea, in carrierborne air attacks. The oiler then provided fuel for the task forces of the carriers USS *Enterprise* and USS *Yorktown* as they prepared for the decisive Battle of Midway in June 1942.

The *Platte* supported U.S. forces off the Solomon Islands from August 10-14, and then again later in the same month before returning to the west coast of the U.S. for essential overhaul before steaming back to the waters off the Solomons. After another visit to San Pedro, the *Platte* headed north on April 9, 1943, for the campaign to regain the Aleutian islands seized

Platte reached her new base, at San Pedro, California, on September 4. For the next 14 months, she worked between San Pedro and Pearl Harbor, where she was berthed when the Japanese attack drew the U.S. into World War II on December 7, 1941.

On January 11, 1942, the *Platte* was with the aircraft carrier USS *Enterprise* to provide under-way replenishment of Task Force 8, centred on this carrier, as it shielded troop and cargo vessels reinforcing the Samoan Islands. During the next months, the *Platte* supported task

by the Japanese. Following several runs between the west coast and Pearl Harbor, the *Platte* was one of 13 oilers supplying the warships and transports used in the Gilbert Islands campaign of November 1943, and operated in the same task for the Marshall Islands campaign of January and February 1944.

On June 6, 1944, the *Platte* steamed from Majuro Atoll with the Fast Carrier Task Force for the Marianas Islands campaign, providing fuel and other support missions up to August 14. The *Platte* loaded fuel and cargo at Eniwetok Atoll, then made passage to Seeadler Harbor on Manus in the Admiralty Islands, where she was based for logistic support of the forces in the Palau Islands, Ulithi in the Caroline Islands, and Leyte and Samar in the Philippine Islands group. This part of the oiler's career lasted to October 1944, when the *Platte* returned to the U.S. for a major overhaul to play a major supporting role in the next phase of the U.S. war against Japan, including the invasion of Iwo Jima during February 1945 and the supporting carrier strikes on Tokyo. The *Platte* next supported the forces involved in the April 1945 invasion of Okinawa, and then supported Task Force 38 in July 1945 as its carrierborne aircraft struck at Honshu in the Japanese home islands. The Japanese surrendered

on August 15, and the *Platte* steamed into Tokyo Bay on September 10 as station tanker for the ships involved in the first stage of the Allied occupation of Japan, before departing for the U.S. on 29 September.

Less than five months later the *Platte* was back in Japan, this time at Yokohama, to support the occupation forces from February 4, 1946. During the next year, the oiler travelled to and from the oil docks of Bahrain and Saudi Arabia for the fuel to support fleet operations in the principal ports of Japan, the Philippines and South Korea, and after that provide logistic support for U.S. Navy vessels in China, Japan and Okinawa. The *Platte* returned to the U.S. for fleet exercises off the west coast, and a refit and overhaul. There followed an other cruise to the Far East. The post-World War II career of the *Platte* included two tours of duty off Korea during the Korean War (1950/53), followed by another return to the U.S. from November 1953. Next came six tours in support of the U.S. 7th Fleet in the Far East between 1954 and 1960.

The *Platte* recorded almost annual deployments to the western Pacific between 1960-68, including extensive operations in Vietnamese waters and the refuelling of the conventional ships of the nuclear-powered USS Enterprise's task group off Korea during the *Pueblo* incident. The *Platte* remained with the Pacific Fleet to 1970, and was sold for scrapping on May 14, 1971.

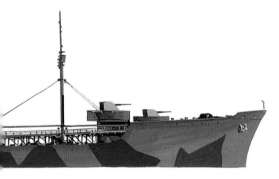

Operating in support of major combat forces, the oiler USS Platte was herself a potential target for submarine, surface ship and, especially, air attack. The vessel always carried defensive armament, which peaked in 1945 with four 5-in (127-mm) guns, two twin 40-mm guns, and two twin 20-mm guns.

USS *Platte*

Type:	fleet oiler
Tonnage:	24,830 tons full load
Dimensions:	length 553 ft (160.0 m); beam 75 ft (22.9 m); draft 32 ft (9.75 m)
Propulsion:	two geared steam turbines delivering 30,400 shp (22666 kW) to two propellers for 18.3 kt
Complement:	304

Building a steel ship in World Wars I and II

From the 1880s, as there emerged major improvements in the design and construction of steam engines, allowing larger ships to be powered effectively, the creation of enlarged hulls was made feasible by the introduction of steel, created by the newly developed Siemens process, as successor to iron as the primary material for ship construction. Offering greater strength per pound than wood or iron, steel paved the way for naval architects to design larger ships. Steel was also much better suited to bearing the increasingly massive weight of the more powerful

steam engines, together with their boilers and furnaces.

The structural members of early steel vessels were riveted together, but gas welding had entered limited use by World War I. The skilled workmen of the world's more modern yards thus traded auger, saw and mallet for pneumatic drill, gas cutting torch, and pneumatic rivet gun, and within the yard itself hoisting shears gave way to massive steam- and later electrically-powered cranes. Yet while it was undeniably true that the steel ship demanded vastly more complicated plans and a more tightly integrated co-ordination of the efforts of the various shops, the ship itself was assembled in much the same way as had been a wooden vessel. From the keel rose the stem, sternpost, and frames to create the basic structure, and to this

When the shipyard of Charleston, South Carolina, started to build steel vessels during 1915, a new ship ways was erected on the site of the shiphouse in which the wooden propeller frigate Merrimack had been built 60 years earlier. The yard built three 475-ft (144.8-m) fuel ships on this shipways between 1917 and 1921, steadily reducing the time between keel laying and launch from two years for the first ship to less than one year for the last.

Building a Steel Ship *continued*

were added the transverse beams, longitudinals, vertical stanchions, watertight bulkheads, decking and plating to complete the hull. The whole structure was held together by a vast number of rivets. In the 1930s electric welding was developed, and this opened the way to lightened construction and the prefabrication of sections which could be moved into position as complete subassemblies only when needed.

Cheaply manufactured steel opened the way to lower-cost but more durable ships, and the high tensile strength of the new steel allowed a weight saving of about 25% in the metal of any hull. This weight saving could be translated into a lower consumption of coal or, later, oil, for a given speed, or in the case of a passenger ship, slightly greater speed on the same engine power. The use of steel was not without its own disadvantages, however, for mild steel corrodes with greater speed than the wrought it succeeded. Yards soon appreciated, therefore, that as soon as the keep had been laid the development of rust was inevitable unless a rust inhibitor, such as a paint based on red lead, was used. Moreover, the need for scraping and painting was constant throughout the life of the ship.

Traditional methods of shipbuilding were based on the concept that the shape of all the plates and other parts of the hull were obtained by having the lines on the plan projected full scale on to a mold loft floor. From these lines full-scale patterns or templates were created and issued to the steel workers. As

With the basic skeleton of a ship complete, the plating of the outer hull could be added, paving the way for the completion of the main part of the hull's interior.

it was made, each item was marked in correspondence with its location on the plan. From the same source are derived the molds or templates for the vessel's stem, sternpost, rudder fittings, engine beds, propeller brackets and other heavy forgings.

The first step in construction is the laying of the keel plate, with its center longitudinal and rider plate, on the building blocks, which are normally given a slight inclination of about 1/30 down to the water to ease the task of launching the vessel. The stem and sternpost are then erected. Next come the frames, which are the vessel's ribs. These fabricated units were based on frame angle bars drawn from the furnace in a state of bright heat and quickly bent to the shape required on pre-shaped bar iron. The reverse bar and connecting floor plate were prepared in basically the same way, and the whole assembly was riveted together to form a complete frame. The completed frames were erected in their proper order across the keel plate, and after being adjusted into their correct position were secured by something akin to scaffolding. The deck beams, fore-and-aft stringers, and keelson plates were lowered into position and riveted to complete the hull skeleton,

to which the outer plating was riveted or welded. The inner plating for the double bottom, ballast tanks, shaft tunnel(s), beween-decks supporting pillars, and watertight bulkheads and other parts were added in sequence according to the methods and custom of the shipyard.

With the hull completed, the construction team set about installing the fresh water and oil fuel systems, air-conditioning and refrigeration plant, water sprinkler fire-fighting system, and all the vessel's "plumbing," all before or just after the launch. Once afloat the vessel was moved to her fitting-out berth where the engines and auxiliary machinery, and the boilers if she were a steamship, were lowered into position by cranes.

PAC Rocket (1941/42)

While aircraft had been only a limited threat to shipping in World War I (1914-18), they became a very major threat from the very beginning of World War II (1939-45) as a result of their larger numbers, increased weight and diversity of the weapon loads, greater accuracy of aiming devices, and use of shallow or steep diving attacks in addition to level bombing. The obvious answers were the provision of greater air cover and the installation on merchant shipping of anti-aircraft guns. Fighter cover was virtually impossible to provide except for coastal convoys and those oceanic convoys for which long-range flying boat or aircraft carrier support could be offered. Anti-aircraft guns were fitted on a number of ships, but there were never enough guns and trained personnel to fit every important merchant vessel with the anti-aircraft fire it needed.

This situation offered great scope for those concerned with the development of "funny" weapons. None of these was "funnier" than a British organization known as the Department of Miscellaneous Weapons Development (DMWD), otherwise known as the "Wheezers and Dodgers." This was adopted, at the urging of Prime Minister Winston Churchill, by the Admiralty during 1940 with Captain G. O. C. Davies as its director and Commander Charles Goodeve as its deputy director.

The DMWD had initially been part of the Inspectorate of Anti-Aircraft Weapons and Devices (IAAWD) as its primary task was to devise methods of defeating air attacks on surface targets, at sea as well as on land.

In March 1941 Churchill's fears about the casualties to the British merchant marine led him to issue a

special directive giving the Admiralty priority for "short-range AA guns and other weapons they can mount upon suitable merchant ships plying in the danger area." The "other weapon" included a version of the land-service Parachute And Cable Rocket (PAC Rocket), which the DMWD had for some time been working to adapt for sea service.

The initial task had been allocated to the well-known Schermuly pyrotechnics company, which had soon designed a rocket able to carry a steel cable up to a height of 500 ft (150 m), from which it descended slowly under a p a r a c h u t e . This allowed an airfield with a battery of such rockets to raise its own emergency "balloon barrage."

The Admiralty soon appreciated that the device might be a valuable deterrent at sea. Aircraft attacking a ship at masthead height could drop their bombs with deadly accuracy, but if thcy wcrc forced to bomb from a greater height accuracy would be decreased.

The DMWD's solution was a 480-ft (146-m) cable with a parachute at each end. In early trials it was found that the bottom parachute often failed to open at the critical moment, but this problem was overcome by the insertion of a special explosive link. The rocket had to be made completely waterproof, and some means had to be found of preventing the wire from kinking. The result was a marvelous apparatus using parachutes made by the soft-furnishing department of a well-known Oxford Street store.

When the first PAC Rockets were fitted on merchant ships, there was an inevitable argument before the Admiralty could persuade anyone to give the new device an operational trial. By the spring of 1941, encouraging reports began to come in. The mate of one small vessel, the *Fireglow*, was standing near the windward PAC Rocket launcher when a heavy air attack developed. Seeing one German bomber diving at his vessel from dead ahead, he pulled the lanyard, and up soared the cable. A large section of the airplane's wing was dragged off by the wire, and the warplane came down in the sea.

The skipper of the *Milford Queen* had a successful encounter with a Dornier Do 17. His guns had hit the bomber on its approach run, and when the PAC Rocket was fired it wrapped itself firmly round the wing of the bomber, which was losing height rapidly as it disappeared into the haze, and a few seconds later, the British crew heard a loud explosion.

Greatly encouraged, the DMWD set to work on larger and more destructive versions including the FAM, with an explosive charge attached to the wire, and the Type J, with a larger parachute and a 5-ton wire which the rocket could loft to 600 ft (183 m).

Early in 1943 the apparatus came off the secret list, and DMWD was able to tell Schermuly's work force something of what the device had achieved. Nine enemy aircraft were known to have been destroyed, and at least 35 ships claimed that they had been saved from destruction by the "spirals" which the German air crews feared so much.

Jervis Bay (1922))

The *Jervis Bay* was a British ocean liner later converted into an armed merchant cruiser in World War II, during which she was lost in an extraordinarily gallant but hopeless action in which she helped to save the convoy she was escorting by drawing the fire of the German pocket-battleship *Admiral Scheer* but was sunk in the resulting one-sided battle.

Named after a bay some 85 miles (137 km) south of Sydney in the Australian state of New South Wales, the *Jervis Bay* was one of five sister ships built for the Australian Commonwealth Line, which named all of its ships after bays, for the line's monthly service between Brisbane and London. The ship was built by Vickers Ltd. at its yard in Barrow in Furness, north-western England, during 1922, and her main trade was the transport of emigrants from the UK to Australia. In 1928, the Bay liners came under the control of

Lord Kylsant's White Star Line Ltd., but this holding company collapsed just five years later, and the ships were taken over by the newly formed Aberdeen & Commonwealth Line, which kept the ships in the trade for which they had been designed and built.

In September 1939, when World War II started, the *Jervis Bay* was at London, and at this point was requisitioned by the British government for conversion and service as an armed merchant cruiser for the patrolling and protection of the sea lanes on which the UK was largely reliant. The ship was hastily fitted with an anti-ship armament of seven 6-in (152-mm) guns, which were obsolescent Mk VII weapons dating from World War I, and an anti-aircraft armament of two 3-in (76-mm) guns. The maximum range of the Mk VII guns was a mere 14,200 yards (12985 m), and the fire-control system was more hopeful than realistic, nothing

Outclassed in every important aspect of naval warfare other than the courage of her captain and crew, the armed merchant cruiser Jervis Bay charges at the pocket battleship Admiral Scheer.

of any genuine value to be achieved in the way of improving the ship's protection against anything but shell splinters, so the real value of the vessel was very small.

The *Jervis Bay* was recommissioned in her new role with her mercantile operating crew and captain supplemented by naval gunners, and was at first deployed in the South Atlantic to watch for German merchant raider vessels which might attack the frozen meat ships plying the route from South America to the UK. In May 1940 the *Jervis Bay* was reallocated to the convoy escort role in the North Atlantic, where German surface, submarine and aircraft depredations were beginning to make a severe dent in the UK's ability to bring in oil, food and war matériel by sea.

Late in October 1940, the *Jervis Bay* was the sole escort for the 37 merchant ships which constituted convoy H.X.84 outward bound from Halifax, Nova Scotia, to the UK.

At about 3:00 p.m. on November 5, 1940, the convoy was intercepted by the *Admiral Scheer*, with a primary armament of six 11-in (280-mm) guns, far superior fire-control systems, good protection and a decided speed advantage, about mid-way in the North Atlantic between Newfoundland and Ireland. Captain S. E. Fogarty Fegen immediately appreciated that only the sacrifice of his own ship could buy the time for the ships of H.X.84 to scatter and so reduce the chances of the German warship destroying the entire convoy. After ordering the convoy to scatter, Fegen therefore steered the vulnerably high and essentially defenseless *Jervis Bay* into a charge that might reduce the range to the point at which his obsolete guns might hit the *Admiral Scheer*. Within 15 minutes, the *Jervis Bay* was dead in the water, and the ship sank at about 8:00 p.m. with the loss of 190 of her crew of 259 men. Although the *Admiral Scheer* was able to sink five of the convoy's scattering ships, the destruction was almost certainly have been considerably greater but for the *Jervis Bay*'s courageous charge. In recognition of the courage displayed by himself and his crew, Fegen was awarded a posthumous Victoria Cross, whose citation read, "Valour in challenging hopeless odds and giving his life to save the many ships it was his duty to protect".

Sixty-five of the *Jervis Bay*'s survivors were rescued by a neutral vessel, the Swedish *Stureholm*.

A monument to the *Jervis Bay* lies at Albouy's Point at Hamilton, Bermuda, one of the locations at which transatlantic convoys assembled in both world wars. A monument to Captain Fegen and the crew of the *Jervis Bay* also exists at Ross Memorial Park in St John's, New Brunswick, Canada, the port in which the *Jervis Bay* was refitted for war service during the summer of 1940.

Jervis Bay

Type:	oceanic liner
Tonnage:	14,164 gross registered tons
Dimensions:	length 549 ft (167.3 m); beam 68 ft (20.7 m); draft 33 ft (10.1 m)
Propulsion:	two geared steam turbines delivering 9,000 shp (6710 kW) to two propellers for 15 kt
Complement:	12 first- and 712 third-class passengers, and 216 crew

"Liberty" ship (1941)

Though intended primarily for mercantile use, replacing Allied tonnage sunk by the combination of German, Italian and Japanese surface warships, submarines, warplanes and mines, the "Liberty" ship was so important to the eventual Allied victory in World War II that it can be regarded in many respects as a weapon. The type was created for mass production in U.S. yards on the basis of a standardized design using an all-welded steel hull. The ships were produced in 18 shipyards located along the Atlantic, Pacific and Gulf coasts of the U.S. between 1941 and 1945, and totalled 2,770 vessels (by far the largest number ever completed to a single design) amounting to some 29.292 million deadweight tons. This total included 24 equipped as colliers, 8 as tank carrier ships, 36 as aircraft transports, and 62 as tankers.

The original design was produced by J. L. Thompson and Sons of Sunderland in the north-east of England as early as 1879, and this design was adopted by the Americans because it emphasized simple design and operation, rapid construction, maximum freight-carrying capability and, as it emerged, an excellent capacity to withstand damage. With the whole of U.S. turbine and diesel engine-building capacity already allocated to combatant vessels, it was decided that the "Liberty" ships would be powered by triple-expansion steam engines, and also use steam for all their auxiliary machinery.

The manufacture of the "Liberty" ship was organized and controlled, on the basis of a major industrial undertaking, by the construction magnate Henry J. Kaiser, most of whose previous experience had been in road and dam building. It is Kaiser to whom the definitive "Liberty" ship concept should also be attributed. Kaiser established the procedures to be used to maximize and streamline the production effort on a truly huge scale, and also performed the task of overseeing the entire process.

The "Liberty" ship was optimized for the carriage of cargo, and was both cheap and simple to build. The concept was based directly on ships ordered by the UK from U.S. yards to replace tonnage lost principally to

Simple and therefore quick and cost-effective to build, the "Liberty" ship was vital to both the early survival of the UK in World War II and the later Allied victory in the European and Pacific campaigns.

German aircraft, surface raiders and, most significantly of all, submarines. The ships were then bought for the U.S. merchant marine and also for delivery to U.S. allies under the terms of the Lend-Lease Act.

The production of the "Liberty" ships echoed, on a much larger scale, the building of the "Hog Island" and other standardized ship types in World War I, and also paved the way for the post-World War II "Victory"ship. This latter was completed to a standard less austere than that of the "Liberty" ship,

and was based on a lengthened and strengthened hull with a forecastle and steam turbine machinery. The standard "Victory" ship had a gross tonnage of 7,607 and speed of 16 kt.

In 1940 the British government ordered 60 tramp steamships from U.S. yards to replace war losses and boost the merchant fleet. The units of this "Ocean" class were simple but fairly large with a single propeller driven by a single 2,500-ihp (1864-kW) reciprocating engine working on the steam generated by coal-fired

"Liberty" ship *continued*

boilers; coal was specified as the UK had an abundance of it but no indigenous oil. The order specified an 18-in (0.45-m) increase in draft to increase the displacement by 800 tons to 10,100 tons; the accommodation, bridge and main engine for located amidships; and to be a long tunnel to connect the main engine shaft with its aft extension to the propeller. The first "Ocean" ship was the *Ocean Vanguard*, launched on August 16,

engineering and construction conglomerate.

The number of Lend-Lease ships was increased to 200 in March 1941, and then in April of the same year to 306, of which 117 would be "Liberty" ships. The ships had a poor public image at the time, and in an effort to swing the public behind the program September 27, 1941 became "Liberty Fleet Day," and the first 14 EC-2 type units were launched on this day.

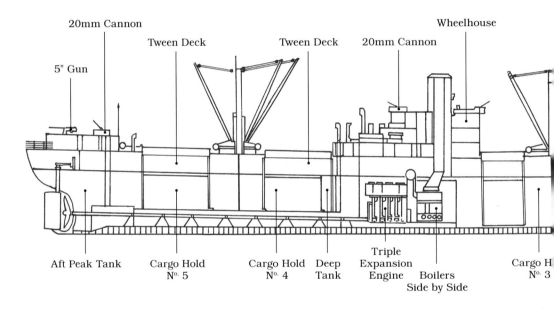

20mm Cannon | Wheelhouse
Tween Deck | Tween Deck | 20mm Cannon
5" Gun

Aft Peak Tank | Cargo Hold Nº. 5 | Cargo Hold Nº. 4 | Deep Tank | Triple Expansion Engine | Boilers Side by Side | Cargo H Nº. 3

1941.

This design was then further developed by the U.S. Maritime Commission in accord with U.S. construction practices and also to simplify them still further for ease and speed of construction. The American version was the variant classified by the U.S. Maritime Commission as the EC2-S-C1 type, in which most of the riveting (one-third of the labour cost) was replaced by welding. The order was given to Kaiser's six-company

The first to enter the water was the *Patrick Henry*, which was launched by President Franklin D. Roosevelt. The president said that the new class of ships would bring liberty to Europe, and this led to the appellation "Liberty" ship.

At first it took about 230 days to build each ship (the *Patrick Henry* took 244 days), but as the process wore on and the work force became more skilled the average dropped finally to a mere 42 days. As a publicity stunt, the *Robert E. Peary* was launched only 4 days and 15.5 hours after the laying of her keel. The ships were made from prefabricated sections joined on an assembly-line basis, and in 1943 three new "Liberty" ships were completed every day. The ships were named mainly for famous Americans, starting with those who had signed the Declaration of Independence in 1775.

A particularly notable "Liberty" ship was the *Stephen Hopkins*, which sank a German commerce raider during 1942, and in the process became the first U.S. ship to sink a German surface combatant.

The "Liberty" ships were often far from perfect. Many suffered hull and deck cracks, and some were lost to such structural problems. During World War II, almost 1,500 serious fracture were reported, and 19 ships broke in half without warning, the latter including the *John P. Gaines*, which sank on November 24, 1943 with the loss of 10 lives. The reasons for this problem were the fact that the ships were built in great haste, often by inexperienced people, in the era before the embrittlement problems of steel were fully comprehended, and the ships were often very considerably overloaded. The losses generally occurred after storms, when the hulls were very severely stressed, but they were among the factors that led to the follow-on "victory" ship being designed with greater strength and less stiffness.

The last "Liberty" ship to be completed was the *Albert M. Boe* delivered on 30 October 1945. Most of the "Liberty" ships survived to become a major element in the post-war cargo fleet.

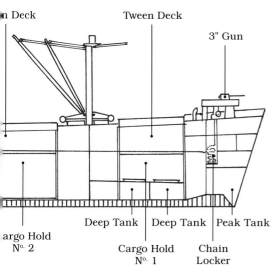

This line illustration highlights the essential features of the typical "Liberty" ship.

"Liberty" ship (typical)

Type:	general-purpose freighter
Tonnage:	14,245 tons displacement
Dimensions:	length 441 ft 6 in (134.6 m); beam 56 ft 11 in (17.35 m); draft 27 ft 9 in (8.45 m)
Propulsion:	two triple-expansion steam engines delivering 2,500 ihp (1864 kW) to two propellers for 11.5 kt
Capacity:	9,140 tons of cargo
Armament:	one 4-in (102-mm) gun, and an assortment of light anti-aircraft gun
Complement:	41

Ohio (1940)

The oil tanker *Ohio* was built for the Texas Oil Company, and at the time was the world's largest tanker. The *Ohio* was launched on April 20, 1940 at the yard of the Sun Shipbuilding & Dry Dock Co. at Chester, Pennsylvania.

The *Ohio* is best remembered for her involvement in "Pedestal," one of the hardest-fought and disastrous end of August, and "Pedestal" was launched in an effort to save the island. The convoy departed Liverpool on August 3, and the most important of its 13 ships was *Ohio*, which had been transferred to the British flag. In "Pedestal" the *Ohio* carried 12,000 tons of diesel fuel and kerosene.

On August 10, the convoy was met

convoy operations of World War II, fought between the convoy and its escort with Axis air and naval units in the central Mediterranean. By the middle of 1942, the British island bastion of Malta, dominating the Axis supply line across the Mediterranean, was on the brink of defeat for lack of food, oil and supplies. Even with severe rationing, it was estimated that the island could hold only to the at Gibraltar by an escort of more than 40 Royal Navy warships including the capital ships HMS *Rodney* and *Nelson*, the carriers HMS, *Eagle*, *Furious*, *Indomitable* and *Victorious*, seven cruisers, 20 destroyers and eight submarines. In the afternoon of the next day the *U-73* torpedoed and sank the *Eagle*, and during the evening of the same day, German bombers attacked without success.

During the following night, further attacks south of Sardinia damaged the freighter *Deucalion*, which was later sunk, and sank the destroyer HMS *Foresight*. At this point, the remaining capital ships and carriers, together with their escorts, turned back to Gibraltar, leaving the convoy and its escort of three cruisers and 10 destroyers to press forward. On the same night, the Italian submarine *Axum* sank the anti-aircraft cruiser HMS *Cairo*, and damaged both the *Ohio* and the cruiser HMS *Nigeria*, the latter turning back to Gibraltar. Next, bombers sank the *Empire Hope* and *Clan Ferguson*, and damaged the *Brisbane Star*, which reached Malta on her own. The Italian submarine *Alagi* damaged HMS *Kenya*.

As they passed through the Skerki Channel at 1:30 a.m. on August 13, the ships were attacked by 10 torpedo boats, which sank the cruiser HMS *Manchester* and the merchant vessels *Glenorchy*, *Wairangi*, *Almeria Lykes* and *Santa Elisa*. Repeated air attacks during the day sank the *Waimarama* and disabled HMS *Dorset* and the *Ohio*, whose crew was transferred to a destroyer until about 6:00 p.m. The badly damaged *Rochester Castle*, *Port Chalmers* and *Melbourne Star* limped into Valetta's Grand Harbor at 4:30 during the afternoon. The *Ohio* and *Dorset* had meanwhile come under attack once more during the evening, the cruiser sinking and the tanker again being abandoned. By the following morning, the *Ohio*'s crew could see Malta, but the tanker's freeboard was less than 3 ft (0.91 m), and even with two destroyers lashed to her, she could steam at no more than 1 kt. The tanker limped into Grand Harbor on August 15, in so precarious a condition that she was deliberately sunk at the dockside so that she would not break up while being unloaded.

The *Ohio* remained at Valetta until 1946, when she was towed out of the harbor and sunk.

The Ohio under attack during "Pedestal," in which the sturdy vessel was severely damaged and twice abandoned, but finally made it to Malta with her all-important cargo.

Ohio

Type:	oil tanker
Tonnage:	9,264 gross registered tons
Dimensions:	length 513 ft 1 in (156.4 m); beam 68 ft (20.7 m); draft 28 ft 6 in (8.7 m)
Propulsion:	one geared steam turbine delivering 10,000 shp (7456 kW) to one propeller for 16 kt
Complement:	not available

Military transport vessels of World War II

Although landing ships and craft of many types were designed and built in very large numbers in the middle and later stages of World War II (1939-45), the war's earlier stages saw the use of adapted merchant vessels. The Landing Ship Infantry was such a mercantile conversion, and the type was subdivided, by size, into LSI(L)s, LSI(M)s, LSI(S)s and LSI(H)s. The greater part of an invasion force was carried in such vessels to the assault area, where the troops and their equipment were transferred to embarked Landing Craft Assault for the assault.

Able to carry upward of 900 troops, the LSI(L) was adapted from an intermediate passenger and cargo liner with a good turn of speed, and had the capability for world-wide deployment. The largest group comprised the 12 "C1-S-AY1" type vessels received under Lend/Lease arrangements, but the three "Glen" class vessels were the most combat-worthy conversions. Able to upward of 375 and 200 troops, respectively, the LSI(M) and LSI(S) had been created for service in sheltered waters, and had to be strengthened and improved in seaworthiness for wide-ranging service. They were fast, but their troop capacity was limited. Whereas nearly all the LSIs carried their LCAs in gravity davits, this was not feasible in some small LSIs, which thus carried their LCAs under projecting spurs and were classed as LSI(H)s.

For large-scale landings, the build-up of stores and equipment ashore was limited by the number of LCMs (Landing Craft Medium) available. Most LSI(L)s carried one or two LCMs, hoisted out by derricks, but the numbers were clearly inadequate,

and means had thus to be devised for transporting LCMs to the assault area. Initially there was not the time to build special ships for this purpose, so conversions were made from available merchant vessels to Landing Ship Stern-chute, Landing Ship Gantry and Landing Ship Carrier standards until purpose-built LSDs (Landing Ships Dock) became available.

The two LSSs were train ferry

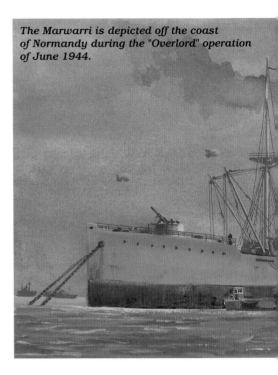

The Marwarri is depicted off the coast of Normandy during the "Overlord" operation of June 1944.

conversions with three rows of LCMs on the deck for launch (from the center row) through a chute cut into the stern stock, as well as landing craft. The three LSGs were Royal Fleet Auxiliary tanker conversions with LCMs in three rows on deck, before and abaft the amidships bridge, from which they were lifted and launched by traveling gantry cranes with hinged booms extending well outboard. The two LSCs were simple adaptations from standard heavy-lift ships with the LCMs deck-stowed for handling by jumbo derricks.

Other merchant ships were also used in a less highly adapted form. Typical was the *Marwarri*. At the start of World War II, this J. 7 T. Brocklebank vessel, completed in 1935, was requisitioned and converted into a vehicle transport, and on October 5, 1939 was damaged by a magnetic mine in the Bristol Channel while on passage to south Wales. The vessel was beached, made watertight, and at Swansea had her three turbines replaced as the original units had been blown out of alignment. She was back in service in January 1940 and used to move vehicles between South Wales and France. The *Marwarri* reverted to the general cargo role for the next two years, but was taken up as a vehicle carrier for the Normandy invasion, in which her capacity was 185 vehicles and 570 troops. The vessel was returned to her owner in 1945.

"Glen" class

Type:	landing ship infantry (large)
Tonnage:	9,800 tons gross
Dimensions:	length 507 ft (154.5 m); beam 66 ft 6 in (20.3 m); draft 30 ft 6 in (9.3 m)
Propulsion:	diesel engines delivering 12,000 bhp (8947 kW) to two propellers for 18 kt
Complement:	1,087 troops, three LCMs, 24 LCAs, and 523 crew
Armament:	three twin 3-in (76-mm) AA guns, one quadruple 2-pdr AA gun and eight 20-mm AA guns

Cable ships

The cable layer is a vessel intended specifically for the laying of underwater telegraph and later telephone cables and, if necessary, their recovery for maintenance and repair. Following the laying of the first successful underwater telegraph cable in 1851, under the English Channel between St Margaret's Bay near Dover and Sangatte in northern France, the succeeding 15 years witnessed the completion of many similar projects in different parts of the world. The first transatlantic telegraph cable had been laid in 1858 but had failed after only a very short time. In this period great strides were made in the manufacture and insulation of underwater cable, and in 1866 the

Great Eastern laid what was in reality the first successful transatlantic underwater telegraph cable. The success of the venture aroused public as well as commercial interest in this medium of communication, and up to the outbreak of World War I in 1914, there followed a major increase in the numbers and routes of cables laid. In this pioneering period the ships used were conversions of ordinary mercantile vessels possessing the power, capacity, stability and seaworthiness for the task. On a gradual basis, though, there began to emerge purpose-built ships.

It was inevitable that, after the 1876 invention of the telephone, underwater cables would be developed

A bow-laying cable ship had most of her forward half, including the volume under the superstructure, devoted to the cable stowage, with handling machinery on or above the deck, and laying sheaves in the bow.

Engine   Boiler
Room   Room   3 Cable Tanks

General arrangement of a cable-laying ship, with the cables accommodated
close to the ship's centre of gravity.

for this new form of communication. Several generally successful experiments were effected, but for technical reasons only comparatively short routes were possible until the invention of the repeater or relay, which was first incorporated in an underwater telephone cable in 1943. Then the road was open for rapid progress. By the 1950s major changes in cable-laying techniques allowed the introduction of larger-diameter cable, and repeaters and amplifiers in the underwater cables. Improved recovery systems and enhanced navigation systems also meant that the laying of long distance underwater telephone links was now possible.

Before the layer could depart, the cable was fed from a shore establishment into large shipboard cylindrical tanks with special features to prevent the cable coils from collapsing or moving more than one coil at a time. As it was loaded, the cable was laid from the outside of the tank to the centre, at which point thin battens were placed across the coils and the cable was taken back to the outside of the tank and the process repeated. When a tank was full the cable was diverted to the next tank and loading continued in the same fashion.

The most important item of equipment for laying or recovering cable was the specially designed winch, or cable engine. Two such winches were installed either on the foredeck or on the deck below. Several turns of cable were taken round the drum before being led to or from the bow sheaves. For telegraph cable these had a diameter of about 3 ft 6 in (1.07 m), of some two to three times that for telephone cable with repeaters. Cable laying over the stern required a different system. As the ship moved forward, the cable was paid out via a large braked drum, which controlled the rate at which the cable was laid. Before reaching the drum, the cable passed through a series of braked jockey pulleys which kept the cable tensioned.

Faraday **(built by Palmers of Newcastle for Siemens Brothers of London in 1923)**

Type:	bow-laying cable-laying ship
Tonnage:	5,533 tons gross
Dimensions:	length 394 ft 4 in (120.2 m) between perpendiculars; beam 48 ft 4 in (14.7 m); draft 34 ft 6 in (10.5 m)
Propulsion:	two triple-expansion steam engines delivering 2,960 ihp (2,207 kW) to two propellers for 12 kt
Complement:	crew not available, and 91,000 cu ft (2577 m³) of cable in four amidships tanks

Hospital ships of World War II

Offering a combination of the facilities more often seen in a well-equipped hospital with the mobility of the more austerely equipped field hospital, the hospital ship has become increasingly common since the time of the American Civil War (1861-65). The hospital of the type that matured from the late nineteenth century is therefore optimized for the treatment of battlefield injuries, but also possesses the facilities to handle other eventualities such as diseases endemic in the type of terrain in which any particular campaign is waged, and also run-of-the-mill matters such as dentistry.

The first major hospital ships were adapted liners whose interiors were most readily converted for the host of specialized departments required in a hospital ship. Typical of this breed was the *Andes*, built in 1913 for the Royal Mail Steam Packet Company. This was part of Lord Kylsant's great shipping empire which crashed in 1932, when the Royal Mail Lines Ltd. was formed and took over the assets of several companies. In World War I (1914-18) the *Andes* had been adapted as an armed merchant cruiser, in 1929 had become a cruise liner with her name changed to *Atlantis*, and in 1939 was requisitioned for use in World War II (1939-45) as a hospital ship. Released from this duty in 1946, the *Atlantis* was adapted for emigrants from the UK to Australasia, a role in which she served from 1948 before being scrapped in 1952.

In World War II the U.S. Navy thought it advisable to operate a small number of dedicated hospital ships. The most important of these were the six "Haven" class vessels, which were based on the Maritime Commission's

"C4-S-B2" type design. These were converted while building, and emerged in 1945 as the *Haven, Benevolence, Tranquility, Consolation, Repose* and *Sanctuary*. These had a standard displacement of 11,140 tons, length of 520 ft (161.25 m) and speed of 18.3 kt on the 9,000 shp (6710 kW) delivered to one propeller by one steam turbine.

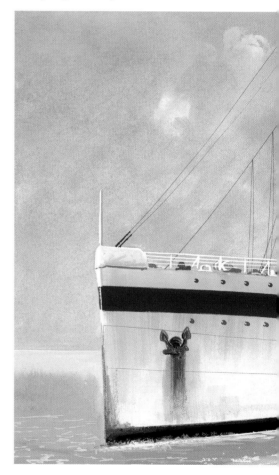

The longest-lived of the vessels was the *Sanctuary*, which was built by the Sun Shipbuilding & Dry Dock Co. of Chester, Pennsylvania, launched in August 1944 and commissioned in June 1945. She was decommissioned in 1946 and handed over to the

Maritime Administration in 1961, but then reacquired in 1966 for service in the Vietnam War. Between December 1971 and December 1972 the ship was converted as a dependent support ship within the context of the U.S. Navy's plan to base an aircraft carrier at Piraeus in Greece, and as such was the first U.S. ship with a mixed crew. The vessel had special facilities for obstetrics, gynaecology, maternity and nursery services, as well as a 74-bed hospital able to grow to 300 beds within 72 hours.

The *Sanctuary* was again decommissioned in March 1974 and laid up. Thought was given but not implemented to her reactivation in 1980 to support the pre-positioning of U.S. equipment in the Indian Ocean for Middle East deployments.

The Atlantis was clearly marked as a hospital ship during her service in World War II.

Atlantis

Type:	hospital ship
Tonnage:	15,135 tons gross
Dimensions:	length 570 ft (173.75 m); beam 67 ft (20.4 m); draft 33 ft (10.05 m)
Propulsion:	geared steam turbine driving three propellers for 16 kt
Complement:	not available, and 143,000 cu ft (13285 m³) of cargo

Royal Eagle (1932)

The origins of the General Steam Navigation Co. Ltd. can be found in 1824, and during the 1960s it was absorbed into the P & O shipping conglomerate. From its beginning, the GSN was a diversified shipping operator which also included deep sea interests and an excursion business in the Thames estuary. This latter proved to be very popular with the people of London, and helped to establish the shores of the estuary, in Essex and Kent, as popular holiday destinations for the urban population of the British capital. For the GSN, this created the type of financial stability which allowed the company to outlast its competitors, although for short spells Belle Steamers and the Victoria Steamboat Association were able to outshine the GSN with their newer vessels. At the hub of the GSN's services were the five so-called "Classical Bird" vessels built in 1887-89, and which were the immediate predecessors of luxurious but ultimately financially crippling vessels such as the Victoria Steamboat Association's paddle steamer *La Marguerite*.

Following an unsuccessful experiment in 1906 with the turbine-powered steamer *Kingfisher*, the GSN reverted to paddle-wheel propulsion in 1909. On the basis of the three "Eagle" paddle-wheelers built between 1909 and 1932, the GSN became the leading operator in the London excursion trade. In 1937 the GSN took over the New Medway Steam Packet Co., which had become its chief rival after World War I (1914-18) and, while they remained nominally independent, the two fleets were then operated in a dovetailed association. During the 1930s a number of large

Paddle Steamer "Royal Star" off Southend Pier, the longest pleasure pier in the world. Artist John Batchelor lived in sight of this pier in the Thames Estuary for the duration of WWII and went aboard this ship.

The Royal Eagle passes under the raised roadway elements of Tower Bridge in London.

pleasure "steamers" (most of them were in fact diesel-powered) were introduced, and despite major losses in World War II (1939-45), the GSN continued to provide services in a fashion very similar to that of the earlier years until the end of 1966, when the company announced its withdrawal from the excursion trade.

The last paddle-wheeler ordered by the GSN was the *Royal Eagle*, which was built by Cammell Laird at Birkenhead and launched on February 24, 1932. The vessel entered service on May 14 for the route from London to Southend, Margate and Ramsgate. There were 310 seats in her saloon, and she was the first GSN vessel with a sun deck and sun lounge. At the start of World War II, the vessel was used initially for the evacuation of London children to East Anglian ports, and then joined other vessels of the GSN fleet at Sheerness. The vessel was used in Operation "Dynamo", the evacuation of the British Expeditionary Force and large numbers of Allied troops from northern France, during May and June 1940 as the Germans broke the back of France's defence, making three trips to recover some 3,000 men from Dunkirk at the end of May. The *Royal Eagle* spent the rest of world War II as a coastal auxiliary anti-aircraft vessel.

The *Royal Eagle* returned to mercantile service in 1946, running services from London to Margate on the northern coast of Kent, and for a few weeks in the summer of 1950, before being laid up, she was operated on a service to Southend and Clacton on the coast of Essex. The vessel was sold in November 1953, and went for scrapping in January of the following year.

Royal Eagle

Type:	excursion side paddle-wheeler
Tonnage:	1,538 tons gross registered tons
Dimensions:	length 289 ft 9 in (88.3 m); beam 36 ft 6 in (11.1 m); draft 11 ft 6 in (3.5 m)
Propulsion:	two triple-expansion steam engines delivering 2,600 ihp (1939 kW) to two side paddle wheels for 17.5 kt
Complement:	2,000 passengers, and crew

Exodus 1947 (1947)

Designed for the carriage of passengers and freight, the *President Warfield* was built in 1928 by the Pusey & Jones Corp. of Wilmington, Delaware, to the order of the Baltimore Steam Packet Co. and named for this operator's late president. The vessel initially operated the Old Bay Line service between Norfolk and Baltimore, with two seasons in Long Island Sound, and on June 12, 1942, was acquired by the War Shipping Administration. After conversion as a transport, she was transferred to the UK on September 21 of the same year. In England she served as a barracks vessel, and was later commissioned into U.S. Navy service for similar use. In November 1945 the vessel was restored to the War Shipping Administration, which sold it on November 9, 1946 to the Potomac Shipwrecking Co. of Washington, D.C., which two days later sold the vessel to the Weston Trading Co. of New York, a front for the Hamossad Le'aliyah Bet. This was the clandestine organization which helped illegal Jewish immigrants to enter Palestine.

The vessel was renamed as the *Exodus 1947*, and on July 11, 1947 departed from a small port near Marseille in southern France with no fewer than 4,515 (or according to some 4,554) Jewish displaced persons on board. The *Exodus 1947* arrived off Palestine on July 18 after being trailed through the Mediterranean by the Royal Navy as the British controlled mandated Palestine for the United Nations. The British boarded the *Exodus 1947* 23 miles (237 km) off the coast. The boarding was challenged by the passengers, and the British therefore used force. Three persons on the vessel were

killed, and 217 others were injured to greater or lesser extents before the British were in control. The British then sailed the vessel into Haifa, where the passengers were removed for deportation back to France rather than the more standard relocation to detention camps on Cyprus. This was intended as a signal to the Jewish community, and also to the European countries which assisted illegal immigration, that illegal immigrants to Palestine would be returned.

The Jewish passengers were transferred to three more seaworthy ships which, with the *Exodus 1947*, left Haifa on July 19 for Port-de-Bouc in southern France, the British insisting that the ship as well as the passengers be returned to their port of origin. When the deportation ships arrived on August 2, the Jews refused to disembark and the French refused to co-operate with British attempts at forced disembarkation.

Media coverage of the human ordeal intensified and the British became pressed to find a solution. After three weeks the ships steamed to Hamburg, which was then in the British occupation zone of Germany, so that the would-be emigrants could be forced off the ships and back to DP camps. Most of the women and children disembarked voluntarily, but the men had to be carried off by force. Within a year, more than 50% of the *Exodus 1947*'s passengers had made another attempt to reach Palestine and were held in camps in Cyprus. When the state of Israel was established in May 1948, all the surviving passengers immigrated to Israel.

The whole of the *Exodus 1947* matter was widely covered by international media, and led to a major embarrassment for the British government, especially after the deportation of the passengers to Germany. The government of the U.S. pressured the British government to return its Palestinian mandate to the U.N., a chance which the British were more than willing to accommodate.

As her passengers were being shipped to Germany, the *Exodus 1947* was returned by the British to Haifa, where she was offered for sale. The vessel was badly damaged by a fire on August 26, 1952, more than three years after a the Jewish state of Israel had come into existence in Palestine. The vessel was finally scrapped in 1963.

The Exodus 1947 is depicted on her vastly overcrowded voyage from the south of France to Palestine.

Exodus 1947

Type:	passenger steamer
Tonnage:	1,814 tons displacement
Dimensions:	length 320 ft (97.5 m); beam 56 ft 6 in (17.2 m); draft 18 ft 6 in (5.6 m)
Propulsion:	one triple-expansion steam engine delivering 2,800 hp (21088 kW) to one propeller for 15 kt
Complement:	300 passengers, and 69 crew (as built)

Caronia (1952)

When World War II ended in 1945, the Cunard Line operated its service between Southampton and New York in two forms, the *Queen Mary* and *Queen Elizabeth* (providing an express service), and the smaller, older and slower *Mauretania* (providing a slower service). In 1946 the company ordered a running mate to the *Mauretania*, a ship of similar speed and proportions for the transatlantic run but, in an astute move, also possessing the capabilities for cruise liner operation in the winter months. Thus the *Caronia* was constructed by John Brown & Co. Ltd. of Clydebank for launch on October 30, 1947 with features such as an outdoor swimming pool and a bathroom in every cabin. Unlike more modern cruise liners, however, the ship offered both first- and cabin- class accommodation. On cruises only the first-class accommodation was used, meaning that the cabin-class berths were not used and therefore generated no revenue.

To distinguish her from the line's other ships, Cunard decided to give the *Caronia* a different colour scheme in different shades of green rather than all-white, resulting in the nickname "Green Goddess." Another striking feature was the very large funnel, which was soon found to catch the wind and so make the ship somewhat difficult to handle.

The *Caronia* departed on her maiden transatlantic voyage on January 4, 1949. There followed another two transatlantic crossings before the ship embarked on her first cruises from New York to the Caribbean. This became the pattern of the *Caronia*'s service for her first years, and in 1951 she made her first world cruise. From 1952 she made transatlantic crossings only during August and September, the rest of the year being dedicated to the cruise market. In the course of her annual refit in November 1956, the ship received complete air-conditioning.

During her annual world cruise in 1958, the *Caronia* suffered the most serious accident of her career. While departing Yokohama at very slow speed in order to avoid collision with a U.S. vessel, she was pushed by the wind against the harbor's breakwater, demolishing a lighthouse in the process. The ship suffered severe damage to her bow, but this was repaired in the U.S. Navy's dry dock at Yokohama.

In 1959 the *Caronia* made regular transatlantic crossings for the last time, most of the trade having now been lost to jet-powered airliners. From this time onward, the vessel's transatlantic crossings were used only for repositioning. By 1963 the *Caronia* was firmly established on a regular schedule of cruises. But by this time other lines were introducing their own purpose-built cruise liners, which were better equipped than the *Caronia*. Cunard therefore decided that from November 1965 the *Caronia* would be dry-docked for two and a half months so that new suites and a lido deck could be incorporated and her interiors modernised. But the writing was on the wall, and 1967 was the first year in which the *Caronia* did not operate at a profit, and Cunard decided to withdraw her at the end of the year.

Early in 1968 the *Caronia* was sold to the Star Line, owned by U.S. and Panamanian interests. She was renamed as the *Columbia* and sailed to Greece to be rebuilt. The

The Caronia was a transitional vessel between the pure transatlantic liner and the cruise ship.

engines needed extensive overhaul, but the owners cut corners and ordered replacement parts from Greek manufacturers rather than the original British companies. As the ship was being rebuilt, Andrew Konstaninidis bought out the other owners of Star Line and renamed the ship *Caribia*. Now painted white, the ship sailed on her first cruise from New York in February 1969, but this was ruined by the failure of her waste system. On the second cruise there was an engine room explosion, and the *Caribia* limped back to New York.

During the next five years, there were constant plans to revive the *Caribia*, but in 1974 she was sold for scrap. A German ocean-going tug was contracted to the *Caribia* to Taiwan, but the vessels were hit by a severe storm near Apra Harbor on Guam, and after the tug had been forced to abandon the tow the *Caribia* was driven against Apra Harbor's breakwater and wrecked. A danger to shipping, the wreck was swiftly cut up.

Caronia

Type:	transatlantic and cruise liner
Tonnage:	34,183 gross registered tons
Dimensions:	length 715 ft (217.9 m); beam 91 ft 4 in (27.8 m); draft not available
Propulsion:	geared steam turbines driving two propellers for 22 kt
Complement:	581 first- and 371 cabin-class passengers, and crew

Andrea Doria (1951)

The *Andrea Doria* was an ocean liner for the Italian Line (Società di Navigazione Italia), and was built by Ansaldo S.p.A. of Genoa in 1953 as Italy was seeking to rebuild its economy and international position after World War II (1939-45). The *Andrea Doria* and her sister ship, the *Cristoforo Colombo*, were the largest, fastest and supposedly safest Italian ships of their time. Launched on June 16, 1951, the ship began her maiden voyage on January 14, 1953. The *Andrea Doria* was neither the largest not the fastest liner on the transatlantic service, but was designed for maximum luxury and as a symbol of Italian design flair.

Intended primarily for South Atlantic services, the *Andrea Doria* was the first ship to feature three outdoor swimming pools, one for each class, and the maximum accommodation was 1,241 on 10 decks. Double-hulled, the *Andrea Doria* was divided into 11 watertight compartments, any two of which could be filled with water without endangering the ship's safety. The *Andrea Doria* also carried enough lifeboats to accommodate all passengers and crew. Furthermore, the ship was equipped with the latest radar. Even with its technological advantages, though, the ship had serious seaworthiness and safety flaws.

During her maiden voyage the vessel encountered heavy storms on the approach to New York but was only very slightly delayed, and the *Andrea Doria* soon became one of Italy's most popular and successful ocean liners, and always carried a near-capacity passenger total. By mid-1956 the vessel was making its 101st crossing of the Atlantic.

On the evening of July 25, 1956 the *Andrea Doria*, carrying 1,134 passengers and 572 crew, was steaming west toward New York in

A popular ship of undoubted luxury, the Andrea Doria had a number of design flaws and was not operated to the safest standards possible.

anticipation of docking during the following morning. At the same time, the Swedish *Stockholm*, a smaller liner which left New York at about midday, was heading on its usual course east to Nantucket Lightship, making about 18 kt in good visibility. The two ships were therefore approaching each other head-on in a congested shipping lane, the *Andrea Doria* in heavy fog through which she was proceeding at a speed cut from 23 kt only to 21.8 kt with her whistle working and her watertight doors closed. The *Stockholm* had yet to enter the bank of fog.

Both ships were navigating by radar, and in the crucial minutes before the two ships collided, the *Andrea Doria* gradually steered to port, rather than to starboard as demanded by the rule of the sea, while the *Stockholm* properly turned about 20° to starboard, an action intended to widen the passing distance of a port-to-port meeting. In fact the two ships were steering toward each other, so narrowing rather than widening the passing distance. In the last moments before impact, the *Stockholm* turned hard to starboard and was in the process of reversing its propellers, while the *Andrea Doria* turned hard to port in an effort to outrun the collision. At about 11:10 p.m. the two ships collided at an almost 90° angle, the *Stockholm*'s raked ice-breaking bow piercing the *Andrea Doria*'s starboard side about halfway along the Italian liner's length, killing 46 persons and cutting into three decks to a depth of some 40 ft (12.2 m). The blow cut open several of the ship's watertight compartments, and also five starboard fuel tanks, which filled with 500 tons of water. With air filling the empty port tanks, the *Andrea Doria* swiftly developed a list which could not be corrected and which prevented the launching of the starboard lifeboats. The ships separated after about 30 seconds.

There were several ships in the vicinity to offer assistance, and by 4:30 a.m. the liner *Ile de France*, the freighter *Cape Ann*, the U.S. Navy transport *Pvt. William H. Thomas* and the *Stockholm* had rescued 1,663 passengers and crew. By this time the *Andrea Doria*'s list had increased to 20°, and in her engine room, the engine team was trying without success to pump water out of the flooding starboard tanks, but could not attempt counter-flooding as the sea water inlets for the port tanks were now well above the water. The *Andrea Doria*'s problems were further compounded by a progressive loss of power.

Though initially her bow was very low in the water as a result of water flooding into the crushed bow, the *Stockholm* soon had matters under control and turned back to New York. Three of her crew had been killed in the collision, and two others later died of their injuries.

The *Andrea Doria* capsized and sank at 10:09 a.m.

Andrea Doria

Type:	transatlantic liner
Tonnage:	29,082 gross registered tons
Dimensions:	length 695 ft 6 in (212.0 m); beam 79 ft 8 in (24.3 m); draft not available
Propulsion:	geared steam turbines driving two propellers for 26 kt
Complement:	218 first-, 320 cabin-and 703 tourist-class passengers, and 563 crew

France (1960)

Ordered by the Compagnie Générale Transatlantique in July 1956, the *France* was constructed by the Chantiers de l'Atlantique at St Nazaire, and launched on May 11, 1960. The ship undertook her sea trials on November 19, 1960, averaging 35.21 kt, and departed on her maiden voyage to New York on February 3,

1961. At the time of her construction the *France* was the longest passenger ship yet built, and was also the last French-built liner.

The *France*'s service mixed six-day transatlantic crossings in the summer with winter cruises and two round-the-world voyages. From July 13-26, 1967, the vessel was docked at the Ile Notre Dame in Montreal, Canada, as a secondary French pavilion at the 1967 World Fair. The *France* worked the North Atlantic run between Le Havre and New York for 13 years, but by the start of the 1970s

the rise of jet-powered air transport and the increasing cost of fuel forced the CGT to rely still more heavily on French government subsidies, which had been paid from the start of the vessel's career.

The versatility of her design meant that the *France* could readily be switched to winter cruises, for which she had initially been thought well suited by features such as her two swimming pools. However, these were enclosed by fixed glass domes, and were therefore not popular on cruises under warm, sun-lit skies, when they became very hot. Another limitation in the cruising role was her limited outdoor deck area, of which much was shielded by thick glass windscreens which prevented the movement of cooling breezes. Even so, the *France* proved to be a popular cruise ship, and undertook her first world cruise in 1972. Too large to pass through the Panama and Suez Canals, she steamed a round Cape Horn and the Cape of Good Hope. By the early 1970s, however, the French government had decided that investment in the Concorde supersonic airliner would be more sensible than further subsidy of the *France*, and the CGT announced that the liner would be retired on October 25, 1974.

This angered the French trade union movement, and the *France*'s crew struck outside Le Havre on September 12, seizing control and anchoring the vessel in the entrance of the port. It was more than a month before the stand-off ended, and by December 7 the ship was moored at a remote quay. By that time the *France* had made 377 transatlantic crossings and 93 cruises, and carried

The great France is aided into her berth by a tug.

588,024 transatlantic and 113,862 cruise passengers.

The ship remained inactive for about four years, with her interiors and furnishings intact. Nothing came of a Saudi Arabian millionaire's offer to buy the ship as a floating museum and casino, and the ship was finally bought in 1979 by Lauritz Kloster, owner of the Norwegian Cruise Line, for a US$80 million conversion into the world's largest cruise ship, the *Norway*, by the Hapag-Lloyd yard at Bremerhaven in Germany. Much changed, the *Norway* entered service on April 14, 1980 with her machinery reduced, her propellers reduced from four to two, and her speed trimmed to just 21 kt. She started her maiden voyage to Miami that same year, amid speculation about her viability in the cruising role, but proved popular and fully demonstrated the concept of the cruise--and not the destination-- being the object of the exercise.

Suffering severe damage in a fire during May 2003 at Miami, the ship was towed to Bremerhaven, and there followed a bemusing series of ownership and name changes, as well as legal battles. Late in 2006, it was reported that the ship's remains were being slowly winched ashore in India for dismantling,

France (as completed)

Type:	transatlantic liner and cruise ship
Tonnage:	66,343 gross registered tons
Dimensions:	length 1,037 ft (316.1 m); beam 110 ft 11 in (33.8 m); draft 32 ft 10 in (10.0 m)
Propulsion:	geared steam turbines driving four propellers for 34 kt
Complement:	407 first- and 1,637 tourist-class passengers, and 1,253 crew

Southern Cross (1955)

At the time of her construction, the *Southern Cross* was innovative among large passenger liners in having her engines located aft, and in having no provision for freight. The latter was the result of the decision of her owner, the Shaw Savill Line (Shaw, Savill & Albion Co. Ltd.) of the UK, to maximize the likelihood of the schedule being met by removing all

offered the opportunity for new concepts in the public spaces and passenger accommodation. The ship's lines included a flush deck and a long superstructure, the latter surmounted by a large bridge structure, a tall, tapered mast and a comparatively small but streamlined funnel placed right aft. The base for the superstructure was the large

The Southern Cross was an innovative passenger ship with all her machinery aft.

connection with cargo, which was often late.

The *Southern Cross* was built and engined by Harland & Wolff, of Belfast, and intended to make four round-the-world voyages each year. On east-bound voyages the vessel steamed via South Africa and returned via Panama, a route reversed on west-bound voyages. The *Southern Cross* was also designed with accommodation for 1,160 tourist-class passengers.

The machinery's aft location

promenade deck, which extended from the stem almost to the stern, and the levels below this were known as the main, saloon, A, B and lower decks. Above the promenade deck rose the lounge, sun and upper bridge decks. The promenade deck was surrounded by a fairly narrow walkway round a volume devoted almost entirely to cabins. The latter possessed anything between one and six berths, and for the most part were disposed six-abreast. This layout was made feasible by the incorporation of

One feature of the Southern Cross which appealed to passengers was her provision of large open decks including a sports area.

large, full-width restaurants. These were located one forward and the other aft of the amidships galley area. Three decks down and at the base of the lift and main staircase was the larger of two swimming pools, the other being high up at the forward end of the sun deck.

The most important single feature of the *Southern Cross*, so far as the passengers were concerned, was the lounge deck centerd on a superb forward-facing room flanked by the smaller library and writing room. Abaft the main staircase were other large rooms such as the smoking room, the tall and galleried cinema/ lounge, and the full-width taverna with its dance floor and bar. At its rear, the taverna had folding doors opening onto the open deck beyond. Above was the sun deck with a swimming pool and lido area, both sheltered by screens. On the lower bridge deck a genuinely novel feature made feasible by the aft location of the machinery and funnel was the sports deck, more than 100 ft (30.5 m) long and also protected by screens. Two other advanced features were Denny-Brown stabilizers and a potent air-conditioning plant.

The *Southern Cross* was retired from British service in 1971, and was then converted as a cruise ship, first as the *Calypso* under the Greek flag and then as the *Azure Seas* under the U.S. flag. In 1992 she became the *Ocean Breeze* for short-duration cruises along the east coast of the U.S..

a third fore-and aft-passage through the cabin volume. Other areas, of different sizes and on different areas, were also allocated on lower decks to more cabins. The saloon deck's two primary features were its pair of

Southern Cross

Type:	oceanic liner
Tonnage:	20,204 gross registered tons
Dimensions:	length 604 ft (184.1 m); beam 78 ft (27,8 m); draft 25 ft (7.6 m)
Propulsion:	geared steam turbines driving two propellers for 20 kt
Complement:	1,160 tourist-class passengers, and crew

United States (1951)

Regarded by many as the most advanced passenger liner ever built, the transatlantic passenger liner *United States* can be regarded as the creation of the celebrated and very successful naval architect William Francis Gibbs more than of any other single person. Ever since the clipper age, the shipping, ship designing and shipbuilding capabilities of the U.S. had been generally inferior to the country's European economic rivals, not only in the UK, which was the major maritime power of the age between 1815 and the late 1930s, but in more recent years also by French. German and Italian interests. This fact was reflected in the knowledge, unpalatable to most Americans, that the last U.S. ship to set a transatlantic speed record was the *Baltic* of the Collins Line, which completed the crossing from Liverpool to Sandy Hook in 9 days and 16 hours during 1854.

Gibbs had embarked on the process of planning a vessel to rival the most powerful and luxuriously appointed European liners in the period before the start of World War II (1939-45). and in many respects his *America* of 1940 can be regarded as his first "take" on the matter of conceiving and creating the ultimate "big ship." World War II, in which the U.S. became embroiled from December 1941, postponed rather than eliminated Gibbs' fascination with the whole concept. The end of World War II ushered in a boom period of considerable economic prosperity and national optimism in the U.S., which was currently the world's only military and economic superpower, and Gibbs re-embarked on his project with enthusiasm.

Gibbs was greatly encouraged and inspired by the excellent service which the British transatlantic liners *Queen Mary* and *Queen Elizabeth* had given in World War II, during which they had safely carried very substantial numbers of troops across the Atlantic to Europe. At much the same time the U.S. government decided that it would be sensible for it to sponsor

The elegant and advanced United States in the waters of New York Harbor.

the construction of a large and very fast vessel intended for use as a liner but also capable of transporting large numbers of soldiers in times of crisis or war. The construction of Gibbs's new liner therefore began to mature as a joint program of the U.S. government and the United States Lines. The U.S. government contributed US$50 million of the US$78 million construction cost, leaving the United States Lines to provide the other US$28 million. In return for its financial contribution to the program, the U.S. government demanded that the resulting ship be readily convertible into a troopship or a hospital ship in the event of war.

The *United States* was built by the Newport News Shipbuilding & Drydock Company at Newport News, Virginia. Her keel was laid on February 8, 1950 in a graving dock, and the hull was floated out of this on June 23, 1951. The *United States* was built to an exacting specification demanded by the U.S. Navy and including a high degree of compartmentalization and wholly separate engine rooms as a means of enhancing her ability to survive should she be damaged in war.

Conscious of the vulnerability to fire revealed in World War II by the U.S. Navy's aircraft carriers, which were characterized by their wooden flight decks, Gibbs' team used no wood in the framing, accessories or decorations of the *United States*. There were no wood interior surfaces, and the vessel's fittings, including all furniture and fabrics, were specially manufactured in glass, metal and spun fiberglass. The process was extended as far as the use of aluminium alloy rather than wooden clothes hangers in the passenger cabins, and indeed the only wooden equipment used in the construction and fitting out of the vessels was in the bilge keels, some of the work surfaces in the galleys, and the ballroom's grand piano, which was made of a rare but fire-resistant wood.

The construction of the ship's superstructure involved the largest use of aluminium alloy in any construction project up to this time, and presented the builder with the difficult technical task of joining a superstructure of aluminium alloy construction to a hull of steel construction. The maximum width of the new liner was fixed at 106 ft (32.3 m) as the maximum able to pass through the locks of the

The United States was driven though the water by four five-blade propellers.

United States continued

Panama Canal, which were just 110 ft (33.5 m) wide. The *United States* also incorporated the most potent engine installation in any merchant vessel of the time and, indeed, the most powerful in any vessel to date, with the exception of the U.S. Navy's recent aircraft carriers.

In overall terms, the *United States* assembled in one package all the recent experience of the Gibbs & Cox company in combination with the technical advances in materials, structures and propulsion for the U.S. Navy in World War II. The *United States* thus began to take shape as a sturdy and very safe vessel which nonetheless offered notably high speed, the capability for realistic competition in accommodation and overall comfort with the larger *Queen Mary* and *Queen Elizabeth*, and low fuel consumption.

In her trials off the coast of Virginia in June 1952, the machinery of the *United States* generated 241,785 shp (180275 kW), resulting in a speed of 39.38 kt or, in one maximum-power sprint, a reported (but in fact inaccurate) 43 kt. In fact, the new liner outpaced an accompanying destroyer of the U.S. Navy. The United States Lines was concerned with keeping its new vessel's real capabilities under wraps for the time being, however, and reported merely that the *United States* had exceeded 34 kt.

On July 4, 1952 the *United States* departed from New York on her maiden voyage across the North Atlantic to Southampton, under command of Commodore Harry Manning. The *United States* then demolished the transatlantic speed record held by the *Queen Mary* for the previous 14 years by more than 10 hours, making her maiden eastbound crossing from the Ambrose Light outside New York harbor to Bishop Rock off Cornwall in the UK in 3 days, 10 hours and 40 minutes at an average speed of 35.59 kt. The vessel then broke the westbound record by returning to the U.S. in 3 days 12 hours and 12

The United States at sea, where she was able to maintain a notably high cruising speed.

minutes at an average speed of 34.51 kt. In just one voyage, therefore, the *United States* had seized both the eastbound and westbound Blue Ribands.

This was a magnificent start to the career of the *United States*, which maintained an average crossing speed of more than 30 kt on the North Atlantic run over her service career of 17 years. During this time her captains were Harry Manning, John Anderson and Leroy J. Alexanderson. The liner was very popular, and was a worthy competitor to the Cunard Line's *Queen Mary* and *Queen Elizabeth* which, though larger, were some 11% to 12% slower than the flagship of the U.S.'s mercantile fleet.

Most voyages included a stop at Le Havre in France, and the *United States* sometimes voyaged as far east as Bremen in Germany. Although the ship embarked fewer passengers than the *Queen Mary* and *Queen Elizabeth*, the *United States* generally had her accommodation occupied to a higher percentage than either of the two British ships. In her first full season, the *United States* filled 90% of her berths and carried 69,231 passengers, whereas the *Queen Elizabeth* carried 70,775 passengers and the *Queen Mary* 63,443.

By the end of the 1950s, though, the *United States* was in the same hazardous position as other transatlantic liners, with most of their potential passengers preferring the speed of jet-powered airliners. At the same time rapidly rising labour costs and a swelling number of strikes rendered the United States Lines economically vulnerable. On November 7, 1969, therefore, the *United States* steamed from New York for what was to have been a routine overhaul at Newport News, but her return to service was then cancelled and the vessel was laid up at Newport News.

In the following years several schemes were mooted for the restoration of the vessel and her return to service, and she was acquired variously by the Federal Maritime Commission in 1973 and the U.S. Cruise Lines in 1978. In 1992, she was purchased by Turkish interests who planned to convert her to a cruise ship. Four years later, she returned to the U.S. and was laid up in Philadelphia. In 1999, the U.S. Foundation and the SS United States Conservancy (at the time the SS United States Preservation Society, Inc.) managed to have the ship placed on the National Register of Historic Places. In 2003 Norwegian Cruise Line bought the ship for its newly announced Hawaiian passenger service. By August 2004 NCL was conducting feasibility studies for restoration of the vessel. In May 2006 the chairman of Star Cruises, NCL's owner, said that the company's next project was the restoration of the *United States*.

United States

Type:	transatlantic liner
Tonnage:	53,329 gross registered tons
Dimensions:	length 990 ft (301.8 m); beam 101 ft 8 in (31.0 m); draft not available
Propulsion:	four Westinghouse geared steam turbines delivering 248,000 shp (184909 kW) to four propellers for 35 kt
Complement:	913 first-, 558 cabin- and 537 tourist-class passengers, and 1036 crew

Moran tugs

Now the largest tug operating company in the world, the U.S. organization now known as the Moran Towing Corporation began its career in 1860 when Michael Moran bought a half share in the tug-boat *Ida Miller* for US$2,700. At this time, the harbor of New York was the scene of huge activity on shore and on the water, where the emergence of the U.S. as a world economic power was reflected in vast numbers of vessels, large and small, from other parts of the country and also from the farthest corners of the earth. An increasing number of these vessels were steam-powered, but most were still worked by sail. The situation was ripe for a man with vision and enterprise, and before long the Moran company had expanded from a single tug to a fleet of such vessels. From the very beginning, the Moran tugs was identifiable by the large white "M" on the sides of its tugs' funnels, and this identifying mark is still used in New York and the number of other major U.S. ports in which the Moran tugs now operate.

During the company's first 75 years, Moran grew steadily in size and capability in reflection of the development of New York's importance as one of the key ports of entry to and exit from the eastern seaboard of the U.S. The company also took every opportunity to develop its image. When, for example, New York celebrated the centenary of the inauguration of George Washington as the U.S.'s first president, Moran undertook the re-enactment of Washington's boat trip to Lower Manhattan. When the New York City subway was built, Moran was responsible for the removal to a dumping site of the spoil from the excavation. By this time the company was spreading its operations well beyond New York, and a Moran tug became the first U.S. vessel to enter Havana harbor after the Spanish-American War of 1898. Another Moran tug sailed around Cape Horn, at the southern tip of South America, to enter the Pacific and play a major part in the removal of earth and other material excavated from the line of the Panama Canal when this was being built between 1904 and 1914. The Moran company provided tugs to the British government in the first stages of World War I (1914-18), and after the entry of the U.S. into this conflict in April 1917, the U.S. government ordered large numbers to support the operation transporting U.S. troops to Europe, and these were based on the Moran tug types.

The Moran company continued to grow and flourish in the 1920s and 1930s despite the Great Depression, and was therefore well placed to make a major contribution to American involvement in World War II (1939-45), when the company operated more than 100 tugs (both its own and

Left: The tug Diane Moran showing fender and bow wave. Photo courtesy of www.morantug.com

Right:
A Moran tug helps to berth a ship in New York.

others under contract from the U.S. government) as part of the U.S. war effort. The company's most significant contribution involved the towage of huge barges across the North Atlantic, effecting a rendezvous with a Moran-operated fleet of tugs in the English Channel transporting artificial "Mulberry" harbors to precise points off the Normandy coast, and finally sinking them close inshore so that heavy equipment could be unloaded straight onto the "Overlord" invasion beaches. It is generally agreed that this operation, though generally little known, was of vital importance in the eventual success of the Allied invasion of German-held Europe.

Its operations in World War II proved decisive in the development of the Moran company, and the period following the end of this conflict saw a considerable expansion in the size and operations of Moran's fleet on the basis provided by its service in a war.

The company was now also in the position to assess the requirements whose fulfilment would allow the achievement of its strategic plans to consolidate its current position as the platform for steady growth. As a result of one of these decisions, the Moran company became one of the first two to switch from steam to diesel propulsion. The company also took an active part in the expansion and consolidation of the harbor tug industry.

The Moran company's first purchases in the period after World War II were centred in the harbor of New York, and on this increasingly firm administrative and economic basis, the company began to extend the geographical scope of its operations to the extent that by the middle of the first decade of the twenty-first century the company had bases of operation in 13 American ports, from New Hampshire in the north to Texas in

Moran tugs *continued*

BHUTAN

MORAN TUG 1950   **25**nu

30th Anniversary International Maritime Organisation

the south.

In the middle of the 1970s, the Moran company started to expand its capability within the marine transportation segment of the towage industry with an steadily implemented program of building and buying tug-barge units. Intended primarily for coastal waters but with an increasing offshore component, the company's fleet of barges provides services for utility companies, municipalities and commercial customers alike in the delivery of bulk commodities such as oil products, grain, fertilizer, metal scrap, steel products and other heavy-lift cargoes of similar types. In more recent years, the Moran Towing Corporation has become the primary provider of offshore contract towing along the eastern seaboard of the U.S.

The tugs of the Moran Towing Corporation have over the years towed very substantial numbers of naval as well as mercantile vessels, carried spent nuclear fuel in special containers on board its barges; delivered commercial container barges on regular schedules; on a contract basis towed the spherical containers for liquefied natural gas, complete and prefabricated oil rigs, oil barges, bridge sections and dry docks; have supported a number of cable-laying operations; and both undertaken and completed many rescue-tows of crippled vessels.

With a long history, extending in an unbroken chain for nearly 150 years, the Moran Towing Corporation is very proud of its services to the U.S. Navy and the mercantile marines of many of the world's shipping nations with links to the U.S. Over this time, the company has developed its own tug designs, large as well as small, allowing it to provide exactly the right vessel for any particular task demanded of it.

In 1998 the Moran company continued its program of growth by acquisition as well as construction by completing a merger with Turecamo Maritime, Inc., together with many of the latter's affiliates. This has further consolidated the Moran company's position as the U.S. leader in the tug and barge industries. At present, the Moran Towing Corporation has three primary strands to its operations, namely ship-docking, contract towage, and marine transportation.

The Moran company's tug fleet has an aggregate power in excess of 298,000 hp (222189 kW), and the types of vessel currently operated by the company include the single-engined single-propeller, twin-engined single-propeller, twin-engined twin-propeller, twin-engined twin Z-drive, twin-propeller pushboat and articulated tugs. At Portsmouth, New Hampshire, are three vessels of between 2,200 and 3,200 hp (1640 and 2386 kW); in the Port of New York, 29 vessels between 1,600 and 7,200 hp (1193 and 5368 kW); at Philadelphia, Pennsylvania, five vessels between 1,750 and 4,200 hp (1305 and 3132 kW); at Baltimore, Maryland, three vessels of between 3,000 and 3,005 hp (2237 and 2241 kW); at Hampton Roads, Virginia, 16 vessels of between 1,400 and 5,100 hp (1044 and 3803 kW); at Charleston, South Carolina, four vessels of between 2,800 and 6,140 hp (2088 and 4578 kW); at Savannah, Georgia, five vessels of between 2,875 and 6,500 hp (2144 and 4846 kW); at Brunswick, Georgia, two vessels of between 2,400 and 2,800 hp (1789 and 2088 kW); at Fernandina, Florida, one vessel of 2,150 hp (1603 kW); at Jacksonville, Florida, five vessels of between 2,150 and 3,200 hp (1603 and 2386 kW); at Miami, Florida, two vessels of between 3,000 and 5,100 hp (2237 and 3803 kW); and at Port Arthur, Beaumont and Orange, Texas, five vessels of between 3,200 and 5,100 hp (2386 and 3803 kW). The company also has 11 5,100-hp (3803-kW) tugs under construction.

Most of the Moran company's tugs have carried a girl's name followed by "Moran."

Mary M. Coppedge (2001)

Type:	tug
Tonnage:	not available
Dimensions:	length 100 ft (30.5 m); beam 30 ft (9.1 m); draft 16 ft 6 in (5.0 m)
Propulsion:	two EMD diesel engines delivering 3,300 hp (2460 kW) to two propellers
Complement:	not available

Savannah (1958)

Named for the *Savannah*, which in 1819 became the first steam-powered vessel to cross the Atlantic Ocean, the *Savannah* of 1958 was the world's first nuclear-powered cargo and passenger ship, and as such one of only four nuclear-powered cargo ships which have been built to date.

During 1955, President Dwight D. Eisenhower proposed the design and construction of a nuclear-powered merchant ship, and in 1966 Congress authorized the program for joint implementation by the Atomic Energy

promotional reasons, the vessel was created with a striking appearance seldom if ever seen before or after on a bulk cargo vessel; so that she could also carry 60 passengers, she had 30 air-conditioned staterooms, each with its own bath, dining facilities, lounge with provision for films, library, veranda and swimming pool.

In many respects the *Savannah* was

Commission, the Maritime Administration, and the Department of Commerce. The vessel was designed by George G. Sharp, Inc., and was laid down at the New York Shipbuilding Corporation's yard at Camden, New Jersey, with the fabrication of the nuclear reactor entrusted to Babcock & Wilcox. The vessel was launched on March 23, 1962 within the context of the U.S.'s "Atoms for Peace" program.

The *Savannah* was schemed as a practical demonstration of the technical feasibility of nuclear propulsion for merchant ships, and was never seen as economically competitive. For

successful, for she had an excellent safety record and her fuel economy was unsurpassed. Moreover, her white color scheme remained unsmudged by exhaust smoke. Between 1965 and 1971, the *Savannah* was leased by the Maritime Administration to the American Export-Isbrandtsen Lines for cargo service. Here the limitations of the vessel, or rather of her conception as a demonstration of technical feasibility, started to become apparent, The cargo was limited to 8,500 tons at a time when most of her commercial rival could carry many times this total. Furthermore, the streamlined hull made it difficult and therefore time-consuming to load the forward holds, and this became a major problem as ports became increasingly automated. Her crew was some 33% larger than that of any comparable oil-fired ship, and had to receive special training. There was of necessity a shore organization to supervise port visits, and a special yard facility.

Under such circumstances the vessel could never have operated at a profit, and this was exacerbated by the fact that the Savannah's passenger space was largely unused and her cargo capacity too small.

The Maritime Administration

decommissioned the vessel in 1972, which was a decision that was valid at a time when oil cost US$20 per ton. Only two years later, though, oil had risen to US$80 per ton, and the Savannah's operating costs would have been no greater than an standard cargo ship. For a time, the Savannah was mothballed in Galveston, Texas, during the 1970s, but in 1981 the vessel was obtained for display at the Patriots Point Naval and Maritime Museum near Mount Pleasant, South Carolina, although ownership remained vested in the Maritime Administration. Once the Savannah had been opened, visitors could tour the cargo holds, view the staterooms and passenger areas, walk the deck, and examine the reactor spaces from an observation window, Even so, the vessel never drew the attention which had been expected, and when an inspection in 1993 revealed the need for expensive repairs, the museum evinced no interest. In 1994 the vessel was dry-docked in Baltimore for the repair, and then moved to the James River Merchant Marine Reserve Fleet near Newport News, Virginia. The reactor fuel had been removed in 1972-73, though some radioactive components remained. Further repair was effected in 2006, and it is planned that the last radioactive elements will be removed, after which the vessel, now a National Historic Landmark, may find a permanent museum home.

The Savannah looked, and indeed was, very advanced, and a notable feature was the absence of any funnel.

Savannah

Type:	nuclear-powered cargo and passenger ship
Tonnage:	22,000 tons displacement
Dimensions:	length 596 ft (181.7 m); beam 78 ft (23.8 m); draft not available
Propulsion:	one nuclear reactor supplying steam to geared turbines delivering 20,300 shp (15136 kW) to one propeller for 24 kt; range 300,000 miles (482790 km) at 20 kt on one fuelling
Complement:	60 passengers, 124 crew, and cargo

Canberra (1960)

The *Canberra* was conceived for service with the British company P&O as an oceanic liner, but later operated in the cruise ship role. The vessel was ordered on December 20, 1956 and laid down on September 23 of the following year at the Belfast yard of Harland & Wolf and, launched on March 16, 1960, was named for the federal capital of Australia. The vessel was completed in May 1961 and departed on her maiden voyage on June 6 of the same year.

P & O ordered the *Canberra* to work the service between the UK and Australia, which was operated jointly by P & O and the Orient Line. The advent of jet-powered airliners had already dented the demand on this route, and in combination with a reduced flow of emigrants and the closure of the Suez Canal as a result of Middle Eastern conflict, dictating a longer passage around the Cape of Good Hope, soon made it impossible to operate the service at a profit.

In 1974, therefore, the *Canberra* was adapted for an oceanic liner into a cruise ship. This type of transformation was often accompanied by major difficulties, but in the case of the *Canberra* was effected without problem and paved the way for a comparatively long, trouble-free and profitable career in the cruise ship regime with 1,737 passengers and a crew of 795. The transformation did not involve any significant external changes, and only very small internal and mechanical alterations.

The single most significant feature of the *Canberra* was arguably her turbo-electric propulsion system. Instead of the standard arrangement, in which they are mechanically coupled to the propeller shafts, the *Canberra* had steam turbines which turned large electric alternators to generate the electrical current that powered electric motors which, in turn, drove the vessel's two propellers. This system was not unique, even in merchant vessels, but was the most powerful installation of its type ever installed in a passenger ship. This type of propulsion arrangement became a standard element of cruise ship design during the 1990s, more than 30 years after the *Canberra* entered service. It should be noted, though, that most modern ships have alternators powered by diesel engines or gas turbines. The *Canberra* also possessed a back-up propulsion system of the same basic concept.

After the Argentine invasion of the Falkland Islands in 1982, the Ministry of Defence requisitioned the *Canberra* for service as a British troopship, a task in which she was invaluable in transporting large numbers of men of the Parachute Regiment and the Royal Marines to the islands, which lie more than 9,000 miles (14485 km) from the UK. The *Queen Elizabeth 2* was used in a similar role, but unlike the *Canberra* was deemed too vulnerable to enter deep into the war zone.

The *Canberra* anchored in San Carlos Water on May 21, 1982 as part of the landings by British forces to retake the islands. Although her size and white color made her an unmistakable target for Argentine air attack, if sunk the *Canberra* would not have been wholly submerged in these shallow waters. As it was, though, the *Canberra* was not badly hit during the landings, the Argentine pilots preferring to tackle the Royal

The Canberra in a typical cruise ship setting, her passengers going ashore by boat.

Navy's frigates and destroyers instead of the supply and troop ships that would have been considerably more useful victims.

With the Falklands war over, the *Canberra* was used to repatriate Argentine prisoners and then steamed back to Southampton and a huge welcome. A lengthy refit was now needed before the *Canberra* resumed her duties as a cruise ship. Her role in the Falklands war had made the vessel very popular, and her passenger numbers rose for several years after the Falklands war. But the ship could not escape the effects of age and steadily rising operating costs eventually caught up with her. The *Canberra* was therefore retired from service in September 1997, and the vessel was sold for scrapping, leaving for Gadani Beach in Pakistan during the following month. Her deep draft meant that the vessel could not be beached as far up as most ships, and in combination with her sturdy construction this meant that the scrapping of the Canberra took almost one year rather than the period of three months which had been estimated.

Canberra (as built)

Type:	oceanic liner and cruise ship
Tonnage:	45,270 gross registered tons
Dimensions:	length 818 ft (249.9 m); beam 102 ft (31.2 m); draft 32 ft 8 in (10.0 m)
Propulsion:	two turbo-alternators powering two electric motors delivering 85,000 hp (63376 kW) to two propellers for 27.5 kt
Complement:	548 first- and 1,690 tourist-class passengers, and 960 crew

Voith-Schneider tug (1965)

The Voith-Schneider propeller is a specialized propulsion system offering extreme agility as it can change the direction of the thrust it generates almost instantaneously. Fitted to the underside of the vessel, the propulsion system is based on a circular table, rotating around a vertical axis and driven by an engine inside the hull at a constant rate. Between this table and a housing below the bottom of the hull on struts, there are a number of vertical hydrofoil blades whose lower ends fit into a freely rotating ring. Each of the blades can be rotated round its vertical axis. The internal gear changes the angle of attack of the blades in synchronisation with the rotation of the table so that each blade can provide thrust in any direction.

Power from the engine goes into the propulsion unit via a gearbox to turn the table from which the propeller blades extend. The sketches (1, 2 and 3) show how the system works. In 1

AN EAGLE *cutaway* DRAWING

by John Batchelor, who was an "Eagle" artist.

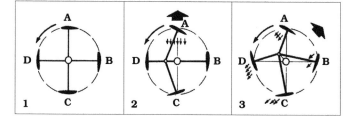

Voith-Schneider tug

Type:	"water tractor" with cycloidal propulsion
Tonnage:	not available
Dimensions:	length 87 ft 6 in (26.7 m); beam 26 ft 6 in (8.1 m); draft 13 ft (4.0 m)
Propulsion:	one Lister Blackstone diesel engine delivering 1,600 hp (1193 kW) to the Voith-Schneider propulsion unit
Complement:	5 or 6 crew

the blades follow each other without any effect. The blades are attached to an adjustable control point (x), and as long as this remains over the center of the "circle," no thrust is produced. If the control point is moved to port, as in 2, the leading edges of the blades on the forward half of the propeller orbit (A) swing outward while those on the other half (C) turn inward. The incidence at A and C causes water to be thrust in the direction of the small arrows, making the vessel move in the direction of the large broad arrow. In 3, the control point has been moved between points A and D, and the blades automatically swing outward and inward at various points round their orbit and generate thrust in the direction of the small

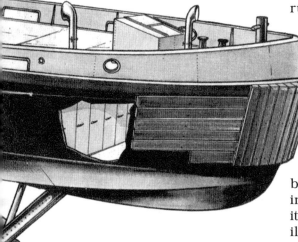

arrows, so causing the vessel to move in the direction of the broad arrow. With the engine running at constant revolutions, many variations of speed can be made in any direction through movement of the control point; the farther this is moved toward the edge of the circle, the greater the incidence of the blades and thus the thrust and speed of the vessel.

Unlike a Z-drive, in which a conventional propeller is tilted on a vertical rudder axis, changing the direction of thrust with a Voith-Schneider drive requires only changes in the pattern of the vertical blades' orientation. In a maritime situation, this creates a drive which can be directed in any direction, and thus removes all need for a rudder. The drive system is very efficient and provides for an almost instantaneous change of thrust direction.

The Voith-Schneider system has become increasingly common since the 1990s for working vessels such as fire-boats and tugs, in which agility is a very desirable factor. The Voith-Schneider system extends below the bottom of the hull, however, increasing the draft and preventing its use in shallow water. The cut-away illustration reveals the details of one of the Voith-Schneider tugs built by Richard Dunston Ltd, in 1965 for the Port of London Authority, which needed four "water tractor" units.

Dockwise ships

The demands of transport by sea can generally be met by standard ships, but the increasing diversity of loads means that there is a need for a few specialized vessels. This is a market niche filled by Dockwise, a Dutch company providing a heavy transport capability with a fleet of 16 semi-submersible vessels. The company serves mainly the marine oil and gas industry, and the company can satisfy very complex transport requirements. Several of the smaller Dockwise vessels have also been modified as yacht carriers to meet the growing demand for transport of yachts, the Dockwise Yacht Transport company offering convenient and frequent services between many popular

the yacht carrier submerges into a "floating marina" to the draft required for loading the yachts and, after the yachts have been moored in their prearranged positions, the carrier starts her docking operation. Once the deck is dry, the yachts are secured to the deck and are ready for a safe crossing. During the voyage, power and fresh water can be made available to the yachts.

Over the years Dockwise has developed innovative concepts and solutions, such as the utilisation of vessels for deck mating operations. Dockwise offers a complete package for float-over and deck-mating operations, followed by transport from construction site to operating

Left:
The Dockwise vessel Swan retrieving HMS Southampton.
Pic courtesy of the Key Agency, Amsterdam.

Right:
The Super Servant 3 carrying a complement of yachts.

destinations. These yacht carriers include spray covers to protect yachts during their movement, and between these spray covers, yachts can be loaded in impressive numbers in the carriers' docks, up to 479 ft (146 m) long.

The semi-submersible yacht carriers can load and discharge using the float-on/float-off method:

location. Distance from construction site to the operating location is no longer an obstacle, which increases freedom of construction site choice.

Very large or large offshore structures for the offshore gas and oil industry are often constructed at a yard distant from the offshore location, and here Dockwise provides the essential transport link with five specialized vessels. The recently "jumboized" *Blue Marlin* of 76,061 deadweight tons provides an integrated system for the movement of ultra-heavy and large production and drilling platforms, which allows oil companies to have integrated units built anywhere in the world and transported to the relevant offshore destination, so reducing hook-up and commissioning times. The heavy transports for the oil and gas industry therefore all have a large and unobstructed deck area to provide a safe platform for a wide variety of large cargoes.

For the movement of floating or non-floating cargoes such as dry docks, dredging equipment, power barges, accommodation hulks and defence equipment, Dockwise offers huge flexibility and load capacity. As a result of Dockwise's ballasting capabilities, many loading and unloading procedures (float-on/float-off, roll-on/roll-off, skid-on/skid-off, lift-on/lift-off or any combination) can be used.

Dockwise has already moved large numbers of fully erected port and container cranes. Moreover, the excellent seakeeping characteristics of the Dockwise vessels means that the need for temporary structural reinforcement and fastenings can be greatly reduced, so reducing cost and speeding loading and discharge.

Over the years Dockwise has extended its capacities. One of these extensions is a mobile dry dock and repair base on board a heavy transport vessel.

Super Servant 3

Type:	float-on/float-off transport vessel
Tonnage:	10,224 gross tons
Dimensions:	length 456 ft 4 in (139.1 m); beam 105 ft (32.0 m); draft 20 ft 8 in (6.3 m) sailing and 47 ft 7 in (14.5 m) for loading/unloading
Propulsion:	two Stork-Werkspoor diesel engines delivering 8,390 hp (6256 kW) to two propellers for 15 kt
Complement:	not available

Heavy-lift cargo ships

Over a long period, cargo vessels sometimes needed to load freight items that are awkward or weighty beyond the limit of their standard outfit of derricks. This demanded the fitting of one or more jumbo heavy-lift derricks, whose tackle imposed severe manpower demands, and at the same time the decks of the ships involved were frequently unsuitable for the task. These problems attracted the interest of Captain Christen Smith, a Norwegian naval officer, who had made his name with the movement of 200 railway locomotives as complete units from the UK to Belgium in two specially fitted steamers after World War I (1914-18), and then designed several types of specialised heavy-lift ships, the so-called "Belships." The first of these was the *Beldis*, completed in 1924. Characterised by heavy derricks and winches, long uncluttered decks and large strengthened hatches, and special arrangements for ballasting, these vessels could carry rolling stock, tugs, barges and even light vessels.

The shipping operators with major interests in the movement of large and/or heavy cargo items also increased the capabilities of their heavy-lift equipment. For example, in 1930 Elder Dempster installed a pair of 100-ton derricks on the *Mary Kingsley*, the eighth and last vessel of its "Explorer" class optimized for the West African trade. Two lines operating to India, the Clan Line of the UK and Hansa of Germany, were also heavily involved in carrying locomotives and wagons, and the German company fitted 120-ton derricks to its four "Lichtenfels" class ships built in 1929-31.

During and immediately after World War II (1939-45), the British government ordered a standard class of 10 standard "Empire" heavy-lift vessels with 120-ton derricks similar in design to the "Belships." Between 1947 and 1956, the Ben Line bought four of these vessels for service as the, *Benledi, Benalbanach, Benwyvis* and *Benarty*. The first two were capable of 15 kt on their steam turbine propulsion arrangements, while the second two were slightly slower on their turbo-electric propulsion arrangements. Key features of the design were large uncluttered decks with extra large hatches, each served by one 150-ton derrick.

As soon as restrictions imposed on Germany after World War II were lifted, the Hansa company, which had lost its entire fleet in the conflict, set

The appearance of the Treuenfels and her sister ships was dominated by the pair of Stülcken masts.

about reviving its heavy-lift capability. Completed in 1951, the *Barenfels* was the first of three sister ships which marked a departure from the company's previous practice in having the bridge well forward and the machinery aft. At 6,974 gross registered tons, the *Barenfels* was at the time the second largest ship built in Germany since World War II, and her heavy-lift capability was vested in a derrick capable of lifting 165 tons, and which was mounted on the main mast behind a notably long hatch.

Further heavy-lift designs, including two built in Japan, followed these initial three units, but then in 1954 Hansa took delivery of a new *Lichtenfels*, the first of a class which eventually totaled eight vessels with a speed of 16 kt and fitted with equipment to handle 120 tons. The key features of the new design were the location of the bridge right forward, in the eyes of the ship, and a new and innovative type of mast designed by the ship's builder, H. C. Stülcken Sohn of Hamburg. This comprised two tall tapering masts, which were angled outward and so permitting the derrick mounted between them to serve the hatches both forward and aft of it. Stülcken masts were fitted to all subsequent Hansa cargo vessels, as well as those of many other cargo specializing companies, and their lifting capacity was steadily increased up to 300 tons. This type was installed in the Blue Star Line's 21-kt *Australia Star* in 1965.

Typical of Hansa's vessels was the *Treuenfels*, of 12,750 deadweight tons. The ship had her bridge located well forward and her machinery aft, but was fitted with two Stülcken masts, each rated at 130 tons but capable of operating in tandem to handle loads up to 280 tons. The ship also had two 5-ton deck cranes, which were mounted on rails to serve all three of the ship's hatches.

Norway (1979)

In 1979 the French Line's flagship, the great transatlantic liner *France*, which was no longer profitable in her designed role, was sold to Lauritz Kloster, owner of the Norwegian Cruise Line (NCL), for just US$18 million. NCL believed that this two-class liner could be converted into a profitable one-class cruise ship, and by August 1979 the *France* had arrived at the Hapag-Lloyd yard in Bremerhaven to be cycled through a US$80 million renovation and conversion effort including the decommissioning of the two forward sets of machinery and the removal of the propellers from the two outer shafts, as high speed was now no longer desirable.

In her new guise the ship was registered in Oslo, Norway, and rechristened as the *Norway* on April 14, 1980. She thus became the first super-liner readied for cruise ship service. The "new" vessel departed on her maiden voyage to Miami later in the same year, and was the subject of intense speculation about her future as a cruise ship: the *France* had been built as a liner optimized for high speed with a long, narrow and deep-draft hull, and with a host of compact cabin shapes and sizes intended for travel rather than leisured cruising. But the *Norway* proved the critics wrong, being very popular right from the start.

The size, capacity for 1,944 single-class passengers, and high degree of comfort and amenities swiftly effected a major shift in the thinking of the cruise industry, and thus triggered a virtual frenzy of new construction. As these newer ships started to eat into her customer base, the *Norway* was refitted to ever higher standards, including the addition of new decks in her superstructure. Some thought this spoiled the vessel's lines, but the new private veranda cabins on the added decks were important in keeping the *Norway* profitable in her later years.

As a cruise ship, the Norway confirmed that the object of most passengers was as much a comfortable cruise as an exotic destination.

Inevitably, though, the competition caught and overtook the *Norway*, which was then relegated to a less-prominent position in NCL's promotions, and the amount spent on her maintenance was curtailed. The ship then suffered a number of mechanical failures, fires, and even safety violations for which she was detained in port until repairs had been effected. Even so, the vessel retained a strong customer appeal, and there were many who claimed that NCL was wrong to reduce the importance of the vessel in its operations, as evidenced by the success of the *Queen Elizabeth 2* as a cruise ship. But the cut-backs continued, and difficulties continued to escalate even as the ship maintained a full passenger list. A fire broke out as the *Norway* entered Barcelona in 1999, and the vessel was out of service for three weeks. Intended for retirement, the *Norway* sailed from New York for the last time on September 21, 2001 bound for Greenock in Scotland, and thence her home port, Le Havre in France. At this time air travel took a severe knock as a result of the terrorist air attacks on New York on 9/11, and the *Norway* was reprieved for low-cost cruises from Miami. Nothing was done to ameliorate the ship's growing mechanical degradation.

On May 25, 2003 the *Norway* was seriously damaged by a boiler explosion which killed seven members of her crew and injured another 17. On June 27 of that year NCL and its ultimate owners decided to move the *Norway*, which was towed from Miami to Bremerhaven, where the decision was taken not to repair the damaged boiler. On March 23, 2004 NCL announced the retirement of the ship, whose ownership was then passed to NCL's parent company, Star Cruises. There followed a period of name and ownership changes, extensive legal battles and protests from environmental groups about the plans to scrap the vessel. The ship was moved from Germany to Malaysia and then India, where the scrapping continues in a desultory fashion.

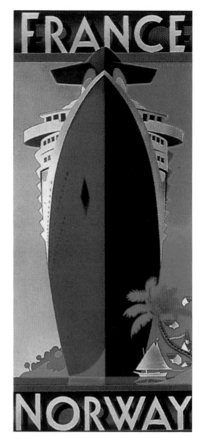

Advertising material for the Norway emphasised the link with glamorous France.

***Norway* (1994 standard)**

Type:	cruise liner
Tonnage:	76,049 gross registered tons
Dimensions:	1,035 ft (316.1 m); beam 110 ft 8 in (33.8 m); draft not available
Propulsion:	two geared steam turbines driving two propellers for 21 kt
Complement:	2,565 passengers, and 875 crew

Ferries on the Bosporus

The Bosporus is the strait separating Rumelia and Anatolia, the European and Asian parts of Turkey. The narrowest strait in the world used for international navigation, the Bosporus provides the essential link between the Black Sea and the Sea of Marmara, the latter connected by the Dardanelles to the Aegean Sea and thence the Mediterranean and the rest of the world. The Bosporus is some 18.6 miles (30 km) long with a maximum width of 2.3 miles (3.7 km) at its northern entrance, and a minimum width of 765 yards (700 m) between Kandilli and Asiyan. The strait is heavily populated on each side as metropolitan Istanbul (with more than 11 million inhabitants) straddles it, and is bridged

in two places, with a third crossing planned.

As a bottleneck in the maritime connection between the Black Sea and the Mediterranean, the Bosporus has been of great commercial and strategic import throughout recorded history. Thus, in the fifth century BC, the city state of Athens on the Greek mainland carefully instituted and maintained alliances with the cities controlling the strait, such as the Megarian colony Byzantium, to ensure the smooth flow of the grain imports from Scythia on which Athens was reliant. Furthermore, it was the strait's strategic significance that helped to persuade Roman emperor Constantine the Great in 330 AD to turn Byzantium

Three views of a ferry typical of those which ply the routes along and across the Bosporus, dividing metropolitan Istanbul into European and Asian sections.
Photos: John Batchelor

The waters of the Bosporus are extremely crowded with larger vessels heading north and south along the strait, as well as smaller craft such as this ferry working the routes across the strait.

into his new capital of Constantinople, which became the hub of the Eastern Roman (or Byzantine) Empire. On May 29, 1453, Constantinople was taken by the Ottoman empire, and in 1930 the Turkish republic prohibited all names but Istanbul.

Early in the twenty-first century the importance of the Bosporus remains as high as ever. Control of the strait has been an objective of a number of modern military campaigns, notably the Russo-Turkish War (1877-78), as well as the ultimate objective of the Allied effort to take Constantinople in World War I (1914-18), which was checked by the allied failure to take Gallipoli and the rest of the Dardanelles in 1915. The types and rights of vessels which may use the Bosporus have been the subject of several treaties, the most important of which was the Montreux Convention Regarding the Regime of the Turkish Straits (1936).

As well as its importance in international affairs, the Bosporus and its western extension, the Golden Horn, have for millennia played a key part in local communications and commerce. Public ferries therefore ply the waters of the Bosporus and Golden Horn in large numbers, and are arguably one of the cheapest and most effective ways to see the city, many of whose magnificent antiquities line the European and Asian shores of the Bosporus. The main ferry terminal on the Rumelian side of the city is sited at Eminönü, just to the east of the Galata Bridge across the Golden Horn, and slow ferries depart from this at about 45-minute intervals, with fast ferries available every 10 minutes or so. Visitors can also take a trip on tourist ships from thoroughly modern vessels to craft styled on Ottoman lines. Larger ferries ply the route south-west from Istanbul to the Princes Islands in the Sea of Marmara, and also to Yalova on the southern side of this land-locked body of water. Smaller vessels also operate services between the European and Asian shores of the Bosporus as far north as Kavagi and Anadolu on the European and Asian sides of the northern Bosporus via 16 and 11 intermediate stops, respectively.

Windsor Castle (1960)

The Union-Castle Line was an important British shipping operator which ran a fleet of passenger liners and freighters between Europe and Africa from 1900 to 1977. A replacement for the ageing *Arundel Castle*, the *Pendennis Castle* was the largest liner built up to that time for the Union-Castle Line and departed on her maiden voyage in 1959. She was followed in 1960 by the even larger *Windsor Castle* which, on her maiden voyage, became the largest vessel then to have visited Cape Town. By 1966 the growing maturity of mass air transport, freight containerization and rapidly rising oil fuel costs were combining to render the traditional maritime service to South Africa increasingly unprofitable. In October 1973 the British & Commonwealth Shipping Company (Union-Castle's parent) and the South African Marine Corporation combined their operations under the name, "International Liner Services Ltd.," but the end was inevitable and the passenger service finished with a sailing from Southampton to Cape Town in September 1977. All of the Union-Castle Line's ships had the suffix "Castle" in their names, and the liners were characterized by their pale lavender hulls and black/red funnels, The ships operated a strongly scheduled timetable between Southampton in the south of England and Cape Town in South Africa: at 4:00 p.m. on every Thursday, a Union-Castle Royal Mail Ship would leave Southampton bound for Cape Town, and at the same time another of the line's vessels departed Cape Town for Southampton.

The *Windsor Castle* was laid down on December 9, 1959 in the Birkenhead yard of Cammell Laird & Co. (Shipbuilders & Engineers) Ltd., and launched in June 23, 1959 by Queen Elizabeth, the Queen Mother. At the time of her launch, the *Windsor Castle* was the largest liner built in England, and owned by the Union-Castle Line, and the first Union-Castle liner built by Cammell Laird. The *Windsor Castle*'s maiden voyage from Southampton began on August 18, 1960, and reached Durban 11½ days later. In the course of her second voyage, the *Windsor Castle* was called upon to aid another of the line's vessels, the *Capetown Castle*, which had suffered an engine room explosion at Las Palmas in the Canary Islands. In December 1967 the *Windsor Castle* completed her 50th voyage, in which she had carried some 35,000 passengers and suffered no schedule delay or mechanical problems. The ship was refitted in 1967 and 1972, increasing her gross tonnage slightly on each occasion. Features of the design which were worthy of note were the interchangeability of part of her accommodation, allowing a reduction in the tourist-class provision for an increase in first-class berths from the standard figure of 191 to a maximum of 241, and the slope of the hull decks which resulted in an apparent misalignment of the ports.

The vessel was the flagship of the Union-Castle Line's fleet, but had only a short career. By the 1970s, with the inroads into sea travel by jet-powered airliners now compounded by the advent of the Boeing Model 747 "jumbo" jet, economy air travel was now available to South Africa and most other parts of the world. The Union-Castle Line therefore began

The pride of the Union-Castle Line's fleet, the Windsor Castle featured a hull in the line's lavender color.

to trim all non-profitable passenger services. On August 12, 1977 the ship left on her 124th and last voyage from Southampton, followed on September 6 by the last departure from Cape Town. The *Windsor Castle* returned to Southampton on September 19 and was then sold to John S. Latsis, a Greek oil and shipping tycoon. She departed Southampton on October 3, 1977 for Greece. Renamed *Margarita L*, the ship was converted at Piraeus as an floating hotel with 852 luxury berths, at Jeddah, the port city for Mecca in Saudi Arabia. The ship was then used as an office and leisure centre for the Latsis-owned Petrola International S.A.'s construction company at Rabegh. In February 1979 she replaced the *Marianna VI* as the hub of a complex with car parks, swimming pools and sports facilities. A helicopter pad was added aft of the former first-class promenade deck pool area.

In 1983 the ship was dry-docked, overhauled and returned to service in the same role. After 1990 she was towed to Eleusis in Greece and laid up, and occasionally used as private quarters by her owner. The *Margarita L* and three other British-built passenger vessels in the Latsis fleet were put up for sale in 1998.

Windsor Castle

Type:	oceanic liner
Tonnage:	37,640 tons gross
Dimensions:	length 783 ft 1 in (238.7 m); beam 92 ft 8 in (28.2 m); draft 32 ft (9.75 m)
Propulsion:	four Parsons geared steam turbines delivering 49,000 shp (36534 kW) to two propellers for 22.5 kt
Complement:	191 first- and 591 tourist-class passengers, and 475 crew

Lenin (1957)

With no major ports free of ice year-round, Russia, in both its Imperial and Soviet incarnations, had a great interest in icebreaking as a means of ensuring that mercantile and naval vessels could enter and leave major ports such as Murmansk and Arkhangyelsk in the Arctic, St Petersburg in the Gulf of Finland, and Vladivostok in the Pacific, even during the frozen winter months.

As it rebuilt its capabilities after World War II (1939-45), the USSR initially relied on old but updated vessels, and then in 1955 ordered three "Kapitan" class state-of-the-art vessels from a Finnish yard. These were successful in the Baltic Sea, and in 1957 the USSR contracted with the same yard for five larger icebreakers for Arctic operations.

Meanwhile, the USSR was completing the design of a wholly novel ship. Built by the Baltic Shipbuilding & Engineering Works in Leningrad, as the Soviets called St Petersburg, for launch in 1957, the *Lenin* was the world's first nuclear-powered surface ship and thus also the first nuclear-powered civilian vessel. The *Lenin* entered service in 1959. Nuclear power offered a host of advantages for an icebreaker, including freedom from the need to refuel frequently, and abundant power for icebreaking. The *Lenin* soon proved that she could make 2 kt steadily through ice 4 ft 7 in (1.4 m) thick, and her capabilities meant that

merchant ship convoys could gain winter access to the northern ports of resource-rich Siberia to bring in supplies and equipment, and to take out raw materials.

When launched in 1957, *Lenin* was powered by three OK-150 reactors. In the February 1965 the vessel suffered a coolant loss accident. After the reactors had been shut down for refuelling, the coolant was removed from the no. 2 reactor before the spent fuel had been removed. As a result,

Fitted with a helicopter operating platform aft for ship-to-ship and ship-to-shore communications, the nuclear-powered Lenin suffered a number of reactor-related problems but fully confirmed her potent icebreaking capabilities.

some 60% of the fuel elements melted or were deformed inside the reactor, and therefore could not be removed. The decision was taken to remove the fuel control grid, and control rods as a single unit: these were then fitted into a special container, solidified, stored for two years, and finally dumped in Tsivolki Bay (near the Novaya Zemlya archipelago) during 1967.

The second accident occurred in 1967 and involved a cooling system leak. Location of the leak's precise position meant that men with sledgehammers were used to break through the concrete and metal containment vessel. The leak was found, but the vessel was so badly damaged that it could not be repaired. Some 30 men died in the episode as a result of radiation sickness. The *Lenin* was abandoned for one year, and then all three OK-150 reactors were removed and replaced by a pair of OK-900 reactors. This was completed in the spring of 1970.

The *Lenin* was finally decommissioned in 1989 as a result of the fact that her hull was worn thin by steady ice friction, and for a time was used as a power station. The vessel was laid up at Atomflot, the base for nuclear icebreakers in Murmansk, and according to *Pravda*, her repair and refurbishment as a museum ship was completed in 2005.

Lenin

Type:	nuclear-powered icebreaker
Tonnage:	16,000 tons displacement without ballast
Dimensions:	length 439 ft 7 in (134.0 m); beam 90 ft 6 in (27.6 m); draft 34 ft 2 in (10.4 m)
Propulsion:	initially three OK-150 90-MW reactors, and later two OK-900 171-MW reactors supplying steam to turbo-alternators providing current for three electric motors delivering 30,200 hp (22517 kW) and later 44,000 hp (32806 kW) to three propellers for 18 kt
Complement:	220

Pendennis Castle (1957)

When the Union-Castle Line made its decision to replace the *Arundel Castle*, built in 1921, it contracted with Harland & Wolff Ltd. to build the *Pendennis Castle* at its Belfast yard in Northern Ireland. The keel of this new oceanic liner was laid in November 1955, just before the January 1956 merger of the Clan Line and the Union-Castle Line. It was soon appreciated that the requirements of the merged companies were different from those of the Union-Castle Line, and as a result there was a major redesign of the new ship.

The *Pendennis Castle* was the best of all the liners operated by the Union-Castle Line in terms of passenger appreciation and mechanical and operating reliability, and the vessel was

also the fastest of any Union-Castle's liners as a result of the decision by the company to upgrade her machinery. She was also the first British liner fitted with stabilizers, and thus required a lengthening of her hull from 748 ft (228.0 m) to 764 ft (232.9 m) while she was still on the stocks in Belfast.

Named after a Cornish castle, the *Pendennis Castle* was named on December 10, 1957 but not launched for another fortnight as a result of a dockyard strike. The vessel was completed and handed over to her owner on November 14, 1958, and departed on her maiden voyage on January 1, 1959. The *Pendennis Castle* was the first British liner to embark waitresses, known at the

time as "stewardettes," for her dining rooms.

The ports served on the *Pendennis Castle's* regular schedule from Southampton to South Africa were Port Elizabeth, East London and Durban, with occasional calls at Madeira. The ship had been completed with a partial air-conditioning system, and in July 1964 the Union-Castle Line revealed that this system would be increased to all of the first-class cabins. At approximately the same time, a further 21 cabins had showers fitted.

The *Pendennis Castle* became known as the "fun-ship" of the Union-Castle Line's fleet as the company steadily incorporated more amusement facilities and improved the standard of the ship's recreational facilities. This was a deliberate ploy by the company to attract a larger percentage of younger travellers in the hope that they would become regulars.

While the *Pendennis Castle* berthed in Southampton during May 1958, she suffered a fire which damaged some of the accommodation in the ship's amidships section. This was the time at which air-transport was starting to make significant inroads into liner traffic, and the Union-Castle Line was determined to adhere as closely as possible to the published schedule. The ship therefore sailed on her next voyage with Harland & Wolff workmen on board to continue the repairs and complete the necessary refurbishment even as the ship steamed south.

The *Pendennis Castle* remained in useful service through the 1960s and into the first half of the 1970s, but the Union-Castle Line's board of directors decided in 1976 to take the ship out of service and place her on the market. The *Pendennis Castle* thus steamed from Southampton on her final passenger-carrying voyage on April 23, 1976, and, on her return to her home port on June 14 of the same year, she was withdrawn from service.

The *Pendennis Castle* was sold to the Filipino-owned Ocean Queen Navigation Corporation. Flying her new owner's flag, the ship left on July 7, 1976 for Hong Kong, which she reached on August 9. Here she was revised in a new livery in place of the Union-Castle Line's distinctive paint scheme, centerd on a lavender hull. She now sported another attractive scheme, based on a white hull and a golden brown funnel. The Filipino corporation's intention was to use the vessel as a cruise ship, but this never happened and the vessel remained at Hong Kong, laid up until 1978. In this year the ship was sold to a Liberian company, Kinvarra Bay Shipping, which renamed her as the *Sinbad I*, but she nonetheless remained laid up. After four years of inactivity, the ship steamed out of Hong Kong in April 1980 for Kaohsiung in Taiwan, where she was scrapped.

The Pendennis Castle was immediately identifiable as a ship of the Union-Castle Line by her combination of a lavender hull and black/red funnel.

Pendennis Castle

Type:	oceanic liner
Tonnage:	28,582 gross registered tons
Dimensions:	length 764 ft (232.9 m); beam 83 ft 6 in (25.5 m); draft not available
Propulsion:	two Parsons geared steam turbines delivering 46,000 shp (34298 kW) to two propellers for 22.5 kt
Complement:	197 first- and 473 tourist-class passengers, and crew

American Queen (1995) and the Mississippi stern-wheelers

Now best remembered as one of the most distinctive features of river transport in the U.S. in the mid-nineteenth century, the stern-wheeler is a steam-powered vessel propelled by a single paddle-wheel in the stern of the vessel and normally extending over the whole breadth of the stern. Such a propulsion arrangement was the first way in which steam power was adapted to propulsion on inland waters, but it was quickly overtaken, especially for sea-going purposes, by the arrangement of two paddle wheels, one on each side of the ship. However, the stern wheel was kept for many years for river service, and its advantage over the propeller was that it could operate effectively in water deep enough only to float the vessel involved. The stern-wheeler was employed for police work on the major rivers of China, in the form of river gunboats; for some of the big excursion vessels on the Mississippi, other major rivers and larger lakes of the U.S.; and for freight and passenger services on rivers in Australia, India, Mesopotamia and the U.S. where major difficulties had to be overcome, including shoals and rapids.

In these circumstances a shallow-draft vessel of the flat-bottomed type was demanded, and here the stern wheel came into its own. The wheel, in this case usually of the simple type with fixed rather than feathering floats, was driven directly by two long-stroke cylinders located on deck level with the paddle shaft and fed with steam from a boiler, or boilers, mounted on the same deck right forward near the bows. Stern wheelers of this concept were

employed on many shallow rivers in Africa, Arabia, Australia, Egypt, India and other parts of the world including North and South America.

In the U.S. about half of all river steamers were of the stern-wheel type, but the larger and faster passenger river boats were almost all of the side-wheel variety. Some steam boats for service, on the larger rivers such as the Mississippi and Ohio, were as much as 5,000 tons gross with five or six decks rising above a flat hull with a bluff bow and square-cut stern. To turn their 40-ft (12.2-m) paddle wheels, a form of walking beam engine was developed in which the moving beam, in full view above the top deck, was constructed, together with the truss-like structure on which it was mounted, primarily from timber and wrought iron supports of local manufacture. This was a type of paddle steamer engine which was not found anywhere else, and as such was a product of U.S. engineering ingenuity which proved perfect for its purpose. In the great steamboat races of the 1870s, vessels such as the *Robert E. Lee* and *Natchez* were able to claim speeds in the order of 18 or 19 kt in the run between Natchez and New Orleans.

A Mississippi steamer of 1884 celebrated on a Bhutan stamp for the 30th Anniversary of the International Maritime Organisation.

In the twentieth century there was a nostalgic resurgence of interest in the stern wheeler for leisure and holiday purposes.

Typical of such vessels are the *Delta Queen* and *Delta King*, sister craft dating from 1926. The 1,650-ton *Delta Queen* has a length of 285 ft (86.9 m), beam of 58 ft (17.7 m) and draft of 11 ft 6 in (3.5 m), and can carry 200 passengers. Its compound steam engine delivers 2,000 hp (1491 kW) to the stern-mounted paddle wheel.

Pre-fabricated by the Clyde-based Isherwood yard in Scotland, the *Delta Queen* and *Delta King* were shipped in pieces to Stockton, California,

where the California Transportation Company assembled the two vessels for its scheduled Sacramento River service between San Francisco and Sacramento, and excursions to Stockton, on the San Joaquin River. The two vessels were, at the time, the most comfortably appointed and expensive stern-wheel passenger vessels yet completed. Rendered superfluous by the construction of a new highway linking Sacramento with San Francisco in 1940, the vessels were laid up, and then bought by Isbrandtsen Steamship Lines for service out of New Orleans. Before this could be inaugurated, however, World War II (1939-45) intervened and the

The American Queen has the type of bow-mounted brows which allowed the original Mississippi vessels to nose up to the bank, discharge passengers, and man portable freight straight onto the shore, or to load payload in the same manner.

American Queen
and the Mississippi stern-wheelers continued

two vessels were requisitioned by the U.S. Navy for use in San Francisco Bay.

In 1946 the *Delta Queen* was bought by Greene Line Steamers of Cincinnati, Ohio, and towed via the Panama Canal and the Mississippi and Ohio Rivers for refurbishment in Pittsburgh. In 1948 the *Delta Queen* began a regular passenger service along the Ohio, Mississippi, Tennessee and Cumberland rivers between cities such as Chattanooga, Cincinnati, Nashville, New Orleans and St Paul, together with a host of smaller river ports between these major cities. The *Delta Queen*'s ownership has changed a number of times during the last half century, and since 1971 the vessel has operated with a presidential exemption to the law banning overnight passenger services by vessels with wooden superstructures. The *Delta Queen* was listed as a National Historic Landmark in 1989.

The *Delta Queen* is currently operated by the Majestic America Line, which bought the vessel,

together with the *American Queen* and the *Mississippi Queen*, from the Delaware North Companies in April 2006. The Majestic America Line also offers river boat cruises on the Columbia and Snake Rivers in Oregon and Washington, as well as cruises through the Alaska Inside Passage.

The *Delta Queen* provides regularly scheduled cruises along the Mississippi and its tributary rivers to points as far distant from each other as New Orleans, Memphis, St Louis, St Paul, Cincinnati and Pittsburgh, to name but a few. The *Delta Queen* is also small enough to navigate waters such as the Arkansas, Red, Black Warrior and Mobile Rivers as well as the Tennessee-Tombigbee Waterway

Another visitor attraction in which the *Delta Queen* is involved is the annual re-creation of historic steamboat races during the Kentucky Derby Festival. In this event she races the *Belle of Louisville* on the Ohio river at Louisville, the winner receiving a trophy of golden antlers, which is

The Delta Queen's stern wheel with the vessel's pair of rudders immediately abaft it.
Photo:
John Batchelor

mounted on the pilot house until the next race. There are also races during the "Tall Stacks" festivals celebrating steamboats, every three or four years in Cincinnati.

Built by the McDermott Shipyard of Amelia, Louisiana, the *American Queen* is the largest stern wheeler ever built. Laid down in July 1993 and completed in May 1995, the vessel is a six-deck recreation of a classic Mississippi river boat, and is operated by the Delaware North Companies, which bought the bankrupt Delta Queen Steamboat Company in 2002.

The *American Queen*'s paddle wheel is 30 ft (9.14 m) wide and 28 ft (8.53 m) in diameter, and has 18 blades (floats). This wheel is powered by a pair of 1928 Norberg double-expansion horizontal reciprocating steam engines supplied with steam by a single oil-fired 400-lb/sq in (28.13-

kg/cm²) water tube boiler.

It should be noted that although the *American Queen*'s stern wheel is indeed powered by a genuine steam plant, her primary propulsion arrangement is in fact vested in a pair of diesel-powered Aquamaster electric Z-drives, one on each side of the stern wheel, delivering 1,000 hp (746 kW) to each of the two four-blade propellers, each with a diameter of 69 in (1.75 m).

This does not detract from the appearance of the *American Queen*, which has the authentic look of a genuine Mississippi stern-wheeler with a side-by-side pair of funnels rising above the pilot house to a height 97 ft 5 in (29.69 m) above the water. The funnels and pilot house can be lowered for an overall height of 55 ft (16.76 m) so that the *American Queen* can pass safely below low bridges.

American Queen

Type:	stern paddle-wheeler
Tonnage:	3,707 tons gross
Dimensions:	length 418 ft (127.4 m); beam 89 ft 4 in (27.2 m); draft 8 ft 6 in (2.6 m)
Propulsion:	two double-expansion steam engines delivering 1,500 hp (1118 kW) to one paddle wheel for 10.4 kt
Complement:	481 passengers, and 180 crew

Queen Elizabeth 2 (1967)

By the mid-1960s, travel across the Atlantic was the province of the jet-powered airliner, and the Cunard Line thus found that its two principal ships, the *Queen Mary* and *Queen Elizabeth*, were becoming unprofitable. Cunard did not wish to abandon passenger services, and therefore decided to invest heavily in a new liner. Cunard decided that its new ship would be smaller and more economical than its predecessors and, after initial consideration of three-class accommodation, was finalized with a two-class arrangement which could readily be adapted to single-class standard for cruising, which would be the primary task of the ship in the winter months.

The result was the *Queen Elizabeth 2*, which was ordered in 1964 and built by Upper Clyde Shipbuilders at the John Brown Shipyard in Clydebank, Scotland. The vessel was laid down in July 1965 and launched on September 20, 1967. As completed, the ship was powered by steam turbines for 28.5 kt, but in 1986 the ship was revised by the Lloyd Werft Shipyard in Bremerhaven with a diesel-electric powerplant to reduce fuel consumption by half.

The *Queen Elizabeth 2* began her maiden voyage from Southampton to New York on May 2, 1969, and in 1970 set a record of 3 days, 20 hours and 42 minutes for an average speed of 30.36 kt. In 1971 she was involved in the rescue of some 500 passengers from the French Line ship *Antilles*, which had caught fire. On May 17, 1972, while steaming from New York to Southampton, she received a bomb threat. She was searched by her crew and a bomb disposal team was parachuted into the sea near the ship, but no bomb was found. In 1973 the vessel made two chartered cruises through the Mediterranean to Israel for the 25th anniversary of the founding of that state.

In 1982 the vessel was requisitioned as a troopship in the Falklands war, transporting 3,000 troops to the south

The Queen Elizabeth 2 underway.

The QE2 sails into New York in happier days. Photo: Cunard.

On November 5, 2004 the *Queen Elizabeth 2* became Cunard's longest serving ship, surpassing the 35 years logged by the *Aquitania*. In May 2005 the ship was replaced on the transatlantic route by the *Queen Mary 2*, but still undertakes an annual world cruise and regular trips around the Mediterranean; and on February 20, 2007, while on a round-the-world cruise, the *Queen Elizabeth 2* met her sister and successor as Cunard flagship, the *Queen Mary 2*, herself on her first world cruise, in Sydney, Australia.

As the *Queen Elizabeth 2* approaches the 40th anniversary of her entry into service, there is interest about her future, the more so as the new Cunard cruise ship *Queen Victoria*, while of a size similar to the *Queen Elizabeth 2*, should enter service in 2007. But the *Queen Victoria* is not an ocean liner, however, and Cunard (owned since 1998 by the Anglo-U.S. Carnival Corporation) is currently committed to retaining the oldest, if no longer the largest, ship in its fleet.

Atlantic. In 1986, her steam machinery was removed after the vessel had steamed 2.622 million miles (4.221 million km), and the conversion also included a larger funnel which altered the ship's look. In 1990 the *Queen Elizabeth 2* made the fastest diesel-powered crossing of the Atlantic in 4 days, 6 hours and 57 minutes for an average speed of 30.16 kt.

In August 1992 the hull of the *Queen Elizabeth 2* ran aground off Cuttyhunk Island near Cape Cod, and had to be dry-docked for repairs. The ship celebrated the 30th anniversary of her maiden voyage in Southampton in 1999. In three decades she had carried more than 2 million passengers. Late in 2001, the *Queen Elizabeth 2* was refurbished with new carpets and furnishings throughout many cabins and public rooms, and also saw minor changes in layout.

Queen Elizabeth 2

Type:	transatlantic liner and cruise ship
Tonnage:	70,327 tons gross
Dimensions:	length 693 ft (293.5 m); beam 105 ft (32.0 m); draft 32 ft (9.9 m)
Propulsion:	nine MAN diesel engines delivering 128,252 hp (95625 kW) to two propellers for 32.5 kt
Complement:	1,756 or, for cruising, 1,892 passengers, and 1,015 crew

"PacifiCat 1000" class (1993)

The 1998 completion, by Catamaran Ferries International, a Canadian subsidiary of Incat of Australia, of the first of BC Ferries' three "PacifiCat 1000" series catamaran ferries marked the emergence of a new era in high-speed ferry services on Canada's west coast from 1999.

BC Ferries decided to adopt a Ro/Ro catamaran type to meet the demands of anticipated growth and also to overcome current as well as future traffic congestion problems at each end of its main routes between the mainland and Vancouver Island. The three ferries, making 18 return trips per day at an average of 37 kt, replace two larger conventional ferries making eight return trips. The simultaneous loading and unloading of the two drive-through vehicle decks is one of the reasons for the ferries' notably short turn-around times in unloading 250 cars and then taking on the same number in some 15 minutes. The lower deck is strengthened for the carriage of up to four coaches.

BC Ferries issued its requirement in 1994, and the fast turn-round time militated a catamaran, which can feature a bow door more safely than a monohull when a high speed is required. Of the 22 proposals which BC Ferries received from design outfits, 14 were catamarans. BC Ferries then opted for a proposal from Incat Designs Pty Ltd based on a proven catamaran hullform. The Australian company was awarded the contract in December 1994 in a joint venture arrangement with a Canadian naval architect, Robert Allan Ltd. The height of the two car decks had to match the terminal infrastructure right through the local 16.4-ft (5-

m) tidal range, which limited the available tunnel height to some 8 ft 2 in (2.5 m).

Special features identified by the designers include a double bottom built into the hulls extending forward of the engine room up to the collision bulkhead. Each hull contains six upper and six lower void spaces, accessible only from above. The forward quarter-length of the hulls has also been strengthened with 0.79-in (20-mm) plate and half-spaced sub-frames to cope with the potential problem of hitting floating logs. The propulsion

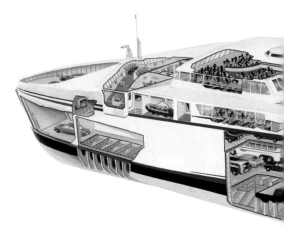

of the "PacifiCat1000" is centred on four MTU diesel engines each driving a KaMeWa waterjet. Seven propulsion concepts were considered, and in addition to weight factors, the final selection was based on the proven ability of the powerplant to provide the power offered at minimum operating costs.

Cars enter the drive-through decks simultaneously via the double-deck linkspan, and there are no internal ramps. Lane widths are 7ft 11 in (2.4 m) on the upper deck and 8 ft 2 in (2.5 m) and 9 ft (2.7 m) on the lower car deck. Allied Shipbuilders built the hinged bow and stern ramps serving the lower vehicle deck, which were fitted to reduce the length of overhangs that would otherwise have been necessary to match the terminal facilities. The larger ramp, at the bow, measures 39.4 x 65.6 x 6.6 ft (12 x 20 x 2 m). The upper vehicle deck is basically an open-ended structure enclosed only by "up and over" garage doors beneath each end of the superstructure.

Passenger access to the public spaces (the passenger deck and overhead observation lounge) includes a central elevator. Foot passengers enter the passenger deck via overhead walkways. The passenger deck, abaft the wheelhouse, is divided into two areas by a central services block. The passenger area was designed to encourage passengers toward the various attractions available and so increase their spending on board the ferry. The accommodation includes 987 seats and 236 tables grouped around a self-service food counter. On one side of the after end of the forward lounge is a coffee shop counter, and on the other side a playroom. A sizeable gift shop at the other end hides an amusement arcade. Central staircases from the forward lounge lead to the observation lounge, which occupies the forward end of the uppermost deck, offers all-round views, and has table seating for around 275 passengers, another coffee shop counter, and a small open deck area aft with benches.

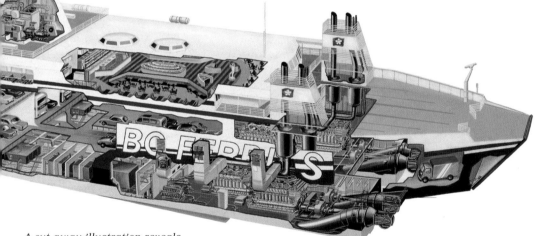

A cut-away illustration reveals the major features of BC Ferries' three "PacifiCat 1000" class fast ferry catamarans.

"PacifiCat 1000" class

Type:	fast catamaran ferry
Tonnage:	532 tons deadweight
Dimensions:	length 400 ft 3 in (122.0 m); beam 81 ft 4 in (24.8 m) excluding sponsons; draft 12 ft 4 in (3.8 m)
Propulsion:	four MTU diesel engines delivering 34,871 hp (26000 kW) to four waterjets for 37+ kt
Complement:	1,000 passengers and 250 cars, and crew

Princess Marguerite (1948)

The Canadian Pacific Railway embarked on the shipping business in 1884, initially with three steamers on the Great Lakes. Built in the UK, these steamed across the Atlantic and up the St Lawrence River to Montreal, where they were each cut in two, towed to Buffalo and there reassembled. In 1886 the CPR began regular passenger services between Montreal and Port Moody, and in 1887 launched a service with chartered vessels between Vancouver on the coast of British Columbia and the Far East. This latter was very successful, and in 1891 the company followed with the introduction of its own "Empress" ships. The CPR bought the Columbia & Kootenay River Navigation Company in 1890, which made it possible to enter the stern-wheeler traffic of the Canadian Rockies' lakes and rivers. During the same year, the CPR began passenger services between Toronto, Montreal and Chicago, following in 1897 with a service linking Victoria and Vancouver, and in 1901 purchased the ships and coastal services of the Canadian Pacific Navigation Company. The CPR spread its wings wider from 1903, when it took over the ships and North Atlantic interests of Elder Dempster & Co. and its subsidiary, the Beaver Line, and in the following year a regular service was inaugurated between Seattle in Washington State and Victoria in British Columbia. More expansion came in the years immediately preceding World War I (1914-18), a service in the Bay of Fundy starting in 1912, and in 1913 the CPR and the Allan Line began a co-operation in victualling and stores depots before the two operators' fleets were merged in 1916.

Most of the CPR fleet was requisitioned for war service in 1914 and in 1915 the Canadian Pacific Ocean Services was formed to operate the combined CPR and Allan

The Princess Marguerite off the coast of British Columbia.

Line fleets. In 1921 the company's operating name was changed to the Canadian Pacific Steamships Ltd. At the outbreak of World War II (1939-45), CPR placed its fleet at the disposal of the government and several vessels were taken over as troopships. In the 1960s the rise of air travel and cargo containerization meant a decline in the CPR's passenger fortunes, so the passenger ships were replaced by container and bulk cargo ships.

The *Princess Patricia* and *Princess Marguerite*, the latter taking the name of a vessel sunk in World War II, were the last CPR "Princess" type passenger vessels in service on Canada's Pacific coast. They were built at the yard of the Fairfield Co. Ltd. in Glasgow, Scotland. The *Princess Marguerite* was launched on May 26, 1948, and arrived in Esquimault, British Columbia, on April 6, 1949. She was soon complemented by her sister ship on the triangular route linking Victoria, Vancouver and Seattle, in the busy summer months of 1949.

Capable of 27 kt but generally cruising at 19 kt, the vessels were intended primarily for day services, and therefore had only limited cabin accommodation. The vessels each had a large coffee shop, rather than the dining saloon of the older ships, from which they also differed in having a cruiser stern and two, not three, funnels. During the 1950s, demand for car capacity increased and, now uneconomic, the triangular route was ended in 1959. Retained for the summer day service to Seattle, the *Princess Marguerite* was retired in September 1974. British Columbia Steamships Ltd. bought the vessel in 1975 and operated her until 1988 before selling her to the Stena Line of Sweden, which sold her in 1989 to a Singapore company for use as a floating restaurant. The ship was scrapped in 1996.

Princess Marguerite

Type:	car and passenger ferry
Tonnage:	5,911 tons gross
Dimensions:	length 359 ft 6 in (109.6 m); beam 56 ft 3 in (17.1m); draft 16 ft (4.9 m)
Propulsion:	two steam-powered turbo-electric engines driving two propellers for 27 kt
Complement:	2,000 day passengers (including 91 in 51 cabins), 50 cars, and crew

Fast ferries of the future

The term HSC (high-speed craft) is used for a high-speed vessel specifically for civilian use, and other terms used for the same type of vessel are "fastcraft" or "fast ferry." The first high-speed craft to enter service were often hydrofoils or hovercraft, but in the 1990s several types of high-speed catamaran and even monohull vessels entered service and became popular for their combination of speed, comfort and safety. While most high-speed craft are of modest

Further down the size ladder is the "HSS 900" class, of which a single unit, the *Stena Carisma*, was built in 1997 by the Westamarin yard of Norway. Able to carry 900 passengers and 208 cars, or alternatively 151 cars and 10 coaches, the 8,631-ton "HSS 900" unit has dimensions including a length of 294 ft 6 in (89.75 m), beam of 100 ft (30,5 m) and draft of 12 ft 9 in (3.9 m). Powered by two ABB-STAL GT35 gas turbine engines delivering 44,930 hp (33500

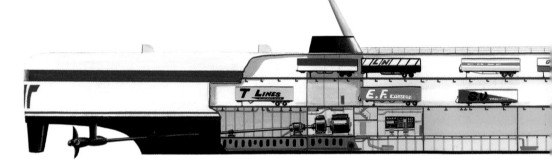

size and operate primarily in the passenger ferry role, there are also a number of large catamarans and monohulls which can carry vehicles up to the size of a lorry or bus. Among the hulled designs are many types powered by water jets rather than propellers.

High-speed Sea Service, or HSS, is the name usually applied to the type of high-speed craft operated by the Stena Shipping Line. Currently, Stena has four catamaran HSS ferries. The "HSS 1500" units are currently the largest fastcraft in service anywhere in the world, with an in-service cruising speed of 40 kt. These three vessels, built by Finnyards of Rauma in Finland during 1996-97, are the *Stena Explorer, Stena Voyager* and *Stena Discovery.*

Finnish yards and operators are among the most far-sighted and ambitious in the world, and this cutaway illustration presents a concept for possible development and construction in the near future. The propulsion arrangement is based on diesel-powered electrical generators below the streamlined bridge structure supplying current to aft-mounted electric motors driving two propellers.

kW) to two propellers, the "HSS 900" type can make 38 kt. The type has proved success in service, but had been beset by corrosion problems in its aluminium hull, but as the yard went into liquidation after completing this catamaran ferry, the Stena Line was unable to claim compensation.

As of the first days of 2007, all four of the vessels remained in service, the three larger units operating from the UK and the single smaller unit from Sweden. Of the larger units, two operate between the UK and Ireland (the *Stena Explorer* between Holyhead on the Welsh island of Anglesey to Dun Laoghaire in the Irish Republic, and the *Stena Voyager* between Stranraer in south-west Scotland to Belfast in Northern Ireland) and the third, the *Stena Discovery*, between Harwich in the east of England and the Hoek van Holland in the Netherlands. The smaller unit, the *Stena Carisma*, works the route between Göteborg in southern Sweden and Frederikshavn in northern Denmark. The high speed of the ferries, and the careful design

that the vessel has now been moved from her base at the Hoek van Holland to Belfast. Her future may involve sale to another operator or retention by the Stena Line as a spare for cannibalization to keep the other two units fully serviceable.

The Stena Line had replaced the HSS service with a twice-daily service using two more conventional super ferries, the *Stena Hollandica* and *Stena Britannica*. The two vessels are to be "stretched" to 787 ft 5 in (240.0 m) in length at the Lloyd Werft shipyard in Germany.

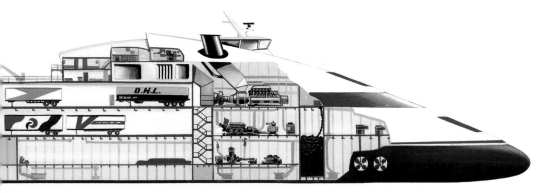

that optimized the speed with which passengers and vehicles can enter and leave the vessels, meant that several round trips could be completed every day.

On January 8, 2007, the *Stena Discovery* was withdrawn from the service across the south-western corner of the North Sea. It is believed

It is believed that the reasoning behind the Stena Line's changes were not any technical problems with the "HSS" class vessels, but rather a decrease in passenger demand at a time when fuel prices have risen sharply and continued operation could by financially justified only by higher load factors.

"HSS 1500" class

Type:	high-speed ferry
Tonnage:	19,638 tons
Dimensions:	length 415 ft 4 in (126.6 m); beam 131 ft 3 in (40.0 m); draft 15 ft 9 in (4.8 m)
Propulsion:	COGAG (combined gas turbine and gas turbine arrangement) with two LM2500 and two LM2500 gas turbines delivering a total of 91,200 hp (68000 kW) for 60+ kt
Complement:	1,520 passengers and 375 cars or 120 cars and 50 freight units totalling 985 lane yards (900 lane m), and crew

"S" class ferry (1993)

British Columbia Ferry Services Inc. otherwise BC Ferries, provides all the most important passenger and vehicle ferry services on the west coast of Canada in British Columbia. Set up in 1960 to provide a substantially better service than those provided by the Black Ball Line and the Canadian Pacific Railway, BC Ferries has become the largest passenger ferry line in North America and the second largest in the world, boasting a fleet of 35 vessels with a total passenger and crew capacity of over 27,000, serving 48 locations on the coast of British Columbia.

which in 2005 carried 2.5 million vehicles and 6 million passengers, the question arose of how these vessels were to be built. Government policy demanded that the vessels be built in British Columbia, but the only company with dry docks of sufficient size and technical experience was in receivership. BC Ferries feared that if a contract were awarded to this firm, funds and/or material connected with

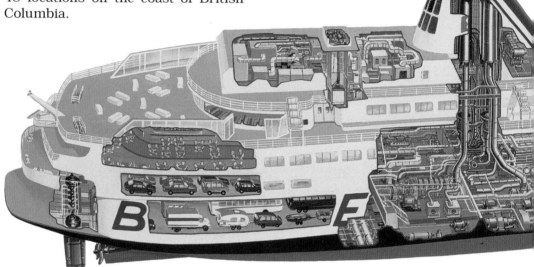

As BC Ferries provides an essential link from mainland Canada to the various islands on its routes, it is subsidised by Transport Canada. The subsidy is adjusted annually to keep pace with the rate of inflation.

In 1989 the BC Ferries' board of directors faced a significant difficulty. With the preliminary design for two "super ferry" sister ships to serve and add capacity on the very busy route linking the Tsawwassen (Vancouver) and Swartz Bay route,

the project might be diverted to the eastern Canadian financial institution administrating the receivership. An ingenious solution was found in the creation of an entirely new entity called Integrated Ferry Constructors Ltd., wholly owned by BC Ferries, itself wholly owned by the government of British Columbia.

The contract was awarded to IFC, which had only a small number of marine architects, engineers and accountants on its books. Thus the

IFC was more a broker and a bank than anything else. Many British Columbian companies were awarded elements of the total contract, this total including the company in receivership that had the dry docks required for final assembly. All the materials were bought by IFC and delivered to the appropriate shipyards, and stage payments were made as construction of each segment progressed. The available funds were therefore never at risk, and the performance of the sub-contractors was never an issue, as jobs could be moved from yard to yard or contractor to contractor

The two vessels have performed flawlessly since entering service in 1993 and 1994, respectively, as the *Spirit of British Columbia* and the *Spirit of Vancouver Island*. These two "S" class units are currently the largest ferries in the BC Ferries fleet. The vessels are largely the same in layout and characteristics. The *Spirit of British Columbia* underwent extensive internal renovation in 2005, and in January 2006 similar refurbishment of the *Spirit of Vancouver Island* was completed.

The vessels sail only on the Highway 17 (Tsawwassen/

Fabricated from sub-contracted subassemblies brought together only for the final assembly of the vessel, the "S" class ferry was built on schedule and below budget, and had since performed excellently.

if performance became an issue. In the event, all the sub-contractors performed admirably, and the two vessels were delivered ahead of time and under budget for about Can. $120 million each.

Swartz Bay) route. The *Spirit of Vancouver Island* is based at Swartz Bay on Vancouver Island and the *Spirit of British Columbia* on the mainland to operate reciprocal services.

"S" class ferry

Type:	vehicle and passenger ferry
Tonnage:	18,747 tons gross
Dimensions:	549 ft 5 in (167.5 m); beam not available; draft not available
Propulsion:	diesel engines delivering 21,394 hp (15951 kW) to two propellers for 19.5 kt
Complement:	470 cars and 2,100 persons (passengers and crew)

Waverley (1946)

In 2007 the *Waverley* is the sole survivor of the Clyde steamers, and, as such, is the world's last sea-going paddle steamer. Maintained to a peak of elegance, the vessel undertakes a full season of cruises every year in the Firth of Clyde, the Thames and the Bristol Channel, and also along the south coast of England. Below decks, a passageway on each side of the engine room allows passengers to watch the workings of the steam engine, built by Rankin & Blackmore Engineers of the Eagle Foundry in Greenock.

The *Waverley*'s cruises are an evocatively nostalgic link with the period in which Glaswegians packed such steamers to go "doon the watter" from Glasgow along the Firth of Clyde to the seaside resorts and little towns of the western Highlands. The vessel was built as a replacement for the 1889 vessel of the same type and name, which had been impressed for

service in World War II (1939-45) as a minesweeper until sunk in 1940 during the Dunkirk evacuation.

The new *Waverley* was launched on October 2, 1946 from the Glasgow yard of A. & J. Inglis, which had built the vessel for the London & North Eastern Railway for services on the Firth of Clyde between Helensburgh and Arrochar via Loch Long. In 1948 the British government nationalised the railway system, and the *Waverley* came into the ownership of the British Transport Commission, which in 1951 passed the vessel to the Caledonian Steam Packet Company.

A revival of steamer fortunes in the 1950s provided for the oil- rather than coal-fired reboilering of the *Waverley* for the 1957 season. A gradual change in Glaswegian holiday habits was taking place, however, and this was reflected in weakening passenger traffic. The Caledonian Steam Packet Company now merged with the ferry

The paddle-wheeler Waverley at sea during one of her many excursion voyages.

Right and below: The Waverley had survived as a working paddle wheeler against all the odds, and now possesses a nostalgia-tinged popularity that ensures her career into the foreseeable future. Note the large boxes which protect the paddle wheels from damage as the vessel nudges her way alongside a pier.
Photos: Gavin Stewart/ Martin Longhurst

company MacBraynes, which in 1973 became Caledonian-MacBrayne Ltd.

The company withdrew the *Waverley* after the 1973 season, but in the next year the Paddle Steamer Preservation Society bought the vessel for £1. A major fund-raising operation proved very successful, and the PSPS set up Waverley Excursions Ltd. to operate the refurbished *Waverley*

from 1975. On April 28, 1977, the *Waverley* left the Clyde to cruise from Liverpool and Llandudno, extended in 1978 to the south of England. On May 12, 1980, she cruised to Cap Griz Nez on the northern coast of France for the 40th anniversary of the Dunkirk evacuation. In 1981 a new boiler was fitted, and in the same year the cruise program was based on a circumnavigation of Great Britain. The *Waverley* visited Dunkirk in 1990 for the 50th anniversary of the evacuation, and in 1998 she received National Heritage Lottery funding for a major reconstruction, the work being undertaken in 2000/03 by George Prior Engineering Ltd. of Great Yarmouth, which largely restored the vessel to her 1947 condition but improved safety provisions.

Waverley

Type:	excursion side-wheel paddle steamer
Tonnage:	693 gross registered tons
Dimensions:	length 239 ft (72.8 m); beam 30 ft (9.1 m); draft 6 ft 6 in (2.0 m)
Propulsion:	one triple-expansion steam engine driving two side paddle wheels for 18.5 kt
Complement:	(as built) 1,350 passengers, and crew

Super-tanker

"Super-tanker" is an unofficial term generally applied only to the world's largest ships, which are tankers with a deadweight of more than 250,000 tons and able to carry between 2 and 3 million barrels of crude oil. Within the shipping industry such vessels are more formally known as VLCCs (Very Large Crude Carriers) of up to 320,000 tons deadweight and ULCCs (Ultra-Large Crude Carriers) of up to 500,000 tons deadweight.

The largest super-tanker, and indeed the largest ship yet built, was the *Jahre Viking*, which was damaged in the 1980s and was repaired to become the permanently moored storage tanker *Knock Nevis*, weighing in at 499,358 tons deadweight.

During the 1950s, tankers with only 10% of this total would have been called super-tankers, but the size and capacity of the vessels needed to carry the quantities of crude oil needed by the world's most advanced industrial nations was already growing rapidly, and presented problems as there were limits of the size of ship which could pass along the Suez and Panama Canals. The former was also closed between 1967 and 1975 as a result of the Six-Day War of 1967 between Israel and its Arab neighbours, and therefore imposed on operators the longer and more costly passage round the Cape of Good Hope. This led shipping companies to opt for the construction of very large tankers

The whole of the accommodation and propulsion machinery for a super-tanker is located right aft, leaving the rest of the vessel clear for its primary task of carrying oil in very large quantities.

offering better economies of scale than older, smaller vessels.

When introduced, the larger tankers were prevented by their size and draft from using many existing docks, and had thus to discharge their cargo into smaller tankers offshore, but the problem has since been alleviated by the development of special deep-water offloading facilities with pipelines to take the oil to land: a good example is the Louisiana Offshore Oil Port.

The super-tanker is a very efficient ship, most such vessels having only one engine driving a single propeller, and are therefore very cost-effective. However, as a result of their great size and inertia, the latter especially significant when loaded, the super-tanker has very poor maneuverability and requires a notably long distance to slow to a halt. Traveling close to shore, the super-tanker is susceptible to running aground and starting to lose oil as, at low speeds, it is slow to respond to the helm and is also resistant to fine control.

In single-hulled tankers the hull is also the wall of the oil tanks, and a hull breach necessarily means a loss of oil. Newer tankers are of double-hulled construction with a space between the hull and the storage tanks to reduce the risk of an oil loss if the outer hull is breached. The volume between the hull and the tanks is used for water ballast when the ship is not carrying an oil cargo. Even so, double-hulled construction is not the whole solution, and such hulls are more prone to suffering an explosion if oil vapor collects in the space between the outer hull and tanks.

The largest known double-hulled tanker in the world is the *Hellespont Fairfax*. Completed in January 2003, it boasts a deadweight tonnage of 442,470 tons.

At 210,258 tons, the Marisa of the Helderline Shell fleet, a VLCC tanker, was completed in 1973.

Hellespont Fairfax (2002)

Type:	ULCC tanker
Tonnage:	435,475 tons deadweight
Dimensions:	length 1,246 ft 9 in (380.0 m); beam 223 ft 1 in (68.0 m); draft 80 ft 5 in (24.5 m)
Propulsion:	one Sulzer 9RTA 84TD diesel engines driving one propeller for 17.9 kt
Complement:	not available

Bulk carriers

"Bulk carrier" is the overall designation applied to any ocean-going vessel used to transport bulk cargo items such as ore, food staples such as grain, and similar cargo. The bulk carrier is characterized by the large box-like deck hatches designed to slide outward for loading/unloading. Within the bulk carrier classification, the two major subdivisions are wet and dry.

It is worth noting that while most lakes are too small to need or accommodate bulk carrier services, such ships have plied the Great Lakes and St Lawrence Seaway of North America for more than a century.

The expansion and more global basis of the world economy since the middle of the twentieth century has been reflected in bulk carriers, as indeed in other types of mercantile vessel, by smaller numbers, very considerably greater size, and increased role specialization. This has helped to promote the growth and capability of highly efficient cargo-handling tools optimized for the needs of specific markets and industries. The low-cost movement of raw materials and basic commodities, the most common bulk cargoes, can

be undertaken only with the use of advanced and fully optimized technologies.

The modern bulk carrier has its origins in solving this problem of moving cargo on and off the ship efficiently. The idea originated with a ship broker named Ole Skaarup, whose New York company repaired and chartered ships for bulk cargoes in the mid-1950s. Appreciating the complete inefficiency of the current system, he conceived a new type of cargo vessel with "wide, clear cargo holds [with the] machinery aft, [and] wide hatch openings to ease cargo handling." Skaarup also wanted a stable and seaworthy vessel, and devised special measures, including wing ballast tanks with sloped interior surfaces, to prevent the tendency of a bulk load to move at sea and thus destabilise the vessel.

Skaarup approached a Swedish shipping company, Nordstrom & Thulin, which was confident that Skaarup was right and helped to finance a 19,000-deadweight experiment, the "OS" type design with sloped wing tanks, the machinery and bridge aft, and cargo holds with smooth sides, sloping bulkheads

A Russian bulk carrier passes along the Bosporus. Photo: John Batchelor.

and large hatches. The resulting *Cassiopeia* was built by the Kockums Shipyard in Sweden and became an immediate success. As a result of its novel features, *Cassiopeia* could be loaded at a cost saving of 50 U.S. cents per ton, a saving which accumulated over a 10-year period in the entire building cost of a vessel intended for a 30-year life.

Other shipping companies soon saw the advantages of Skaarup's concept, and by the middle of the twenty-first century's first decade almost 7,000 ships of the "OS" type had been built, carrying the vast majority of the world's dry bulk cargoes.

As with other types of modern cargo ships, the bulk carrier has grown in size over the years. There are currently four main types of bulk carriers, namely the Handysize of between 10,000 and 40,000 tons deadweight, the Handymax of between 40,000 and 60,000 tons deadweight, the Panamax of between 60,000 and 100,000 tons deadweight, and the Capesize of more than 100,000 tons deadweight, which has to pass round the Cape of Good Hope or Cape Horn as it is too large to traverse the Suez and Panama Canals.

At 320,000 tons deadweight, the Bergeland is slightly smaller than the Bergestahl, but operates on the same service, delivering Brazilian iron ore to Rotterdam for the German steel industry. Both vessels were built by Hyundai in South Korea.

Bergestahl (1986 and the world's largest dry bulk carrier)

Type:	iron ore bulk carrier
Tonnage:	364,767 tons deadweight
Dimensions:	length 1,125 ft 4 in (343.0 m); beam 208 ft 4 in (63.5 m); draft 75 ft 6 in (63.5 m)
Propulsion:	one Italiani-Sulzer diesel engine delivering 19,900 hp (12601 kW) to one propeller for 13 kt
Complement:	not available

Queen Mary 2 (1999)

The *Queen Mary 2* is a Cunard Line ocean liner named after the earlier Cunard liner *Queen Mary*. At the time of her construction in 2003, the *Queen Mary 2* was the longest, broadest and tallest passenger ship ever built, and at 148,528 gross tons, also the largest. She lost that last distinction to the 154,407-gross ton *Freedom of the Seas* in April 2006, but the *Queen Mary 2* remains the largest ocean liner rather than cruise ship ever built. The *Queen Mary 2*'s features include 15 restaurants and bars, five swimming pools, a casino, a ballroom, a theatre, and a planetarium.

November 2000 Cunard contracted with the Chantiers de l'Atlantique of St Nazaire in France for the construction of the vessel, which was laid down on July 4, 2002, in Saint-Nazaire. The ship was floated out on March 21, 2003, and undertook her sea trials on September 25-29 and November 7-11 of the same year.

Cunard took delivery on, December 26, 2003 at Southampton, and, on January 12 of the following year, the new liner departed on her maiden voyage to Fort Lauderdale,

The *Queen Mary 2* is Cunard's flagship, and, as such, makes regular transatlantic crossings. The vessel was built as the successor to the *Queen Elizabeth 2*, which was Cunard's flagship between 1969 and 2004, on the transatlantic route.

Cunard undertook the design for a new class of 84,000-ton liners, capable of carrying 2,000 passengers in 1997-98 but, on comparing its thoughts with those of the Carnival Cruise Lines' 100,000-ton "Destiny" class and Royal Caribbean's 137,200-ton *Voyager of the Seas*, immediately began a major revision and began inviting construction tenders. In

Florida, with 2,620 passengers. During the 28th Olympics in Athens, the ship was berthed at Piraeus as a floating hotel vessel for VIPs and others. The *Queen Mary 2* started on a voyage round South America in January 2006, but the ship struck the side of a channel on departing Fort Lauderdale, damaging one of her propeller pods. The ship could continue, albeit at reduced speed, but this persuaded Cunard not to call at some promised ports of call on the way to Rio de Janeiro. The anger of many passengers led Cunard to offer refunds. The voyage continued, and it was only after the ship had returned to Europe in June that the damaged pod was removed. Repaired, it was reinstalled in November 2006. At the same time both bridge wings were lengthened outboard by 6 ft 8 in (2.0 m) to improve the bridge crew's field of vision.

On January 10, 2007, the *Queen Mary 2* departed on her first round-the-world cruise, circling the globe in 81 days.

A running mate is planned, to be known as the *Queen Victoria* and entering service in 2007.

Like many other liners, the *Queen Mary 2* has a promenade deck right

lower bow section to reduce drag and thereby increase speed, range and fuel economy.

As her size prevents the *Queen Mary 2* from docking in most ports, passengers are ferried to and from the ship in boats which, while the vessel is at sea, are stored in davits alongside the lifeboats. To transport passengers to shore, the boats come alongside four loading stations, which each have a large hull door that hydraulically opens outwards to form a boarding platform, complete with railings and decking.

In a reversal of tradition, the *Queen Mary 2* has her main public rooms on the lowest passenger decks with the cabins stacked

round Deck 7. The promenade passes behind the bridge screen and allows passengers to walk completely round the deck while sheltered from the strong wind of the ship's full-speed passage through the water. A feature which has attracted some criticism is the stern's counter. Her chief designer wanted the ship to have a stern profile similar to that of the *Queen Elizabeth 2*, but the mounting of the propeller pods required a flat transom. The compromise was a stern combining the traditional cruiser stern with a contemporary box-like transom stern. Like many modern ships, the *Queen Mary 2* has a bulbous

A cutaway illustration of the Queen Mary 2 reveals the ship's propulsion arrangement with four podded propulsor pods as well as maneuvering units in the underside of the bow, and extensive passenger spaces on 14 decks with the public rooms located low and the cabins high.

above. This paved the way for larger rooms to be contained within the stronger hull, as well as for more cabins to have private balconies. The designer sought to create a central axis to the two decks accommodating the main public rooms, but a full lengthwise view is broken by various public rooms extending across the hull's full beam. The dining rooms

were placed farther aft, and other features include a shopping arcade, champagne bar, wine bar, nightclub, winter garden, buffet dining area transformed at night into four themed restaurants, three grill rooms, several restaurants, large library, book shop and two spas.

The *Queen Mary 2*'s CODAG (combined diesel and gas turbine) propulsion system is based on four 16-cylinder Wärtsilä 16V46C EnviroEngine diesel engines delivering 90,120 hp (67200 kW) and two General Electric LM2500+ gas turbines delivering 66,700 hp (49731 kW) for economical cruising at lower speed and the capability for sustained higher speeds as and when required. The *Queen Mary 2* is the first passenger ship with CODAG propulsion, Water propulsion is the province of four Rolls-Royce Mermaid

podded propulsion units, each with a forward-facing KaMeWa propeller of the low-vibration type with bolted-on blades. The forward pair is fixed, but the after pair can rotate through 360°, obviating the need for a rudder.

As in most modern cruise ships, the *Queen Mary 2*'s propulsion machinery is electrically decoupled

inside the podded propulsor units and therefore entirely outside the ship's hull.

Another novel feature is the fact that the gas turbines, which are comparatively light and compact, are not housed with the diesel engines in the engine room deep in the hull, but are instead located in a soundproofed

Top left:
The Queen Mary 2's first Master, Commodore Ronald Warwick.
Photo: Cunard.

Bottom left:
Construction underway.
Photo:
John Batchelor.

Right:
The QM2 on her maiden voyage.
Photo: Cunard.

from the propeller shafts, so the ship's propulsion arrangement should perhaps be more accurately be described as "CODAG-electric." In this system the Diesel engine and gas turbines drive electrical generators, which provide the power to drive four 28,836-hp (21500-kW) electric motors made by Alstom (parent company of the yard which built the ship) located

special compartment directly below the funnel. This arrangement was selected as it allowed the design team to supply the oxygen-hungry turbines with the means to aspirate their air from nearby inlets without having to provide ducts through the complete height of the ship, which would have been a major waste of invaluable interior space.

Queen Mary 2

Type:	oceanic liner and cruise ship
Tonnage:	148,528 tons gross
Dimensions:	length 1,132 ft (345.0 m); beam 131 ft (39.9 m); draft 32 ft 10 in (10.0 m)
Propulsion:	CODAG arrangement with four diesel engines delivering 90,120 hp (67200 kW) and two gas turbines delivering 66,700 hp (49731 kW) to electric generators delivering current to four 28,836-hp (21500-kW) electric motors driving four propellers for 30 kt
Complement:	2,620 passengers, and 1,253 crew

Future submarine merchant ship

The idea of a nuclear-powered submarine for mercantile purposes had been a staple of imaginative fiction for more than 60 years, and has also drawn the attention of more serious thinkers. The basic concept of a mercantile submarine had an almost venerable history, for although only two submarines have yet been completed for mercantile purposes, naval submarines had been used, in standard or adapted forms, for the transport of small quantities of high-value cargo, especially in war.

The only pair of mercantile submarines were built in Germany during World War I (1914-18). They were designed to evade the Allied blockade of Germany with raw materials essential to the German war effort. The boats were built in 1916 by the Deutsche Ozean-Reederei, a shipping company created for the purpose, and were designed to operate between Germany and the U.S. which, in 1916, was still neutral.

The *Deutschland* could carry 700 tons, much of it outside the pressure hull. On its first journey to the U.S., departing on June 23, 1916, the *Deutschland* carried 163 tons of expensive chemical dyes, medical drugs and mail. The boat reached Baltimore, Maryland, on July 8, 1916 and returned to Germany with 348 tons of rubber, 341 tons of nickel and 93 tons of tin, arriving back in Bremerhaven on August 25, 1916. A second trip, between October and December of the same year, was also successful. A third trip was cancelled when the U.S. entered the war on the Allied side. The *Bremen* departed on her first voyage in August 1916, but disappeared at sea. The Deutsche Ozean-Reederei was building another

six boats at the time of the U.S.'s declaration of war, when their construction was halted or completed to create submarine cruisers. In World War II (1939-45), Germany used some of its submarines to maintain a physical link with Japan, exchanging high-value equipment and raw materials.

The USSR planned cargo submarines in World War II and during the Cold War. In World War II the Soviets used submarines to supply the besieged Crimean port of Sevastopol. Drawing on this, the Soviet naval command initiated a transport submarine program. The initial *Project 605* was a submarine barge to be towed by a standard submarine. This idea was discarded as a result of technical problems. The *Project 607* cargo submarine, to carry up to 300 tons of solid cargo and two folding cargo cranes, was later suggested, but this too was dropped in 1943.

The USSR envisaged and almost started construction of several types of large cargo submarines during the 1950s and 1960s, though these would not have been mercantile boats but rather the means to deliver troops. In the 1990s, a Russian design bureau proposed plans for submarines capable of transporting oil products or freight containers in or through Arctic regions. The proposed tanker and container models would be based on nuclear-powered naval submarines, with the tanker variant carrying almost 30,000 tons of petroleum, to be loaded and discharged from surface or underwater terminals. It was conceived that the container variant would carry 912 standard freight containers. In the period since the end of the Cold War, there have been several U.S. schemes for nuclear-powered submarine oil tankers to exploit Arctic oilfields in Alaska and Siberia.

The cargo vessel, tanker and bulk carrier of the future? With a pair of propellers driven by steam turbines powered by nuclear reactors, such a boat could have the standard hydroplanes for control in patch together with blow and stern thrusters for control in yaw under command of an automatic system based in an inertial system with satellite update and upward-, downward- and side-looking sensors. This would allow safe high-speed voyages below ice and adverse weather.

Merchant submarine

Type:	mercantile submarine
Tonnage:	105,000 tons gross
Dimensions:	length 1,200 ft (365.75 m); beam 100 ft (30.5 m); draft 35 ft (10.7 m) on the surface
Propulsion:	two nuclear reactors supplying steam to four geared steam turbines for 35 kt submerged and 12 kt surfaced; range at least 280,000 miles (450604 km); diving depth 700 ft (213 m)
Complement:	48

Newcastle, 1909

Index